Moodle 3 E-Learning Course Development
Development
Fourth Edition

Create highly engaging e-learning courses with Moodle 3

Susan Smith Nash
William Rice

BIRMINGHAM - MUMBAI

Moodle 3 E-Learning Course Development
Fourth Edition

Commissioning Editor: Amarabha Banerjee
Acquisition Editor: Larissa Pinto
Content Development Editor: Flavian Vaz
Technical Editor: Vaibhav Dwivedi
Copy Editor: Shaila Kusanale
Project Coordinator: Devanshi Doshi
Proofreader: Safis Editing
Indexer: Pratik Shirodkar
Graphics: Jason Monteiro
Production Coordinator: Aparna Bhagat

First published: June 2008
Second edition: August 2011
Third edition: June 2015
Fourth edition: May 2018

Production reference: 1250518

Published by Packt Publishing Ltd.
Livery Place
35 Livery Street
Birmingham
B3 2PB, UK.

ISBN 978-1-78847-219-7

www.packtpub.com

To the memory of my mother, Mona Margaret Wicker Smith, for her continual support, encouragement, and belief in education and the importance of sharing knowledge

– Susan Smith Nash

`mapt.io`

Mapt is an online digital library that gives you full access to over 5,000 books and videos, as well as industry leading tools to help you plan your personal development and advance your career. For more information, please visit our website.

Why subscribe?

- Spend less time learning and more time coding with practical eBooks and Videos from over 4,000 industry professionals

- Improve your learning with Skill Plans built especially for you

- Get a free eBook or video every month

- Mapt is fully searchable

- Copy and paste, print, and bookmark content

PacktPub.com

Did you know that Packt offers eBook versions of every book published, with PDF and ePub files available? You can upgrade to the eBook version at `www.PacktPub.com` and as a print book customer, you are entitled to a discount on the eBook copy. Get in touch with us at `service@packtpub.com` for more details.

At `www.PacktPub.com`, you can also read a collection of free technical articles, sign up for a range of free newsletters, and receive exclusive discounts and offers on Packt books and eBooks.

Contributors

About the authors

Susan Smith Nash has been designing and developing online courses and programs for more than 15 years for education, training, and personal development. In addition to *Moodle 3.x Teaching Techniques*, *Packt Publishing*, she is the author of a number of Moodle books and training videos, including *Moodle Course Design - Best Practices* and *Moodle for Training and Professional Development*. Other *Packt Publishing* instructional videos include two on the *Canvas Virtual Learning Environment*. She has also authored *Video-Assisted Mobile Learning for Writing Courses*.

William Rice is an e-learning professional from New York City. He has written books on Moodle, Blackboard, Magento, and software training. He enjoys building e-learning solutions for businesses and gains professional satisfaction when his courses help students.

His hobbies include writing books, practicing archery near JFK Airport, and playing with his children.

William is fascinated by the relationship between technology and society, how we create our tools, and how they shape us in turn. Married to an incredible woman who encourages his writing pursuits, he has two amazing sons.

About the reviewers

Donald Schwartz has been designing and managing Moodle since 2003. He is an expert on video e-learning course presentation and delivery to large and disparate clients. His clients include medical societies (AOA), engineering schools, a startup med-tech school, a distributed recruitment firm, and many of the ENR top 50 for their CAD software training.

Don is the Principal of VectorSpect LLC, a New Hampshire USA based e-learning consultancy.

Don has reviewed two other *Packt* publications: *Gamification with Moodle* and *Moodle Administration Essentials*.

John Walker is a licensed professional engineer in industrial engineering and currently a licensed full-time teacher in computer science at Cleveland High School in Portland, OR. He has worked on *GameMaker Essentials* and the *GameMaker Cookbook* for *Packt Publishing*. John has used Moodle since 2005 and beyond administering Moodle and creating courses, has created Open Educational resources using Moodle.

Packt is searching for authors like you

If you're interested in becoming an author for Packt, please visit authors.packtpub.com and apply today. We have worked with thousands of developers and tech professionals, just like you, to help them share their insight with the global tech community. You can make a general application, apply for a specific hot topic that we are recruiting an author for, or submit your own idea.

Table of Contents

Preface

This book will guide you in setting up a course and also use Moodle's unique attributes and platform. It will take you on a journey from conception to actualization. After working through this book, you will be able to design, launch, and administer courses in Moodle using effective instructional design that is both attractive and engaging. You will be able to configure your courses so that they incorporate success strategies for students, flexible and high-quality materials, and learning objectives-focused assessment strategies.

Who this book is for

This book is for educators, e-learning professionals, and teachers who want to get the best out of Moodle. Experienced Moodle users will find powerful insights into developing successful educational courses.

What this book covers

This book is intended to be a useful companion as you create your courses in Moodle. It provides step-by-step instructions, and it also gives illustrative examples. At the same time, the book should instill confidence so that you feel free to experiment and create resources and activities that include your own special views and personality. With Moodlecloud and on-premise installations, you have the chance to create *sandbox* courses where you can play, experiment, build, and create your own unique learning world.

Chapter 1, *A Guided Tour of Moodle*, is a guided tour of Moodle and what makes it unique. This chapter is an overview and should give you a good idea of what is possible. We hope you feel inspired to experiment and create after you read this chapter. In this chapter, you will begin building a plan to create your learning site, and how to do it in a way that incorporates Moodle's unique philosophy of learning, which rests on a foundation of interaction and the idea that people learn from each other. You will learn about the way Moodle is structured and its basic architecture. We will review how to get started and describe how you can begin to explore ways to make the "Moodle Experience" uniquely engaging for both students and instructors.

Chapter 2, *Installing Moodle*, teaches how to install Moodle on a server (on-premise) and also to use cloud-based Moodle (MoodleCloud). If you are a small institution or an individual teacher who would like to create a few courses to experiment with the form, or even to set up your own courses or tutoring services, in this chapter, you will find step-by-step instructions for installing Moodle. You will also learn how to access and use Moodle through the cloud so that you do not have to install Moodle on-premise. In learning about MoodleCloud, you'll find out how Moodle makes it easy for individuals to experiment in a friendly, free environment.

Chapter 3, *Configuring Your Site*, focuses on getting your site ready for use, whether you are using on-premise or a Moodle's cloud-based solution. We will cover the basics of Moodle navigation, and we will introduce the administrative functions for site administrators as well as instructors.

Chapter 4, *Creating Categories and Courses*, takes a close look at content administration in Moodle. This stage is important, because it involves planning and integrating your institution's mission and vision with the way that you structure and administer your courses. We will discuss how to effectively plan your course and how to align the course with your institution's vision and mission. We'll learn how to set up the framework for creating courses and also learn how to enroll users, including teachers, students, and guests.

Chapter 5, *Resources, Activities, and Conditional Access*, says that as you begin to build your courses, it's important to take a look at your curriculum as a whole and then standardize in order to have consistent courses. We will discuss the way to develop your course frameworks and provide an overview of the kinds of resources and activities that are available in Moodle. You will learn how to design your course so that it achieves learning goals, with learning objectives at the center. You will also learn the mechanics of customizing the courses and their functionality.

Chapter 6, *Adding Resources*, covers the kind of resources you can utilize in Moodle, and it describes ways to customize them and organize the course so that your resources are aligned with your course goals. You will learn how to add different kinds of resources, which include text files, embedded media files, URLs, and links to different types of libraries and open source repositories.

Chapter 7, *Adding Assignments, Lessons, Feedback, and Choices,* outlines developing the instructional strategy you will use for your courses. In addition, you'll find the best way to build courses around your learning objectives so that you can clearly map your content and activities to them. Also, you'll learn about different ways to motivate your students and keep them engaged. We review writing learning objectives and developing assessments with Bloom's taxonomy in mind. We will also look at competency learning, including micro-competencies. You will learn how to incorporate certificates and badges in Moodle so that they are automatically generated when mastery has been demonstrated.

Chapter 8, *Evaluating Students with Quizzes,* deals with assessment and assuring that learning objectives have been mastered. We will review how to set up quizzes, and we will include engagement strategies that involve recognizing student achievement. You will learn how to build different types of quizzes and tie them to mastery / competencies.

Chapter 9, *Getting Social with Chats and Forums,* informs that collaboration and interaction are important in Moodle, and in many learning settings, they constitute the backbone of the entire educational experience. We will learn how to set up effective social platforms in Moodle that encourage learning objective-focused engagement. We focus on an interaction-based instructional strategy that emphasizes learning from each other, and uses forums and chat rooms.

Chapter 10, *Collaborating with Wikis and Glossaries,* takes you through learning activities involving collaboration that are very important because they give learners an opportunity to employ numerous skills and also learn from each other. In this chapter, we will look at using collaboration as an instructional strategy, and we will discuss when and where to best employ it. We will go into detail and provide examples. For example, we will look at a wiki that we call the *Shark Tank Wiki,* because it deals with evaluating pitches for start-up funding (as in the popular television show, *Shark Tank*). Another good example of using Moodle for collaboration is in planning an event such as a fund-raiser.

Chapter 11, *Running a Workshop,* demonstrates that using Moodle for an interactive workshop with group projects is a good strategy, because Moodle has unique attributes that make student interaction and content sharing very easy and effective. In this chapter, we discuss why and when to use a workshop and how to select a topic for a project that is ideal for a group workshop. Then, we review the four phases of a workshop and discuss the best strategies.

Chapter 12, *Groups and Cohorts,* says that students learn from each other in the course as a whole and also within groups and subgroups. Many groups are formed for specific purposes, such as peer review or to develop a wiki or glossary entry. In this chapter, you learn how to set up and manage groups and cohorts in Moodle.

Chapter 13, *Extending Your Course by Adding Blocks,* informs that developing content in the form of a block can be very effective for managing and delivering materials. In this chapter, we will discuss the use and management of blocks. We will cover examples of blocks and discuss how to configure a block and control where it appears. We will learn about standard as well as custom blocks.

Chapter 14, *Features for Teachers,* says that Moodle has several different types of tools that make the teacher's life easier, which include customizable logs and reports. We learn how to manage them in this chapter.

To get the most out of this book

These are the things you'll need to keep in mind in order to get the most of this book:

1. You need to be able to use basic HTML
2. You'll need a good text editor, such as Google Docs or Microsoft Word
3. You'll need to be able to use photo editing programs, either Cloud-based (GIMP, for example), or installed on-premise (MS-Paint, for example)
4. You'll need to be able to use spreadsheet programs (Excel or Google Sheets) for importing and exporting student records and questions to test banks in quiz

Conventions used

There are a number of text conventions used throughout this book.

CodeInText: Indicates code words in text, database table names, folder names, filenames, file extensions, pathnames, dummy URLs, user input, and Twitter handles. Here is an example: "Note the full course name in the <title> and <meta> tags. Many search engines give a lot of weight to the title tag. If your Moodle system is open to search engines, choose your course title with this in mind."

A block of code is set as follows:

```
<head>
      <title>Course: Non-Surgical Anti-Aging Services </title>
      <link rel="shortcut icon"
href="http://localhost/moodle/theme/image.php/standard/theme/1359480837/fav
icon" />
      <meta http-equiv="Content-Type" content="text/html;
      charset=utf-8" />
      <meta name="keywords" content="moodle, Course: Non-Surgical Anti-
Aging Services" />
```

When we wish to draw your attention to a particular part of a code block, the relevant lines or items are set in bold:

```
<head>
      <title>Course: Non-Surgical Anti-Aging Services </title>
      <link rel="shortcut icon"
href="http://localhost/moodle/theme/image.php/standard/theme/1359480837/fav
icon" />
      <meta http-equiv="Content-Type" content="text/html;
      charset=utf-8" />
      <meta name="keywords" content="moodle, Course: Non-Surgical Anti-
Aging Services" />
```

Any command-line input or output is written as follows:

```
$ git clone -b MOODLE_{{Version3}}_STABLE
git://git.moodle.org/moodle.git
```

Bold: Indicates a new term, an important word, or words that you see onscreen. For example, words in menus or dialog boxes appear in the text like this. Here is an example: "To use conditional activities, your system administrator must enable the feature **Enable conditional access** under **Site administration** ∣ **Advanced Features**."

Warnings or important notes appear like this.

Tips and tricks appear like this.

Get in touch

Feedback from our readers is always welcome.

General feedback: Email feedback@packtpub.com and mention the book title in the subject of your message. If you have questions about any aspect of this book, please email us at questions@packtpub.com.

Errata: Although we have taken every care to ensure the accuracy of our content, mistakes do happen. If you have found a mistake in this book, we would be grateful if you would report this to us. Please visit www.packtpub.com/submit-errata, selecting your book, clicking on the Errata Submission Form link, and entering the details.

Piracy: If you come across any illegal copies of our works in any form on the Internet, we would be grateful if you would provide us with the location address or website name. Please contact us at copyright@packtpub.com with a link to the material.

If you are interested in becoming an author: If there is a topic that you have expertise in and you are interested in either writing or contributing to a book, please visit authors.packtpub.com.

Reviews

Please leave a review. Once you have read and used this book, why not leave a review on the site that you purchased it from? Potential readers can then see and use your unbiased opinion to make purchase decisions, we at Packt can understand what you think about our products, and our authors can see your feedback on their book. Thank you!

For more information about Packt, please visit packtpub.com.

A Guided Tour of Moodle ¹

Moodle is a free, open source learning management system that enables you to create powerful, flexible, and engaging online learning experiences. I use the phrase *online learning experiences* instead of *online courses* deliberately. The phrase *online course* often connotes a sequential series of web pages, some images, maybe a few animations, and a quiz put online. There might be some email or bulletin board communication among the teacher and students. However, online learning can be much more engaging than that.

Moodle's name gives you an insight into its approach to e-learning. The official Moodle documentation on `http://docs.moodle.org` states the following:

> *"The word Moodle was originally an acronym for Modular Object-Oriented Dynamic Learning Environment, which is mostly useful to programmers and education theorists. It's also a verb that describes the process of lazily meandering through something, doing things as it occurs to you to do them, an enjoyable tinkering that often leads to insight and creativity. As such, it applies both to the way Moodle was developed and to the way a student or teacher might approach studying or teaching an online course. Anyone who uses Moodle is a Moodler."*

The phrase *online learning experience* connotes a more active, engaging role for students and teachers. It connotes, among other things, web pages that can be explored in any order, courses with live chats among students and teachers, forums where users can rate messages on their relevance or insight, online workshops that enable students to evaluate one another's work, impromptu polls that let the teacher evaluate what students think of a course's progress, and directories set aside for teachers to upload and share their files. All these features create an active learning environment, full of different kinds of student-to-student and student-to-teacher interactions. This is the kind of user experience that Moodle excels at and the kind that this book will help you create.

Moodle's philosophy of learning

For those of you who are interested, the underlying learning philosophy for Moodle is that of "connectivism." Basically, it means that people learn from one another, and Moodle's framework is structured to maximize interactivity with other students and the content itself. When Moodle first debuted, the philosophy usually involved forums, with some potential for real-time chat. However, with the ability to include webinars using BigBlueButton and other add-ins, the possibilities of synchronous (real-time) and asynchronous interactivity have expanded.

One thing to keep in mind as you develop a course that incorporates connectivistm as learning philosophy is that you'll be working with the affective (the emotional) as well as the cognitive domain. This means that you will be engaging the emotions (which is good for motivation). Connectivism also means that you can also encourage the sharing of experiences and allow people to build on prior knowledge and experience. In fact, building courses that allow students to scaffold their knowledge with experiential and prior learning can give rise to a very solid approach. Your students will be able to do more with the knowledge, particularly if the course has to do with applied knowledge and skills.

In this chapter, we will learn the following:

- How to launch a plan to create your learning site
- How Moodle's philosophy of connectivism creates conditions for learning
- The fundamental architecture of Moodle
- The way people learn with Moodle
- What makes Moodle unique

A plan to create your learning site

Whether you are the site creator or a course creator, you can use this book to develop a plan to build your courses and curriculum. As you work your way through each chapter, the book provides guidance on making decisions that meet your goals for your learning site. This helps you create the kind of learning experience that you want for your teachers (if you're the site creator) or students (if you're the teacher). You can also use this book as a traditional reference manual, but its main advantages are its step-by-step, project-oriented approach and the guidance it gives you about creating an interactive learning experience.

Moodle is designed to be intuitive to use, and its online help is well written. It does a good job of telling you how to use each of its features. What Moodle's help files don't tell you is when and why to use each feature and what effect it will have on the student experience, and that is what this book supplies.

One of the most exciting new developments with Moodle is that Moodle now has a cloud-based **virtual learning environment (VLE)**, which is called **MoodleCloud**. It is free for you to use if you have fewer than 50 registered users (students, instructors, and so on). You can still customize the course, and you can build in a great deal of flexibility and functionality. It does not have the same number of options as an on-premise local installation, but it saves a great deal of time and money. MoodleCloud allows you to experiment with designs and also to start small, with the intention of growing. It also makes it easy for individuals and organizations to develop new kinds of training, collaboration, and education, and then scale up when needed.

Step-by-step instructions to use Moodle

When you create a Moodle learning site, you usually follow a defined series of steps. This book is arranged to support that process. Each chapter shows you how to get the most from each step. Each step is listed with a brief description of the chapter that supports the step.

As you work your way through each chapter, your learning site will grow in scope and sophistication. By the time you finish this book, you should have a complete, interactive learning site. As you learn more about what Moodle can do and see your courses taking shape, you may want to change some of the things that you did in the previous chapters. Moodle offers you this flexibility. Also, this book helps you determine how those changes will cascade throughout your site.

Step 1 – Learning about the Moodle experience

Every **learning management system (LMS)** has a paradigm, or approach, that shapes the user experience and encourages a certain kind of usage. An LMS might encourage very sequential learning by offering features that enforce a given order on each course. It might discourage student-to-student interaction by offering few features that support it, while encouraging solo learning by offering many opportunities for the student to interact with the course material.

In this chapter, you will learn what Moodle can do and what kind of user experience your students and teachers will have, using Moodle. You will also learn about the Moodle philosophy and how it shapes the user experience. With this information, you'll be ready to decide how to make the best use of Moodle's many features and plan your online learning site.

Step 2 – Installing Moodle

Chapter 2, *Installing Moodle*, guides you through installing Moodle on your web server. It will help you estimate the amount of disk space, bandwidth, and memory that you will need for Moodle. This can help you decide the right hosting service for your needs.

Step 3 – Configuring your site

Most of the decisions you make while installing and configuring Moodle will affect the user experience. Not just students and teachers, but also course creators and site administrators are affected by these decisions. While Moodle's online help does a good job of telling you how to install and configure the software, it doesn't tell you how the settings that you choose affect the user experience. Chapter 3, *Configuring Your Site*, covers the implications of these decisions and helps you configure the site so that it behaves in the way you envision.

Step 4 – Creating the framework for your learning site

In Moodle, every course belongs to a category. Chapter 4, *Creating Categories and Courses*, takes you through creating course categories and then creating courses. Just as you chose site-wide settings during installation and configuration, you choose course-wide settings while creating each course. This chapter tells you the implications of the various course settings so that you can create the experience that you want for each course. It also shows you how to add teachers and students to the courses.

Step 5 – Making decisions about common settings

In Moodle, course material is either a resource or an activity. A resource is an item that the student views, listens to, reads, or downloads. An activity is an item that the student interacts with or that enables the student to interact with the teacher or other students. In Chapter 5, *Resources, Activities, and Conditional Access*, you will learn about the settings that are common to all resources and activities and how to add resources and activities to a course.

Step 6 – Adding basic course material

In most online courses, the core material consists of web pages that the students view. These pages can contain text, graphics, movies, sound files, games, exercises—anything that can appear on the **World Wide Web (WWW)** can appear on a Moodle web page. Chapter 6, *Adding Resources*, covers adding this kind of material, plus links to other websites, media files, labels, and directories of files. This chapter also helps you determine when to use each of these types of material.

Step 7 – Making your courses interactive

In this context, *interactive* means an interaction between the student and the teacher, or the student and an active web page. Student-to-student interaction is covered in a later chapter. This chapter covers activities that involve interaction between the student and an active web page, or between the student and the teacher. Interactive course material includes lessons that guide students through a defined path, based upon their answers to review question and the assignments that are uploaded by the student and then graded by the teacher. Chapter 7, *Adding Assignments, Lessons, Feedback, and Choices*, tells you how to create these interactions and how each of them affects the student and teacher experience.

Step 8 – Evaluating your students

In Chapter 8, *Evaluating Students with Quizzes*, you'll learn how to evaluate the students' knowledge with a quiz. The chapter thoroughly covers creating quiz questions, sharing quiz questions with other courses, adding feedback to questions and quizzes, and more.

Step 9 – Making your course social

Social course material enables student-to-student interaction. Moodle enables you to add chats and forums to your courses. These types of interactions will be familiar to many students. Chapter 9, *Getting Social with Chats and Forums*, shows you how to create and manage these social activities.

Step 10 – Adding collaborative activities

Moodle enables students to work together to create new material. For example, you can create glossaries that are site-wide and those that are specific to a single course. Students can add to the glossaries. You can also allow students to contribute to and edit a wiki in class.

Moodle also offers a powerful workshop tool, which enables the students to view and evaluate one another's work.

Each of these interactions makes the course more interesting but also more complicated for the teacher to manage. The result is a course that encourages the students to contribute, share, and engage. Chapter 10, *Collaborating with Wikis and Glossaries*, and Chapter 11, *Running a Workshop*, help you rise to the challenge of managing your students' collaborative work.

Step 11 – Managing and extending your courses

Chapter 12, *Groups and Cohorts*, shows you how to use groups to separate the students in a course. You will also learn how to use cohorts, or site-wide groups, to mass enroll students into courses.

Every block adds functionality to your site or your course. Chapter 13, *Extending Your Course by Adding Blocks*, describes many of Moodle's blocks, helps you decide which ones will meet your goals, and tells you how to implement them. You can use blocks to display calendars, enable commenting, enable tagging, show navigation features, and much more.

Step 12 – Taking the pulse of your course

Moodle offers several tools to help teachers administer and deliver courses. It keeps detailed access logs that enable the teachers to see exactly what content the students access, and when. It also enables the teachers to establish custom grading scales, which are available site-wide or for a single course. Student grades can be accessed online and can also be downloaded in a variety of formats (including spreadsheet). Finally, teachers can collaborate in special forums (bulletin boards) reserved just for them. This is a part of `Chapter 14`, *Features for Teachers*.

Applying the Moodle philosophy

Moodle is designed to support a style of learning called **social constructionism**. This style of learning is interactive. The social constructionist philosophy believes that people learn best when they interact with the learning material, construct new material for others, and interact with other students about the material. The difference between a traditional philosophy and the social constructionist philosophy is the difference between a lecture and a discussion.

Adding static content

Moodle does not require you to use the social constructionist method for your courses. However, it best supports this method. For example, Moodle enables you to add several kinds of static course material. This is the course material that a student reads but does not interact with, such as the following:

- Web pages
- Links to anything on the web (including material on your Moodle site)
- A folder of files
- A label that displays any text or image

Interactive and social course material

However, Moodle enables you to add even more kinds of interactive and social course material. This is the course material that a student interacts with, by answering questions, entering text, or uploading files, which includes the following:

- Assignment (uploading files to be reviewed by the teacher)
- Choice (a single question)
- Lesson (a conditional, branching activity)
- Quiz (an online test)

Creating activities

Moodle also offers activities in which the students interact with one another. These are used to create social course material, such as the following:

- Chat (live online chat between students)
- Forum (you can have none or several online bulletin boards for each course)
- Glossary (students and/or teachers can contribute terms to site-wide glossaries)
- Wiki (this is a familiar tool for collaboration with most younger students and many older students)
- Workshop (this supports peer review and feedback of the assignments that the students upload)

In addition, some of Moodle's add-on modules add even more types of interaction. For example, one add-on module enables the students and the teachers to schedule appointments with each other.

The Moodle experience

As Moodle encourages interaction and exploration, your students' learning experience will often be non-linear. Moodle can enforce a specific order upon a course, using something called **conditional activities**. Conditional activities can be arranged in a sequence. Your course can contain a mix of conditional and non-linear activities.

In this section, I'll take you on a tour of a Moodle learning site. You will see a student's experience from the time the student arrives at the site, enters a course, and works through some material in the course. You will also see some student-to-student interaction and some functions used by the teacher to manage the course. Along the way, I'll point out many of the features that you will learn to implement in this book and how the demo site is using those features.

The Moodle front page

The front page of your site is the first thing that most users will see. This section takes you on a tour of the front page of a demonstration site.

Probably, the best Moodle demo sites are `http://demo.moodle.net/` and `http://school.demo.moodle.net/`. Many of the screenshots in this book are from `http://school.demo.moodle.net`. The contents of that site are graciously offered by **Moodle Pty Ltd**, under the Creative Commons—Attribution-ShareAlike 3.0 Unported License.

Arriving at the site

When a visitor arrives at the demonstration learning site, the visitor sees the front page. You can require the visitor to register and log in before seeing any part of your site.

Alternatively, you can allow the anonymous visitor to see a lot of information about the site on the front page, which is what I have done in the following screenshot:

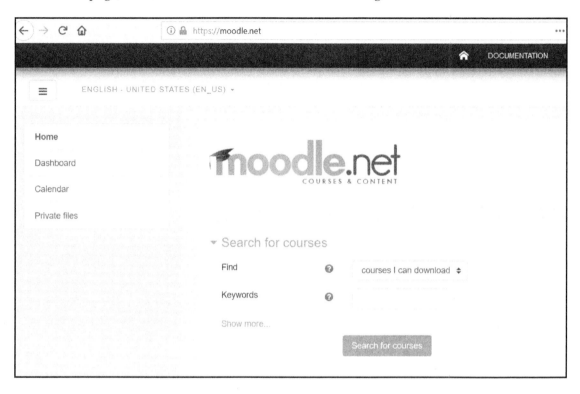

One of the first things that a visitor will note is that you can search for courses to download and use. You can enter keywords, and you'll be able to select from different options. For example, I entered the word literature, and I was able to find a number of modules that I can use in my courses. All I have to do is provide proper attribution. Several options are available, as seen in the following screenshot:

Using moodlecloud.com

Moodle has created a cloud-based Moodle, which allows you to set up courses, develop a *sandbox*, and launch the courses. It is located at `http://www.moodlecloud.com`, and, depending on the number of users, your cost can range from absolutely free to higher costs, seen as follows, and also as described on the information page at `https://moodlecloud.com/app/en/`:

- **Free**: It allows you to develop as many courses as you'd like and develop as many as 50 users. Your idle courses are not archived, so you need to log in often. Your account will be deleted if you do not access it regularly.

- **Starter**: It allows you to have the same number of users as the **Free** option, but you also have access to more applications such as document converters and certificate generators. However, you're limited with respect to themes and other utilities. It costs 80 AUD per year.

- **Moodle for School**: It has different levels and pricing, depending on the number of users and storage space. With packages that can scale up to 500 users, it's ideal for a small school, but does not work for a large school.

The main menu

Logging into MoodleCloud, note the **My new Moodle site** in the upper-left corner in the following screenshot. It includes **Dashboard**, **Site pages**, and **My courses**. It tells the user about the courses you have created and also those made available by Moodle. It includes **Introduction to Moodle**, which is an introductory guided tour that all new users should explore.

In Moodle, the icons tell the user what kind of resource will be accessed by a link. In this case, the icon tells the user that the first resource is a PDF (Adobe Acrobat) document and the second is a web page. Course material that a student observes or reads, such as web or text pages, hyperlinks, and multimedia files, is called **resources**. In Chapter 5, *Resources, Activities, and Conditional Access*, you will learn how to add resources to a course.

Blocks

In the side bars of the page, you will find **Blocks**. For example, the **Main menu**, **Calendar**, and **Tags** blocks. You can choose to add a block to the front page, to all the pages in the site, or to an individual course.

Other blocks display a summary of the current course, a list of courses available on the site, the latest news, who is online, and other information. At the bottom-right side of the front page, you see the **Login** block. Chapter 13, *Extending Your Course by Adding Blocks*, tells you how to use these blocks.

 Your site's front page is a course!—you can add these blocks to the front page of your site because the front page is essentially a course. Anything that you can add to a course, such as resources and blocks, can be added to the front page.

The site description

On the right-hand side of the front page, you see a **Site Description**. This is optional. If this were a course, you could choose to display the **Course Description**.

The **Site Description** or **Course Description** can contain anything that you can put on a web page. It is essentially a block of HTML code that is displayed on the front page.

Available courses

You can choose to display the available courses on the front page of your site. You can also customize the appearance of your front page. You can do that by clicking on **Dashboard** and then customizing the descriptions of the courses, and you can also indicate whether you want to make the default page your home page. If you do not, you can search for a different page and select it.

The following screenshot shows what your dashboard looks like after you've clicked on it and how to customize the descriptions:

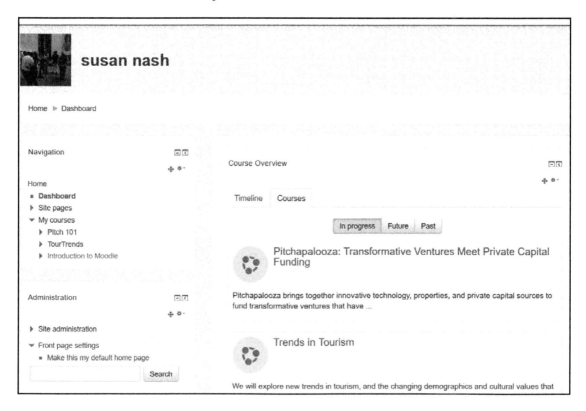

When a course is displayed in a list, clicking on the information icon next to a course displays its **Course Description** in a pop-up window. Clicking on a course's name takes you into the course. If the course allows anonymous access, you are taken directly into the course. If the course allows guest access or requires registration, you are taken to the login screen.

Inside a course

Now, let's take a look inside a course:

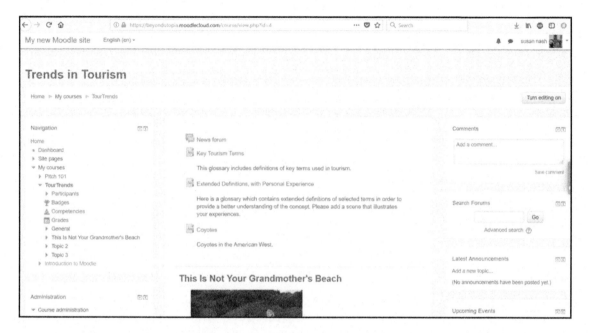

We will be examining the typical elements that you'll find in a course, starting with the navigation used to help you move through it. Then we'll look at blocks, sections, and the places where we can put content.

The navigation bar

In the preceding screenshot, the user has logged in as the **Administrator** and entered the **Trends in Tourism** course. Note the breadcrumbs trail (the **Navbar**) in the top-left corner of the screen, which tells us the name of the site and the short name of the course.

At the upper-right side of the screen, we see a confirmation that the user has logged in. That is not a part of the **Navbar**, but it usually appears next to it. There is also a box that allows you to turn on editing.

Blocks

Like the front page, this course uses various blocks. The most prominent one is the **Navigation** block on the left. Let's talk more about navigation.

The navigation block

The **Navigation** block shows you where you are and where you can go in the site. In the demonstration, you can see direct links to the topics in the course. This enables the student to jump to a topic that is much further down on the page, without scrolling.

At the bottom of the **Navigation** block is a link to the **My courses** page. If you click on each course link, you will see an outline of the main units in that course. It helps the student navigate quickly and easily.

We will cover how to create assignments in `Chapter 7`, *Adding Assignments, Lessons, Feedback, and Choices.*

Sections

Moodle enables you to organize a course by **Week**, in which case each section is labeled with a date instead of a number. Alternatively, you can choose to make your course a single, large discussion forum. Most courses are organized by **Topic**, such as the one seen in the next screenshot:

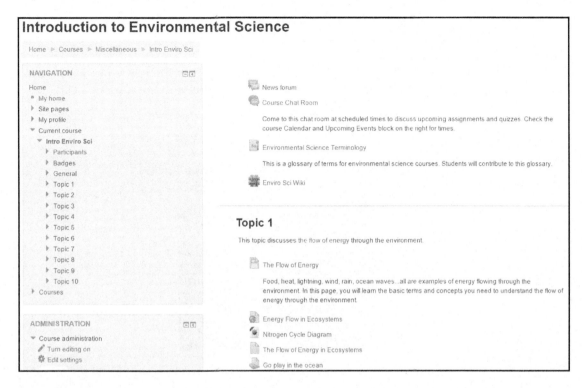

Note that the first topic is not numbered. Moodle allows you the first topic as the course introduction.

Teachers can hide and show sections at will. This enables a teacher to open and close resources and activities as the course progresses.

Topics are the lowest level of organization in Moodle. The hierarchy is **Site | Course Category | Course Subcategory (optional) | Course | Section**. Every item in your course belongs to a Topic, even if your course consists of only **Topic 0**.

Joining a discussion

Clicking on the link for any discussion takes the student into the forum. Clicking on a **Discussion** thread opens that thread in the forum. You can see, in the following screenshot, that the teacher started with the first post. Then, a student replied to the original post:

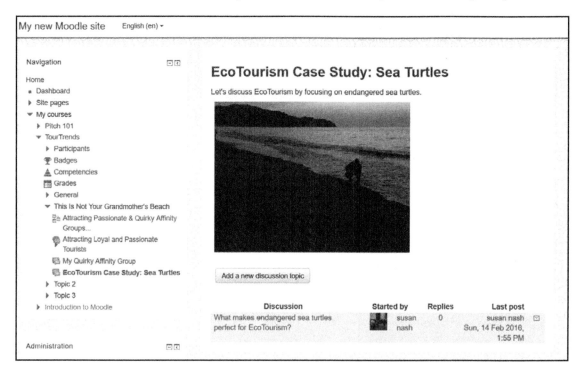

As Moodle supports an interactive, collaborative style of learning, students can also be given the ability to rate forum posts and the material submitted by other students. You'll find out more about forums in `Chapter 9`, *Getting Social with Chats and Forums*.

Completing a lesson

Next, the student will enter a workshop called **Attracting Passionate & Quirky Affinity Groups: Save the Sea Turtles, Stand-Up Paddleboarding, ZombieNights, and more.**

In this lesson, the learner works through different kinds of course materials and assessments. The lesson starts with an article and then includes a multichoice activity to assess the student's mastery. Note that they must go through the content in the proper sequence:

In this book, we will go through the creation of lessons as well as the individual components, which include Content and Activities. Note the online editor that the student uses to write the assignment. This gives the student basic **What You See Is What You Get (WYSIWYG)** features. The same word processor appears when the course creators create web pages, when students write online assignment entries, and at other times when a user is editing and formatting text.

Moodle can be configured to use several different kinds of editors. Depending upon your exact version and how your site administrator configures your site, yours might differ slightly from what is shown here.

Editing mode

We've been looking at Moodle from a student's perspective. Students usually don't edit course material. Let's see what happens when you turn on the editing mode to make changes.

Normal mode versus editing mode

When a Guest user or a registered student browses through your learning site, Moodle displays the pages normally. However, when someone with a course editing privilege enters a course, Moodle offers a button to switch into editing mode:

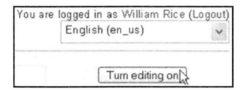

Clicking on **Turn editing on** puts Moodle into editing mode:

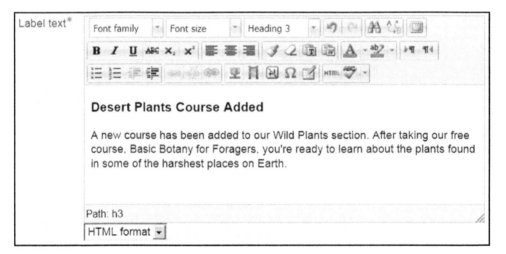

Let's walk through the icons that become available in editing mode.

The Edit icon

Clicking on the Edit icon enables you to edit whatever that icon follows. In this example, clicking on the Edit icon that follows the paragraph enables you to edit the section description. An example of a description is shown as follows:

Clicking on the Edit icon takes you into the editing window for that quiz. In that window, you can create, add, and remove quiz questions, change the grading scheme, and apply other settings to the quiz.

The Delete icon

Clicking on the Delete icon deletes whatever item the icon follows. If you want to remove an item from a course but are not sure whether you'll want to use it later, don't delete the item. Instead, hide it from view. Hiding and showing are explained in the next paragraph.

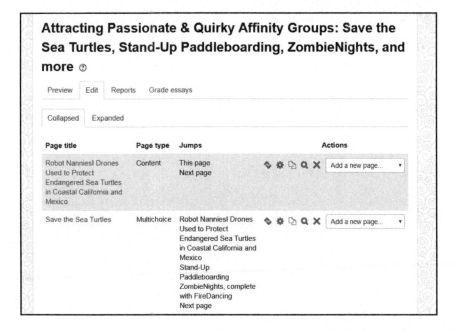

The Hidden/Shown icons

I call these the Hidden/Shown icons, instead of Hide/Show, because the icons indicate the current state of an item, instead of indicating what will happen when you click on them. The Hidden icon indicates that an item is hidden from the students.

Clicking on it shows the item to the students. The Show icon indicates that an item is shown to the students. Clicking on it hides the item from the students.

If you want to remove an item from a course while keeping it for later use, or if you want to keep an item hidden from students while you're working on it, hide it instead of deleting it.

The Group icons

The Group icons indicate what group mode has been applied to an item. Groups are explained in `Chapter 12`, *Groups and Cohorts*. For now, you should know that you can control access to items based upon which group a student belongs to. Clicking on these icons enables you to change that setting.

Resources and activities

The course material that a student observes or reads, such as web or text pages, hyperlinks, and multimedia files, are called **resources**. Course materials that a student interacts with, or that enables interaction among students and teachers, are called **activities**. Now, let's look at how to add some resources and activities to your Moodle site or course.

In editing mode, you can add resources and activities to a course. Moodle offers more activities than resources, such as chat, forum, quiz, wiki, and more.

Adding resources and activities

You add resources and activities using the drop-down menu that appears in editing mode, as seen in the following screenshot:

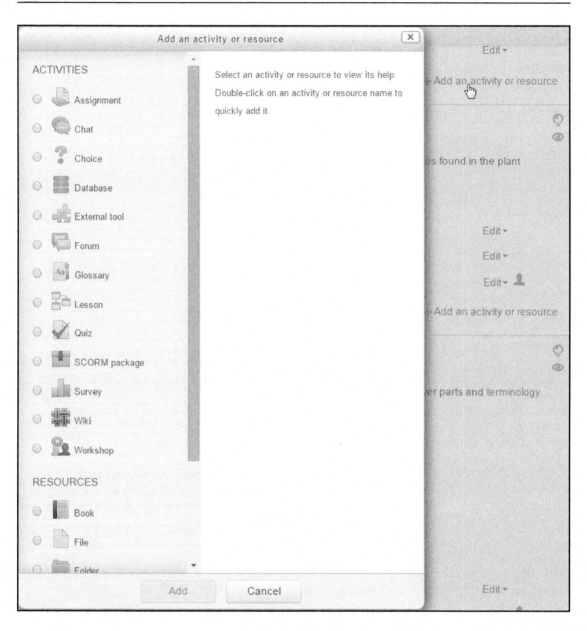

Selecting an item brings you to the editing settings page for that type of item. For example, selecting **URL** displays the window seen in the following screenshot. Note that you can do much more than just specify a hyperlink. You can give this link a user-friendly name, a summary description, open it in a new window, and more.

Every resource and activity that you add to Moodle has a description. This description appears when a student selects the item. Also, if the item appears in a list (for example, a list of all the resources in a course), the description will be displayed.

When building courses, you will spend most of your time in the **Edit settings** pages for the items that you add. You will find their behavior and appearance to be very consistent. The presence of a description is an example of that consistency. Another example is the presence of the help icon ⑦ next to the title of the window. Clicking on this icon displays an explanation of this type of item.

Also, the edit settings pages are divided into sections. Some sections are present for almost every resource and activity that you add. These sections are covered once in this book, to avoid repetition.

The administration menu

The contents of the **Administration** menu change depending upon who is logged in. For example, the next screenshot shows the **Administration** menu when a student is in one of our courses:

The following screenshot shows the teacher's view of the **Administration** menu:

The choices on this menu apply to the course itself. If a teacher, administrator, or course creator selects an activity or resource in the course, the user is taken inside that activity/resource. Then, the **Administration** submenu for that item will appear. In the example seen in the following screenshot, the teacher has selected an assignment and is looking at the **Administration** submenu for that assignment:

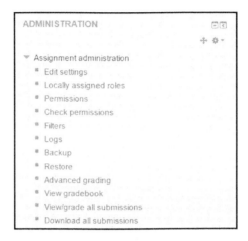

This short tour introduced you to the basics of the Moodle experience. The following chapters will take you through installing Moodle and creating courses. If you work through those chapters in order, you will discover many more features that are not mentioned in this tour. Also, because Moodle is open source, new features can be added at any time. Perhaps, you will be the one to contribute a new feature to the Moodle community.

The Moodle architecture

Moodle runs on any web server that supports the PHP programming language and a database. It works best, and there is more support, when running on the Apache web server with a MySQL database. These requirements—Apache, PHP, and MySQL—are common to almost all commercial web hosts, even the cheaper ones.

The Moodle learning management system resides in three places on your web host:

- The application occupies one directory, with many subdirectories for the various modules
- Data files that the students and teachers upload—such as photos and assignments submitted by students—reside in the Moodle data directory
- Course material that you create with Moodle (web pages, quizzes, workshops, lessons, and so on), grades, user information, and user logs reside in the Moodle database

The Moodle application directory

The following screenshot shows you my Moodle application directory. Without even knowing much about Moodle, you can guess the function of several of the directories.

For example, the `admin` directory holds the PHP code that creates the administrative pages, the `lang` directory holds translations of the Moodle interface, and the `mod` directory holds the various modules.

The `index.php` file is the Moodle home page. If a student was browsing my Moodle site, the first page that the student would read is the `http://moodle.williamrice.com/index.php` file.

As each of Moodle's core components and modules are in its own subdirectory, the software can be easily updated by replacing the old files with new ones. You should periodically check the `https://www.moodle.org` website for news about updates and bug fixes.

The Moodle data directory

Moodle stores the files uploaded by the users in a data directory. This directory should not be accessible to the general public over the web, that is, you should not be able to type in the URL for this directory and access it using a web browser. You can protect it either using a `.htaccess` file or by placing the directory outside of the web server's documents directory.

The Moodle database

While the Moodle data directory stores the files uploaded by students, the Moodle database stores most of the information in your Moodle site. The database stores objects that you create using Moodle. For example, Moodle enables you to create web pages for your courses. The actual HTML code for these web pages is stored in the database. Links that you add to a course, the settings, the content of forums and wikis, and quizzes created with Moodle, are all examples of data stored in the Moodle database.

The three parts of Moodle—the application, data directory, and database—work together to create your learning site. Backup and disaster recovery are obvious applications of this knowledge. However, knowing how the three parts work together is also helpful when upgrading, troubleshooting, and moving your site between servers.

Summary

Moodle encourages exploration and interaction among students and teachers. As a course designer and teacher, you will have the maximum number of tools at your disposal if you work with this tendency, which will make your learning experiences as interactive as possible. Creating courses with forums, peer-assessed workshops, surveys, and interactive lessons is more work than creating a course from a series of static web pages. However, it is also more engaging and effective, and you will find it worth the effort to use Moodle's many interactive features.

When teaching an online course in Moodle, remember that Moodle generally enables you to add, move, and modify course material on the fly. If it's permitted by your institution's policies, don't hesitate to change a course in response to student needs.

Keep in mind that if you're using the cloud-based virtual learning environment version of Moodle, MoodleCloud, you will have built-in options and may not be able to modify the course in the way you could if you had a custom or local (on-premise) installation.

Finally, learn the basics of Moodle's architecture, and at least read over the installation and configuration in Chapter 2, *Installing Moodle*. Don't be afraid of the technology. If you can master the difficult art of teaching, you can master using Moodle to its full potential.

2
Installing Moodle

Even if you don't install Moodle yourself, you should skim this chapter for information that will be helpful to you as a course manager and creator. This is because the choices made during Moodle's installation can affect how the system works for people who create, teach, and take courses on that system.

Installing Moodle requires you to secure space on a web server, create subdomains, unpack Moodle, create the data director, create the Moodle database, and select front page settings.

Each of these is covered in the following sections. In addition, at the end of this chapter, we will discuss MoodleCloud, which is a hosting service from the makers of Moodle, which has the advantage of being cloud-based and more of a virtual learning environment than simply a learning management system. While using a hosted solution is not for everyone, it is an ideal option for individuals, small organizations, and solution developers.

Installation step 1 – Requirements

Moodle is run from a web server if you prefer to use Moodle on-premise rather than cloud-based. You upload or place Moodle in your directory on the server. Usually, the server is someone's computer. If you're a teacher, or work in the corporate world, your institution might have its own web server. If you're an individual or have a small business, you will probably buy web-hosting services from another company. In either case, we are assuming that you have an account on a web server that offers Apache, PHP, and MySQL.

If you must install your own Apache web server and MySQL software, the easiest way to do so is to use another open source tool—XAMPP from http://www.apachefriends.org. Apache Friends is a non-profit project to promote the Apache web server. XAMPP is an easy, all-in-one installer that installs Apache, MySQL, PHP, and Perl. It is available for Linux, Windows, Mac, and Solaris. If you would like to create a test environment for Moodle, installing XAMPP onto your computer will install the web server with the components required to support a Moodle installation.

You can also download a package containing Moodle and the other software needed to make it run: Apache, MySQL, and PHP. Go to the official Moodle website (`https://moodle.org/`), and, under **DOWNLOADS**, look for installer packages. You can install Standard Moodle (requires a web server with PHP and a database), and you can add many plugins from the plugins directory. It's possible to download Moodle Mobile with the Moodle Mobile app, which you can also experience with Moodle Desktop. Moodle is open source under the GPL license, and you may download, use, and share it for free. Here's the site for downloads: `http://moodle.org/downloads`.

Hardware

It's a good idea to start with a smaller installation and as you gain confidence, you will be able to expand it.

Disk space

A fresh Moodle installation will occupy less than 200 MB of disk space, which is not much. However, it's better to budget for 5 GB because of plugins. The content that is added while the users create and take courses will probably grow larger than that. Base your decision on how much space to obtain upon the kinds of courses that you plan to deliver. If the courses contain mostly text and a few graphics, you'll need less space than if they contain music and video files. Also, consider the disk space occupied by files that the students will upload. Will the students upload small word processing files? Large graphics? Huge multimedia files? When determining how much disk space you will need, consider the size of the files that your courses will serve and that your students will submit. The size of files that can be uploaded is controlled by the site administrator using a setting under **Security** | **Site policies** | **Maximum uploaded file size**. It is also controlled by a setting on the web server that is hosting Moodle. The lower of these two settings—the Moodle setting and the server setting—determines the size of the files that can be uploaded through Moodle.

Bandwidth and data transfer limits

Moodle is a web-based product, so course content and assignments are added over the web. Whenever a reader or a user connects to a website, they're using bandwidth. When a user reads a page on your Moodle site, downloads a video, or uploads a paper, they use some of your bandwidth. The more courses, students, activities, and multimedia your Moodle site has, the more bandwidth you will use.

Most commercial hosting services have a limit of data transfer in their service. If your account uses more bandwidth or you transfer more data than what is allowed, some services will cut off your site's access. Others keep your site up, but automatically bill you for the additional bandwidth or data transfer. The second option is preferable in case of unexpected demand. When deciding upon a hosting service, find out how much bandwidth they offer and what they do if you exceed that limit.

In the tip below, consider hosting your videos on YouTube or Vimeo to avoid having to use up server space and bandwidth, which can be expensive.

Are you serving videos with your course?

If your course includes many videos, or if you'll be serving videos to many users, that can use up a lot of the bandwidth that your hosting company provides. Instead of hosting those videos on your Moodle server, consider hosting them on a dedicated video hosting site like http://www.vimeo.com or http://www.youtube.com. Then, you can just embed them in your Moodle page. Vimeo, YouTube, or whoever hosts the video will take care of the bandwidth.

Memory

It is recommended that you use a 2 GHz dual core or more processor. Although you can potentially get started with 1 GB of memory, 8 GB or more is a good idea, especially on a production server. For the best possible performance, visit Moodle's page that contains the latest recommendations for hardware as well as software. Detailed recommendations can be found at https://docs.moodle.org/34/en/Performance_recommendations.

Ensuring minimum prerequisites

Check with your hosting service to ensure that you will be given the following minimum prerequisites:

- Enough disk space for the Moodle software, your course material, and the files that the students will upload.
- FTP access to your server.
- Enough bandwidth to serve your course files and for the students to upload their files.
- PHP version 7.

- The ability to create at least one database or to have it created for you.
- The ability to create at least one database user or to have it created for you.
- Enough shared or dedicated memory to run Moodle's automated backup routines. You may not know how much that is until you've tried it.

When you can confirm that you have those items, you are ready to proceed with the installation.

Many hosting services also offer automated installation of Moodle. Search for hosting services using the terms *fantastico* and *moodle*, or *one-click install* and *moodle*. These are usually shared hosting services, so you will have the same performance limitations as if you installed Moodle yourself on a shared host. However, they simplify the installation and thus provide a fast and inexpensive way to get a Moodle site up and running.

Automated installations are not always the latest version. Also, they often limit the ability to install additional plugins and to customize your site. Check with your hosting company about when they roll out new versions and the limits on customizing it.

 You should also research the services offered by the official Moodle partners. You can find out more about Moodle partners on http://www.moodle.com (note the .com and not .org address).

Installation step 2 – Subdomain or subdirectory?

A subdomain is a web address that exists under your web address and acts like an independent site. For example, my website is www.williamrice.com. This is a standard website, not a Moodle site. I could have a subdomain, http://www.moodle.williamrice.com, to hold a Moodle site. This subdomain would be like an independent site. However, it exists on the same server, under the same account, and they both count toward the disk space and the bandwidth that I use.

In this example, Moodle is installed in the http://www.moodle.williamrice.com subdomain.

Using a subdomain offers you several advantages. Having a site to test updates and add-ons may be helpful if uninterrupted service is important to you. Later, you'll see how easy it is to copy a Moodle installation to a different location, change a few settings, and have it work. If you want to do this, ensure that the hosting service you choose allows subdomains.

If you want to keep things simpler, you can install Moodle into a subdirectory of your website. In the next step, you will see how Moodle can automatically install itself into a subdirectory called /moodle. This is very convenient, and you'll find a lot of websites with Moodle running in the /moodle subdirectory.

 Decide if you want to install Moodle into a subdirectory or a subdomain. If you choose a subdomain, create it now. If you choose a subdirectory, you can create it later, while uploading the Moodle software.

Installation step 3 – Getting and unpacking Moodle

Get Moodle from the official website, http://www.moodle.org/. Go to the **Moodle downloads** page and select the version and format that you need.

Choosing a Moodle version

For a new installation, the *latest stable branch* is usually your best choice. The *last build* information tells you when it was last updated with a bug fix or a patch. This is usually irrelevant to you; the version number determines which features you get, not the build time.

For a production server, do not use the standalone packages mentioned earlier. They are insecure, because they are meant for use by a Moodle developer for experimentation and development. To make the development of a site easier and faster, security settings that would slow down development have been turned off by default. Standalone packages are a good choice if you want to experiment or develop a Moodle site on your local (non-networked) computer.

For a production site, instead of the standalone packages, use the latest stable branch.

The quick way – Upload and unzip

Moodle is downloaded as a single, compressed file. This compressed file contains the many small files and directories that constitute Moodle. After downloading the compressed file, you can decompress (or unzip) the file. Unzipping it on your local PC will extract many files and directories that you must place on your server.

If you're using a hosting service, they may have the ability to decompress the file on the server. If so, you can just upload the entire ZIP file, tell the server to decompress it, and all your Moodle files will be in place. This is much faster than decompressing the ZIP file on your computer and uploading the many files that it creates.

Uploading and decompressing the ZIP file on the server

1. Go to `http://www.moodle.org/` and download the Moodle package (ZIP or TAR file) to your local hard drive.
2. Upload the file to your hosting service. You may wish to pull the code from the Git repository, which is the best option for developers because it makes upgrading very easy. Here is code:

   ```
   $ git clone -b MOODLE_{{Version3}}_STABLE
   git://git.moodle.org/moodle.git
   ```

3. Secure the Moodle files. Ensure that your files are not writeable by the web server user.
4. If your hosting service gives you the option to create a new directory for the unzipped files (*Create subdirectory* in the preceding example), you can select not to do so. Moodle's compressed file will automatically create a subdirectory called `moodle` for the unzipped files.

Installation step 4 – Creating an empty database

Create a new, empty database for your installation. Refer to moodle.org for updated information, and as you do so, you will need to find and make a note of your database server hostname, username, and password for use during the final installation stage:

- dbhost: This is the database server hostname. It is usually localhost if the database and web server are the same machine, or it can be the name of the database server.
- dbname: This is the database name. It is usually moodle.
- dbuser: This is the username for the database. Use what you assigned, which is usually moodleuser. Be sure not to use the root/superuser account. Create an account with the minimum permissions needed.
- dbpass: This is the password for the moodleuser.

If your site is hosted, you should find a web-based administration page for databases as part of the control panel (or ask your administrator). For everyone else, or for detailed instructions, refer to the page for your chosen database server:

- PostgreSQL (recommended)
- MariaDB (recommended)
- MySQL
- MS SQL

On your server, create a directory to hold the Moodle data. This can be a directory outside of the Moodle directory or a subdirectory.

Installation step 5 – Creating the (moodledata) data directory

While the Moodle data directory stores files uploaded by students and some larger files, the Moodle database stores most of the information in your Moodle site. By default, the installer uses the moodle database name and the moodleuser username. Using these default settings gives any hacker a head start on breaking into your site. When creating your database, change these to something less common. At least make the hackers guess the name of your database and the database username.

You should also choose a strong password for the Moodle database user. The following are some recommendations for strong passwords:

- Include at least one number, one symbol, one uppercase letter, and one lowercase letter
- Make the password at least 12 characters long
- Avoid repetition, dictionary words, letter or number sequences, and anything based on biographical information about yourself

You will need to create the Moodle database and the database user before you run Moodle's installation routine; otherwise, the installation process will stop until you create the required database.

Creating the database

Moodle can use several types of databases. The recommended type is MySQL. There are many ways to create a database. If you are using a shared hosting service, you may have access to phpMyAdmin. You can use this to create the Moodle database and the database user.

For detailed instructions, refer to `https://docs.moodle.org/34/en/Installing_Moodle#Requirements`.

Installation step 6 – Installing Moodle

Configuration settings and variables tell Moodle where the database is located, what the database is called, the database user and password, the web address of the Moodle system, and other necessary information. All of these configuration settings must be correct for Moodle to run. They are stored in a file called `config.php` in Moodle's home directory.

The next step is to run the installer to create the database tables and configure your new site.

Moodle recommends using the command-line installer. If this does not work and you need another way (for example, on a Windows server), you can use the web-based installer.

To run the command-line installer, start by running the command line. It should be as your system's web user. Ensure that you know what it is—refer to your system's documentation (for example, Ubuntu/Debian is www-data and Centos is apache)

Here's an example of using the command line as root—substitute www-data for your web user:

```
# chown www-data /path/to/moodle
 # cd /path/to/moodle/admin/cli
 # sudo -u www-data /usr/bin/php install.php
 # chown -R root /path/to/moodle
```

The chown commands allow the script to write a new config.php file. More information about the options can be found using this:

```
# php install.php --help
```

You will be asked for other settings, but all you have to do is to accept the defaults.

For a full discussion, check out **Administration via command line** at https://docs. moodle.org/34/en/Installing_Moodle#Requirements.

Web-based installer

For ease of use, you can install Moodle via the web. Configure your web server so that the page cannot be accessible to the public until the installation is complete.

To run the web installer script, just go to your Moodle's main URL using a web browser.

The installation process will take you through a number of pages. Along the way, you should be asked to confirm the copyright, observe the database tables as they are generated, supply administrator account details, and supply the site details. The database creation can take some time—prepare to be patient. You should eventually end up at the Moodle front page with an invitation to create a new course.

You should prepare to download the new config.php file and upload it to your Moodle installation—just follow the onscreen instructions.

Installation step 7 – Final configuration

Take a look at the settings within Moodle and review the options within the **Moodle Site administration** screens (accessible from the **Site administration** tab in the **Administration** block).

You will be able to include plugins and set up email and authentication:

- **Administration** | **Site administration** | **Plugins** | **Message outputs** | **Email**: Set your SMTP server and authentication if required (so that your Moodle site can send emails). The support contact for your site is also set on this page.
- **Administration** | **Site administration** | **Server** | **System paths**: Set the paths to du, dot, and aspell binaries.
- **Administration** | **Site administration** | **Server** | **HTTP**: If you are behind a firewall, you may need to set your proxy credentials in the **Web proxy** section.
- **Administration** | **Site administration** | **Location** | **Update timezones**: Run this to ensure that your time zone information is up to date.

If you have any problems along the way, it's a good idea to visit Moodle's Installation FAQ. It is quite complete, and it is maintained so that it responds to users' commonly encountered issues. You can find it at https://docs.moodle.org/34/en/Installation_FAQ.

This is for version 3.4.

It is important to keep in mind that Moodle updates are accompanied by updated Moodle doc pages.

MoodleCloud basics

MoodleCloud is a cloud-based solution that allows you to create your own account and start building courses and working with students for free (for upto 50 users). MoodleCloud allows you to develop an unlimited number of courses and activities, so it makes a very nice *sandbox*. It's important to keep in mind that there are several companies that offer hosting for Moodle. What makes MoodleCloud different is the fact that it was developed by the makers of Moodle and always has the latest, most stable version.

Getting started with MoodleCloud

The first step is to create a new account. Go to the `https://moodlecloud.com/en/signup/ chooseuser?plan=free` and click on **Create new account**. Refer to the following screenshot:

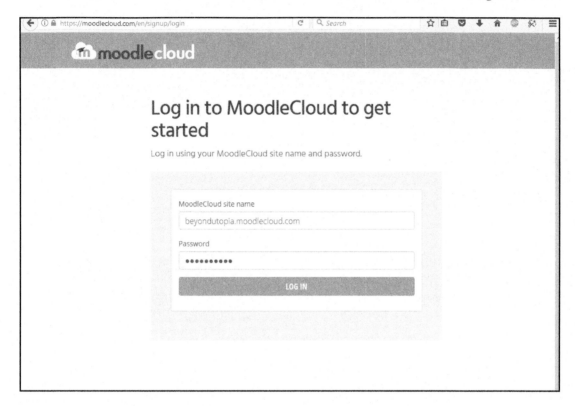

After you've created an account, you can choose a plan with MoodleCloud that accommodates the number of users you plan to have and how you'll need to organize your content. Keep in mind that with MoodleCloud, you have no limits with the number of courses you can develop.

MoodleCloud options

After you've set up your account, you'll have a number of options as you think of the universal settings you'll need for your courses.

There are several different plans, each of which gives you more users, access to plug-in packages, and the ability to automatically generate customizable certificates.

There are a number of things to consider:

- Storage is limited (200 MB to 1 GB), which means that you will need to host your media in the cloud and link or embed a player
- Certificates are only available with the paid plans
- Plugin options are limited with the free plan
- Users are limited with the free plan

Following is an image showing the various plans offered:

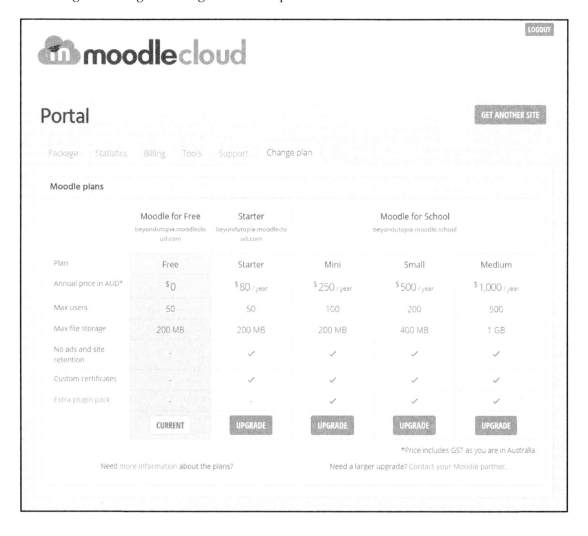

MoodleCloud can be an excellent solution if you're trying out Moodle for the first time or you need to experiment. It's also ideal for organizations that are using Moodle in innovative ways, such as event planning and project management.

Summary

From here, you can create user accounts, configure your site, add content to your site's front page and create courses.

You can do these in any order, but I usually use the order presented in this chapter. Also, don't be intimidated into thinking that they must be perfect the first time. They can be changed and edited at any time. So, start with whatever you're most comfortable with, develop some momentum, and build your learning site.

In the next chapter, we'll cover how to configure your site to create the kind of environment and experience that you want.

Configuring Your Site

3

Many settings that are made after the installation process affect the student and teacher experience in Moodle when they use the site. The focus of this chapter is on helping you create the user experience that you want by choosing the right settings. By configuring your site to enhance the user experience, you'll enhance their learning experience as well. In this chapter, you will learn how to configure your Moodle site. Specifically, we will learn how to set permissions, select default options, enable site administration, configure permissions, and enroll students.

Note that in this book I will be using the MoodleCloud *clean* theme, although I will demonstrate other themes as well, particularly *boost*, since it is a default. The right column can be configured to add a block, such as a calendar.

Here's a screenshot using the MoodleCloud clean theme showing the front page, with the navigation bar on the left and available courses in the center:

Being mindful of user experience

As you prepare to consider your user experience, take a moment to reflect on how the user experience affects the student's ability to learn. You'll want to keep the learning objectives and outcomes first and foremost in the learner's mind. Then, you'll want to ensure that you clearly map the learning objectives to the course content, activities, and assessment. They need to make sense, and your learner should have an idea of how the activity or content will lead to the ability to perform the task and demonstrate skill or mastery.

An easy way to maintain mindfulness of the user experience is to think of the mnemonic **CORN**:

C Clear: Your outcomes should be clear, as should the process of working through the course. Think of a map and how it guides one to a final destination. A clear map contains just the right amount of information, is not superfluous, and provides help when needed.

O Outcome-focused: Ensure that you're always tied to the learning outcomes, which are clearly stated at the outset. Then, ensure that each unit or module also contains objectives. Also ensure that you organize your course in a way that provides sufficient scaffolding so that the sequence makes sense.

R Relevant: Although it can be interesting to include materials or activities that are not totally related to the course as *enrichment*, keep in mind that you could confuse or derail the student. The material should tie directly to the learning outcomes and should help students successfully complete the assessments. Likewise, the assessments need to be relevant and meaningful.

N Needs-based: Provide the tools your students need to be able to perform their tasks. Also, ensure that their learning preferences are acknowledged and you're focused on meeting their needs. A prime determinant of user satisfaction is the degree to which the student feels in charge of their own destiny, something that requires one to develop a high degree of self-efficacy and an "I can do it!" attitude. Further, to motivate your students, you'll need to satisfy their needs. They may need a sense of recognition, and so building in rewards and recognition will be part of the way you configure your site.

In this chapter, we're focusing on the settings. Later, we'll go into more depth about how to design and arrange the content, activities, and assessments.

In all of these, you have choices.

Many of the choices in settings that you make will be easy to decide. For example, will you allow your users to select their own time zone? Other choices are not so obvious. You can spend a lot of time trying different settings to see how they affect the user experience. These are the settings that we will focus on in this chapter. The goal is to save you time by showing you the effects that key settings will have on your site.

 If your system administrator or webmaster has installed Moodle for you, you may be tempted to just accept the default configuration and skip this chapter. Don't do that!

Even if you did not install Moodle or are using MoodleCloud instead of Moodle on-premise, we encourage you to read the configuration sections in this chapter. If you want, work with your system administrator to select the settings that you want. Your administrator can create a site administrator account that you can use for configuring Moodle, or they can make these configuration settings for you.

On-premise versus MoodleCloud

This chapter primarily focuses on an on-premise installation that is fully customizable. However, what if you're using MoodleCloud, Moodle's cloud-based solution? The good news is that MoodleCloud is extremely customizable, and you will have a great deal of flexibility in the site administration area of the course.

MoodleCloud (http://www.moodlecloud.com) is very economical and is a perfect site for teachers, instructional designers, and instructional technologists to develop templates, try out new designs, and pilot an entirely new curriculum or approach. In MoodleCloud, there is no limit to the number of courses you can set up. Your only limitation is the number of active users. Moodle is free for up to 50 users. After that, the pricing increases based on the number of users. For the free version, you will need to allow ads to appear.

MoodleCloud is cloud-based, as the name indicates, and so you do not have to install anything on your computer or on a server. You will need the latest versions of your browser (Chrome, Internet Explorer, Firefox, and Safari). Ensure that cookies are enabled for your site. MoodleCloud has been designed to be very efficient, and it is also responsive.

One advantage of MoodleCloud is that you always have the latest version of Moodle, and when new capabilities emerge, you will be able to use them. For example, you are now able to configure your courses to be compatible with smartphones as well as with tablets, laptops, and computers, for a truly mobile solution.

A potential disadvantage of MoodleCloud is that you do not have the same number of design options because there is a limited number of built-in themes, as opposed to an on-premise solution.

Even though there are a few limitations, MoodleCloud includes features that are valuable to all designers, and you can add a wide array of multimedia resources and activities that include assessment and automatic badge and certificate generation.

Preparing to experiment

While this chapter describes the effects of different configuration choices, there is no substitute for experiencing them yourself. Don't be afraid to experiment with different settings.

You can try the following method:

1. While installing Moodle, you created an account for the site administrator. Now, create test accounts for at least one teacher and three students.
2. Install three different browsers in your computer; for example, Firefox, Chrome, and Internet Explorer.
3. In the first browser, log in as an administrator. Use this account to experiment with the settings that you read about here.
4. In the second browser, go to your site as a teacher. Each time you change a configuration setting, refresh the teacher's browser and observe the change to see how the teacher version of it works.
5. In the third browser, go to your site as a student. Each time you change a configuration setting, refresh the student's browser and observe how it changes the student's experience.

Instructions for each of these tasks are discussed in detail in the following sections.

Creating test accounts

These instructions begin where the installation ended—with you at the home page of your new site, logged in as the administrative user.

To create test accounts for your site, do the following:

1. Before you go into Moodle, launch your note pad or a blank email. You'll use this to take notes.
2. If you're not logged in as the administrative user, log in now. Use the **Login** link in the upper-right corner of the page.
3. You should be looking at the home page of your new Moodle site now.
4. In the **Administration** menu on the left of the page, click on **Site administration**. This expands the **Site administration** menu.
5. Click on **Users** and then on **Accounts**.
6. Click on **Add a new user**. Moodle displays the **Add a new user** page.

7. The following table gives information to help you decide how to fill out each field on this page. Some fields are required. Moodle indicates those fields with a red asterisk:

Field	Notes
Username	For the username, you may find it easiest to use the role that you are testing, so create usernames such as `teacher1`, `teacher2`, `student1`,...`student4`, and such.
Choose an authentication method	For your test accounts, this should be set to **Manual accounts**.
New password	Use your institution's password policy. To ensure that you type the password correctly, click on the **Unmask** checkbox. This enables you to see the password as you type it. In MoodleCloud, it is automatically unmasked.
Force password change	For your test accounts, leave this blank.
First name and Surname	By default, when Moodle lists users, it sorts them by name. Often, it is convenient to have your test accounts appear next to each other in the list of users. Also, if they are at the top of the list, you don't need to scroll or search to find them. For your test users, consider using a last name like `AATest`, which will put them at the top of the list with just one click.
Email address	The email address of every user in Moodle must be unique, so if you are creating six test accounts, you will need six different email addresses.
Email display	Do you want other users on your site to see the email address for this test account? For a test account, set this to **Hide my email address from everyone**, unless you have a good reason for your students to know the email address of your test accounts. Also, you don't want a real student to get confused and email a test teacher account instead of their real teacher.
Email activated	You want your test account to receive emails while you are developing courses, so set this to **This email address is enabled**.
Email format	To test how your site sends emails, you can set your odd-numbered users to pretty HTML format and your even-numbered users to plain text format.

Field	Notes
Email digest type	When a user is subscribed to a forum, Moodle usually sends that user emails about new forum postings. This setting determines how often those emails are sent and what they contain. For testing, leave this to **No digest**. That way, you'll know within a few minutes whether a forum is sending out messages like it should. If your test user starts getting a lot of messages from a forum, you may want to set this to a daily email.
Forum auto-subscribe and Forum tracking	For testing, you can leave these settings to **Yes**. If your test user starts getting a lot of messages from a lot of forums, you may want to set one or both of them to **No**, and then unsubscribe the test user from those forums.
When editing text	To test the behavior of Moodle's HTML editor, you can leave this to **Use HTML editor**.
AJAX and JavaScript	You should find out from your IT department whether the users in your organization have these enabled in their browsers.
Screen reader	For some functions, Moodle offers an interface that is more accessible for sight-impaired users. If you are testing your site for a visually impaired user, set this to **Yes** for one of your test accounts.
City/town and Select a country	These fields are required. If you use names that sound real for your test accounts, consider giving your test accounts a fictional city, like `Testville`. It may make it easier to find the test accounts later.
Timezone	This determines what time is displayed to the user.
Preferred language	This determines what language Moodle uses for its interface. There is a site-wide setting that allows and forbids users to select their own language. If you plan to allow users to select their own language, their selection will overwrite what you choose here.
Description	Most sites allow users to enter their own description in their user profile. You can enter a starting description here. MoodleCloud also offers a chance to upload a profile picture. Gravatar is enabled on MoodleCloud, which will automatically search for an image. Your users can create their own Gravatar that will follow them (similar to how Google profile images appear on all Google applications).

8. The remaining user fields are self-explanatory. Usually, they are filled out by the user.

9. In your notes, take note of the user's username, password, and email address; you'll need these later.

10. At the bottom of the page, click on the **Update profile** button. This saves the profile.

11. Repeat this for each of your test users. When you finish, you will see them listed under **Administration** | **Site administration** | **Users** | **Accounts** | **Browse list of users**:

Installing several browsers

You cannot log into Moodle with two different usernames from the same browser, at the same time. For example, if you want to log in as both `teacher1` and `student1`, you can't do that from the same browser; you need two separate browsers or browser sessions.

Consider installing several browsers on your computer to enable you to log in as several different users at once. For example, you can install the following:

- **Firefox**: Use this as the site administrator
- **Opera**: Use this as a teacher
- **Chrome**: Use this as a student

Also, don't forget Safari and Internet Explorer.

Teaching you how to install these browsers is beyond the scope of this book.
The following table lists the websites where you can get these browsers. If your
organization has your computers secured so that you cannot install your own software, you
will need their help to install more browsers:

Browser	Source	Suitable OS
Firefox	`http://www.mozilla.com`	Windows Macintosh Linux
Opera	`http://www.opera.com/`	Windows Macintosh Linux
Chrome	`http://www.google.com/chrome`	Windows Macintosh Linux
Safari	`http://www.apple.com/safari/`	Windows Macintosh
Internet Explorer Microsoft Edge	`http://www.microsoft.com/windows/internet-explorer/` `https://www.microsoft.com/en-us/windows/microsoft-edge`	Windows

Exploring the site administration menu

After installing Moodle, I like to set some basic configuration options. Some of these
settings determine how the site functions, such as how users are authenticated, what
statistics the site keeps, and which modules are turned off and on. Other settings just affect
the user experience, such as which languages are available, the color scheme, and what is
displayed on the front page. All these settings are available through the **Site administration**
menu. The MoodleCloud **Site administration** menu is similar, but it also includes a setting
for the mobile application so that your users can easily use their phones or tablets. If your
on-premise installation does not include the **Mobile App** menu, ensure that you select a
Theme that is responsive, which means it will work on all devices automatically.

To access the **Site administration** menu, you must be logged-in as an administrative user. Under the **Administration** menu, click on **Site administration** to expand the menu:

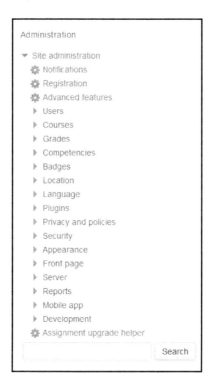

In this chapter, on configuring your site, we'll cover some of the settings under the **Site administration** menu. Others will be covered as we build our courses, teach, calculate grades, and update our site.

 The important idea here is that unlike many other applications, in Moodle, the **Site administration** menu isn't something that you *set and forget*. You return to the configuration settings as your site develops.

Now, let's go through the settings you use to configure your site for the kind of user experience that you want to create.

Configuring authentication methods

Authentication is what happens when a user is logging into your site. When a user is created, an authentication method must be chosen for that user. This can be changed for the user later.

Moodle offers a variety of ways to authenticate users. You'll find them under **Administration** | **Site administration** | **Plugins** | **Authentication** | **Manage authentication**. Each of the options is briefly explained by clicking on **Settings** for that option:

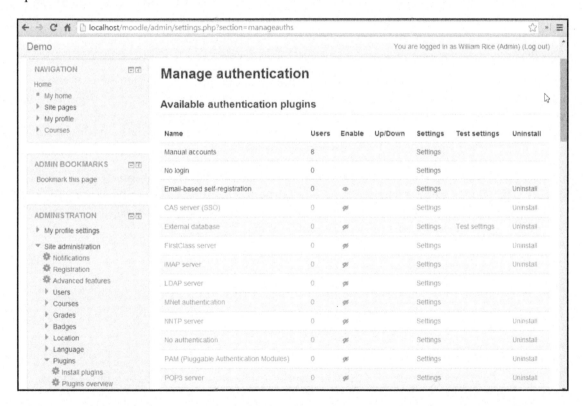

The following subsection will fill in some key information to make it easier for you to work with these authentication methods.

Manual accounts and no login methods

In the preceding screenshot, which shows the authentication methods, note that two methods cannot be disabled: **Manual accounts** and **No login**. These methods are always available to the site administrator.

Manual accounts enables the administrator to create user accounts. You used this method to create your test users.

Even if you are authenticating against an external database, you can still use this method to create users. For example, suppose your company or school uses Moodle and authenticates against your organization's IMAP email server. Since everyone at your organization has an email account, this ensures that your colleagues, and only your colleagues, have accounts in Moodle.

However, what if you have a guest or a consultant teaching one of your courses? If your organization doesn't want to give that person an official email address at your organization, then the guest teacher won't have an entry in the IMAP server. In that case, you can manually create the guest's account in Moodle. Their account will exist only in Moodle and will not be checked against the IMAP (or other) server.

 No login enables the administrator to suspend a user's account. Suspending a user takes away that person's ability to log in but keeps all the work that the person did in the system, such as their blog and grades. Deleting a user removes the account and the user's data.

Manually creating a new user

If you created test accounts at the beginning of this chapter, you manually created user accounts. Follow the instructions under the *Creating test accounts* section.

Suspending a user's account

The end result of this procedure is that the user's authentication method is changed to *no login*:

1. From the Administration menu on the left of the page, click on **Site administration** | **Users** | **Accounts** | **Browse list of users**. The **Users** page is displayed. On this page, you will search for the user.
2. In the **New filter** area, enter all or part of the user's name.

3. Click on the **Add filter** button. The user appears in the list at the bottom of the page.

4. Next to the user's name, click on the **Suspend user account** icon. If you are unsure of which icon that is, hover over the icons until you see the name displayed, as seen in the following screenshot:

Enabling email-based self-registration

This method enables people to register themselves at your site. When someone fills out the new user form at your site, Moodle sends them an email to confirm their account.

You must turn on email-based self-registration in two places.

To enable email-based self-registration, follow the given steps:

1. Under **Administration** | **Site administration** | **Plugins** | **Authentication** | **Manage authentication**, click to open the eye for **Email-based self-registration**:

Manage authentication

Available authentication plugins

Name	Users	Enable	Up/Down	Settings	Test settings	Uninstall
Manual accounts	31			Settings		
No login	0					
MoodleCloud	1	👁	↓			
Email-based self-registration	0	👁	↑	Settings		
LTI	0	⌀				
MNet authentication	0	⌀		Settings	Test settings	
No authentication	0	⌀		Settings		
OAuth 2	0	⌀		Settings		
Shibboleth	0	⌀		Settings	Test settings	
Web services authentication	0	⌀				

Please choose the authentication plugins you wish to use and arrange them in order of failthrough.
Changes in table above are saved automatically.

2. On the same page, further down, for the **Self registration** drop-down list, select **Email-based self-registration**.
3. If you want to increase the security of your site, under the **Settings** for **Email-based self-registration**, enable the **reCAPTCHA** function.
4. At the bottom of the page, click on the **Save Changes** button.
5. Return to the **Manage Authentication** page.
6. If you want to limit self-enrollment to only people at your company or school, consider using the **Allowed email domains** function further down on this page. This will restrict self-enrolment to people who have an email address from your company or school.

Authenticating against an external source

Moodle can look to a different database, or another server, to determine whether a user can log in. This is called **authenticating against an external source**. In the following screenshot, the authentication method for an LDAP server is being enabled:

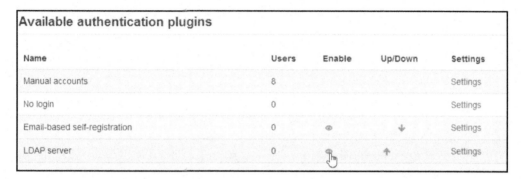

External databases and external servers have some things in common; we'll look at these common features and how to use them for authenticating your users.

Connecting to an external database or server

When you choose to authenticate against an external database, you must tell Moodle how to connect to that database. To get to these settings, click on the **Settings** link for the source.

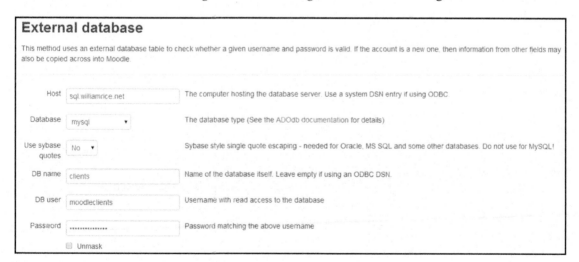

The exact settings that you need to connect are a little different for each type of database. The best way to obtain the information that you need is to ask the administrator of the database that you want to authenticate against. You can take a screenshot of the **Settings** page for the authentication method and send it to the database administrator.

What happens when users are deleted from the external database?

When you authenticate with an external source, by default, each time a person logs in, Moodle looks to the external source for that person's username and password. If the username is removed from the external source, Moodle can do one of the following actions:

- **Keep the user active in Moodle**: This means that although the person was removed from the external source, they can still log in because their profile and login information is still in the Moodle database
- **Suspend the user in Moodle**: The person's records will still be in Moodle, but they cannot log in
- **Delete the user from Moodle**: The person's records will be completely deleted from Moodle

This is controlled by the **Removed ext user** setting:

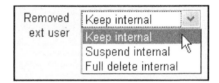

This is an important decision, because you are deciding how Moodle will handle people who have left your organization. **Suspend internal** is the safest option.

For example, suppose you are authenticating Moodle users with your company's human resources database. When a person leaves your organization, that person is removed from the email server. Do you still want that person to be able to log into Moodle? Do you want to suspend their account, but keep a record of everything they did in Moodle, or do you want to completely delete that person's records from Moodle? You should work with your system administrator to make this decision and select the right option for your organization.

What happens when usernames are changed in the external database?

After Moodle checks an external source and determines that a user has access, Moodle creates an account for that user in the Moodle database. Although Moodle looks to the external source for the username and password, records for the user's activity are kept in Moodle. The user's grades, blog entries, history and so on, are all kept in Moodle, under that person's username.

If the username changes in the external source, there will be no connection between the old username in Moodle and the new username in the external source. For example, if you changed a person's username in your external database from `jsmith1` to `jsmith2`, Moodle would not know that the `jsmith2` in your external database is the old `jsmith1`. When the user logs in to Moodle for the first time with their new username, `jsmith2`, Moodle will create a new account for that username. The account for `jsmith1` will still be in Moodle, but it will not be used.

 When changing a person's username in your external source, if you want to keep their records in Moodle synchronized with their new username, you should also change their username in Moodle.

To change a username in Moodle, perform these steps:

1. From the **Administration** menu on the left of the page, click on **Site administration | Users | Accounts | Browse list of users**. The **Users** page is displayed, and you will search for the user on this page.
2. In the **New filter** area, enter all or part of the user's name.
3. Click on the **Add filter** button. The user appears in the list at the bottom of the page.
4. Next to the user's name, click on the **Edit** link. This displays the **Edit profile** page for that user.
5. In the **Username** field, enter a new username for the person.
6. At the bottom of the page, click on the **Update profile** button; this saves the change.

If the user wants to change their password, it must usually be done in the external source and not in Moodle.

When you authenticate users with an external database server, you can allow them to change their passwords through Moodle. You can also make Moodle use the external database server's password expiration feature, forcing users to change their passwords periodically. These are two features that you get when authenticating against LDAP but not when authenticating against an external database. Each type of authentication method offers unique advantages and disadvantages.

Granting access to courses with enrollment choices

Enrollment is different from authentication. In authentication, you grant a user access to your site, and in enrollment, you grant a user access to a course. That is, authentication answers the question, *Are you a member of this site?*, and enrollment answers the question, *Are you enrolled in this course?*

You have several options for managing student enrollment. They are found under **Settings | Site administration | Plugins | Enrolments | Manage Enrol Plugins**:

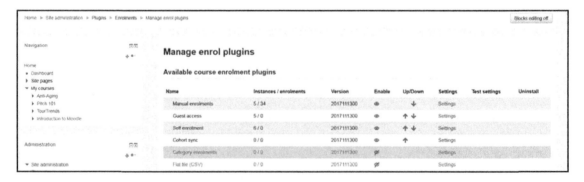

Note the column labels across the top of the list in the preceding screenshot. Let's discuss the meaning of each label and then discuss each enrollment method.

Name

This is the name of the enrollment method:

Manage enrol plugins

Available course enrolment plugins

Name	Instances / enrolments	Version	Enable	Up/Down	Settings	Test settings	Uninstall
Manual enrolments	4 / 32	2017111300	👁	↓	Settings		
Guest access	4 / 0	2017111300	👁	↑ ↓	Settings		
Self enrolment	5 / 0	2017111300	👁	↑ ↓	Settings		
Cohort sync	0 / 0	2017111300	👁	↑	Settings		
Category enrolments	0 / 0	2017111300	⌀		Settings		
Flat file (CSV)	0 / 0	2017111300	⌀		Settings		
IMS Enterprise file	0 / 0	2017111300	⌀		Settings		
Publish as LTI tool	0 / 0	2017111300	⌀		Settings		
Course meta link	0 / 0	2017111300	⌀		Settings		
MNet remote enrolments	0 / 0	2017111300	⌀		Settings		
PayPal	0 / 0	2017111300	⌀		Settings		

Instances/enrollments

Instances activity tells you how many courses have this enrollment method added to them. However, just because a course has an enrollment method added to the course doesn't mean that course is using the enrollment method.

For example, the **Trends in Tourism** course has three enrollment methods added to it:

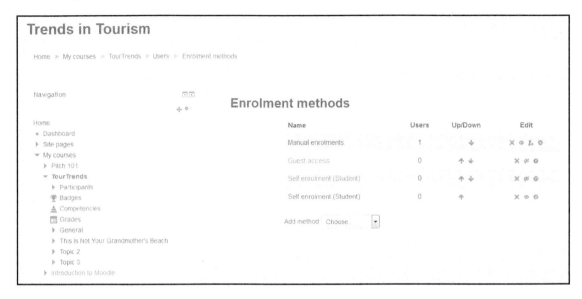

Note in the preceding screenshot that while **Guest access** and **Self enrolment** are added to this course, they are not available, that is, they are not enabled. The teacher or administrator will need to enable those enrollment methods for this course.

Note that self-enrollment is not the same as self-registration. Self-registration enables a person to join your site. Self-enrollment enables a person who is a member of the site to enroll in a course.

In this example, while we configured our site, we turned off guest access and self-registration for the site. However, those methods had already been added to this course; that's why those methods still appear in this course. They can be turned on for just this course, but they cannot be added to any new courses.

The specific overrides the general:
In Moodle, as in most systems, settings for a specific area override settings for a more general area. Many default settings that apply to your whole site can be overridden by settings in a specific course. Also, many settings that apply to a whole course can be overridden by settings in a specific activity.

Enable

This setting determines whether the enrollment method is available to your courses. To make a method available, click on the Eye icon to open it. To make it unavailable, click on the icon to close it.

Up/down

Use the up and down arrows to put the enrollment methods in the order that you want Moodle to use them. The first enrollment method that contains the username that is trying to log in will determine whether the user is authorized.

Settings

Many enrollment methods have a separate page for settings where you configure that method.

If you enable an enrollment method, you should at least look at the **Settings** page for that method and determine whether you need to change any of them.

Manual enrollments

Manual enrollment is the default form of enrollment. When this is selected, a teacher or administrator can enroll the student.

Manually enrolling a student in a course

You can manually enroll a student in a course as follows:

1. Enter the course as a teacher or administrator.
2. From within the course, select **Administration** | **Users** | **Enrolled users**.

3. In the upper-right corner of the page, click on the **Enrol users** button. The **Enrol users** window is displayed:

4. To find a user, enter any part of the user's name into the **Search** field and then press *Enter* or *return* on your keyboard.
5. To enroll a user, click on the **Enrol** button next to the user's name. The display of that user's name will change to indicate that they are enrolled.
6. When you finish enrolling users, click on the **Finish enrolling users** box for this window. You will return to the **Enrolled** users page and see the user added to the list of enrolled users.

Here's a brief summary of users and privileges. There is a complete list in the section entitled *Roles*, which appears later in this chapter:

- **Administrators**: Full privileges. They can create new users and enroll them into a course.
- **Teachers**: Limited privileges. They can only enroll users into a course.
- **Users**: Most limited privileges. They can enter a course.

Remember that teachers can enroll users into a course, but they can't create new users.

Unless you override Moodle's default settings, teachers cannot create new users. They can only enroll the existing users. By default, only a site administrator can manually create new users. In the following screenshot, the site administrator is logged in with the browser on the left. Note that **Site administration** | **users** | **Accounts** | **Add a new user** is available for the administrator. A teacher is logged in with the browser on the right, and the **Site administration** menu is not available to the teacher.

Guest access

Your Moodle site has a special user called **Guest**. This user can be granted access to courses, without requiring them to be enrolled. Essentially, you are allowing anonymous users to access your site and/or course.

In the following screenshot, the **Login as a guest** button indicates that guest access has been enabled for this site. If you disable guest access, this button does not appear:

Who is this guest?

Who is your guest visitor? You will probably never know! That's because the guest account can be used by anyone, even multiple people at the same time. Therefore, you won't know the guest's name. When you look at your site logs and see the activity for the guest, you are looking at the activities performed by every visitor who used the guest account.

The **Settings** page for the **Guest access** method contains some settings for a password:

Guest access

Guest access plugin is only granting temporary access to courses, it is not actually enrolling users.

Require guest access password enrol_guest	requirepassword	☐ Default: No Require access password in new courses and prevent removing of access password from existing courses

Use password policy enrol_guest	usepasswordpolicy	☐ Default: No Use standard password policy for guest access passwords

Show hint enrol_guest	showhint	☐ Default: No Show first letter of the guest access password

Enrolment instance defaults

Default enrolment settings in new courses.

Add instance to new courses enrol_guest	defaultenrol	☑ Default: Yes It is possible to add this plugin to all new courses by default.

Allow guest access enrol_guest	status	No ▼ Default: No Allow temporary guest access by default

Save changes

It may seem odd to set a password for an anonymous guest. However, there is a good reason for requiring a password for the guest user. It prevents automated software, such as web crawlers and spam harvesters, from entering your course. Requiring a password for the guest ensures that the user entering the course is a human and not a piece of software.

If you require a password for guest access, you'll need to tell your guests what the password is; you can add that to the course description that the visitors see on the front page of your site.

Enabling Guest access for a course

First, ensure that the guest authentication method is available, and that guest enrollment is activated:

1. Enter the course as a teacher or administrator.
2. Select **Administration** | **Course administration** | **Users** | **Enrolled users** | **Enrolment methods**.

3. If the **Guest access** enrollment method is not listed on this page, use the **Add method** drop-down list to add it. If it's not available under that list, have your system administrator add it.

4. Once the **Guest access** enrollment method is listed, activate it. Under the **Edit** column, click on the Eye icon to open it.

5. Now, enable this method under the course settings.

6. Select **Administration** | **Course administration** | **Edit settings**. The **Course settings** page is displayed.

7. For the **Allow guest access** drop-down list, select **Yes**.

8. If you require a password for guest access, enter it into the **Password** field.

9. At the bottom of the page, click on the **Save changes** button.

Self enrolment

This allows users to enroll themselves in courses. As with guest access, you must enable this method under **Site administration** for your entire site and also activate it for a specific course.

On the **Settings** page for **Self enrolment**, you can choose to require an enrollment key:

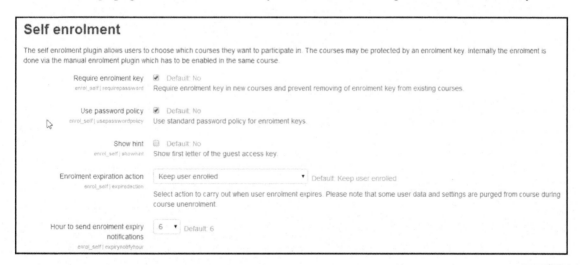

The **enrolment key** is a code that the user must enter when enrolling in a course. Once the user is enrolled, the **enrolment key** is no longer needed.

You can allow self-registration on your site and then require users to have an **enrolment key** for a course. The self-registration removes the burden of you creating accounts for users. The **enrolment key** ensures that only those to whom you give the key can enter your course.

Cohort sync

In a Moodle course, you can add students to a group. Then, you can manage that group's access to activities and resources in the course instead of managing the students one at a time. Moodle also enables you to create site-wide groups. These are called **cohorts**.

The cohorts sync enrollment method enables you to enroll a cohort into a course. This enrolls everyone in that cohort in one go.

 Inside a course, a teacher can create a group. However, because a cohort is a site-wide group, by default, only your site's administrator can create a cohort and enable cohort sync in the enrollment methods. After these are enabled, a teacher can add a cohort into a course.

Creating a cohort

1. Log in to your site as an administrator.
2. Select **Administration** | **Site administration** | **Users** | **Accounts** | **Cohorts**. The cohorts page is displayed.
3. Click on the **Add** button. The **Edit Cohort** page is displayed.
4. Give the cohort a **Name** and **ID**. You will probably leave the **Context** set to **System** so that you can use the cohort throughout your site.
5. Optionally, add a **Description**.
6. Click on the **Save Changes** button. You are returned to the cohorts page, where your new cohort is listed.

Adding users to a cohort

At any time, you can add or remove users from a cohort. This subsection shows you two methods.

Adding a user from the cohort page

As long as we are on the cohort page, let's add some users. This method assumes that you have logged in to your site as an administrator and that you are at the **Administration** | **Site administration** | **Users** | **Accounts** | **Cohorts** page. The cohorts page is displayed, and the list of cohorts is on this page.

1. Next to the cohort to which you want to add users, click on the person icon:

2. The **Search** screen is displayed, where you can search among all the users in the system:

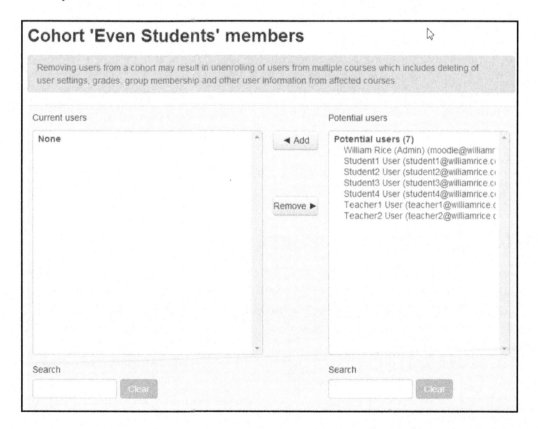

3. Note that on this screen, you can search only for the first name, last name, and email address. If you need to find and enroll students on some other criteria, try the bulk user method described next.

4. After finding and adding the students that you want, at the bottom of the page, click on the **Back to cohorts** button to return to the cohorts page.

Adding a student using the bulk action method

When you search for students using the bulk action page, you get more search fields than just the first name, last name, and email. This can help you find the students that you are looking for. To add students to a cohort using the bulk action page, do the following:

1. Log in to your site as an administrator.
2. Select **Site administration** | **Users** | **Accounts** | **Bulk user actions**. The bulk user actions page is displayed.
3. Under the **New filter** section, select and/or enter the search criteria for your students.
4. Click on the **Add filter** button. Under the **Users** in the list section, the users that meet the criteria will be displayed in the left column.
5. Select the users that you want in the cohort.
6. Click on the **Add to selection** button. The users will be added to the right column.
7. Under **With selected users...** select **Add to cohort**, and then click on the **Go** button.
8. A page listing the cohorts available is displayed. Select the cohort and then click on the **Add to cohort** button.

Enrolling a cohort in a course

1. Enter the course as a teacher or administrator.
2. Select **Administration** | **Course administration** | **Users** | **Enrolled users**.
3. Click on the **Enrol cohort** button (by default, this button doesn't appear for teachers, but only for administrators). A pop-up window appears. This window lists the cohorts on the site.
4. Next to the cohort that you want to enroll, click on **Enrol users**. The system displays a confirmation message.
5. At the confirmation message, click on the **OK** button. You are taken back to the enrolled users page.

Category enrollments

If you used a previous version of Moodle and enrolled students in courses using the category roles, activating this enrollment method will enable you to import those enrollments into the new Moodle. If you're not importing category roles from a previous version, you can leave this enrollment method deactivated.

In MoodleCloud and Moodle on-premise, an easy way to manage your enrollments (including ones using PayPal, and such) is found using the following path:

Administration | Site administration | Plugin | Enrolments | Manage enrol plugins

The flat file

A **flat file** is a text file that contains information from a database. The flat file method of student enrollment causes Moodle to read in a text file and use that as the source for enrollment information. The flat file method is especially useful if you need to enroll a large group of people who have records in another system.

For example, suppose that all the nurses at your hospital need to be trained in patient privacy laws. We can assume that the nurses have records in the hospital's human resource or payroll system. Alternatively, suppose all the teachers at your school need to be trained on new educational standards. These teachers will probably have records in the school's email or human resource system. If you can get a flat file, or text file, containing a list of everyone who needs to be trained, and that file contains their Moodle ID numbers, you are well on your way to enrolling them all at once. When you speak to the system administrator of the other system, you may ask them for an *extract* from the system.

The file

The flat file has the following format:

```
operation, role, ID number of user, ID number of course
```

Here, keep the following in mind:

- `operation`: It can be add or delete. These enroll and unenroll the user from the course.
- `role`: It is the role, or function, that the user will have in the course; for example, **student** or **teacher editing**.

- `ID number of user`: It is a unique identifier for the user (note that this is not the same as username).
- `ID number of course`: It is a unique identifier for the course (note that this is not the same as the course short name).

Moodle periodically reads in this file and modifies its enrollment data according to what the file says. Consider this example:

```
add, student, 007, EM102
```

The preceding line will add the **student** with the **ID number** of **007** to the course with the **ID number** of **EM102**.

The flat file is read into Moodle on the schedule that is set up under **Administration** | **Site administration** | **Server** | **Scheduled tasks**.

Place this file in a directory that is accessible to your web server. For example, you can put it inside the Moodle data directory.

Student ID number required

Before you can enroll a person into a course, that person needs to be a member of your site, that is, the person needs to be authenticated. In this case, your first step is to authenticate the users using one of the methods discussed in the *Authenticating against an external source* section.

If you use a flat file to enroll students in a course, the file will identify each student by their ID number. Whatever method you use to authenticate your users, it should include a unique ID number for each user. This number should consist of only digits and should be up to 10 characters in length. In the user profile page as seen in the following screenshot, you can see that **ID number** is an optional field:

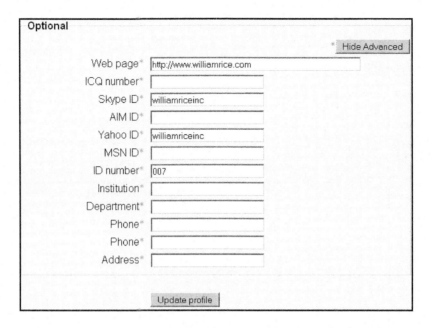

This **ID number** will match the student in Moodle to a record in the enrollment file. For example, the following line from the file enrolls student `007` into the course with the ID of `EM102`:

```
add, student, 007, EM102
```

In the Moodle database, you will find the student's **ID number** in the `mdl_user` table in the `idnumber` field, as seen in the following screenshot:

If you want to use a flat file to mass-enroll a group of students and your users don't have ID numbers, speak to your administrator about loading those numbers directly into the Moodle database. They may be able to use a database command to fill that field.

If your database administrator cannot add ID numbers for your users, you will need to edit each user's profile manually and add the ID numbers.

Course ID required

If you use a flat file to enroll students in a course, the file will identify each course by its ID number. The example we used earlier was as follows:

```
add, student, 007, EM102
```

This ID can consist of any alphanumeric characters, not just digits, and be up to 100 characters in length. In the **Edit course settings** page, you can see that **CourseID number** is an optional field:

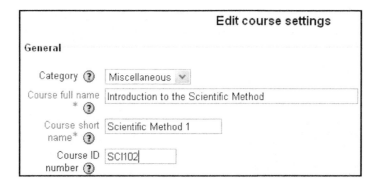

In the Moodle database, you will find the CourseID number in the `mdl_course` table in the **idnumber** field:

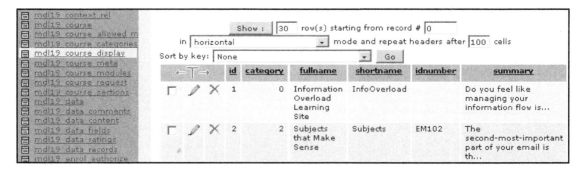

If you want to use a flat file to mass-enroll a group of students and your courses don't have ID numbers, you can add them in the **Edit course settings** page for each course. If you need ID numbers for a lot of courses, your database administrator may be able to use a database command to fill that field.

Role

A user's role in a course determines what the user can do in that course. Later in the book, we'll discuss Moodle's built-in roles in detail, how to customize roles, and how to create new ones. For now, let's look at the built-in roles that Moodle gives you in a standard installation:

Manage roles	Allow role assignments	Allow role overrides	Allow role

Role ⑦	Description	Short name
Manager	Managers can access course and modify them, they usually do not participate in courses.	manager
Course creator	Course creators can create new courses.	coursecreator
Teacher	Teachers can do anything within a course, including changing the activities and grading students.	editingteacher
Non-editing teacher	Non-editing teachers can teach in courses and grade students, but may not alter activities.	teacher
Student	Students generally have fewer privileges within a course.	student
Guest	Guests have minimal privileges and usually can not enter text anywhere.	guest
Authenticated user	All logged in users.	user
Authenticated user on frontpage	All logged in users in the frontpage course.	frontpage

A user can have a role in the site and a role in a course.

When you use a flat file to enroll students in a course(s), the file specifies what role each user will have in the course. Let's return to our example:

```
add, student, 007, WP102
```

The preceding line from the file specifies that the user ID number `007` will be added as a `student` to the course ID number `WP102`.

Note that the flat file uses *student* with a lowercase *s* while the role is called *Student* with a capital *S*. They don't match exactly because the flat file uses the short name of the role. To find out the short name of a role, go to **Administration** ǀ **Site administration** ǀ **Users** ǀ **Permissions** ǀ **Define roles**.

Summary of flat files

A flat file is an effective way to mass-enroll a large group of students into one or multiple courses at once. Remember that this method requires you to have a student ID number and course ID number. You'll need to populate those fields in your student records and course settings manually or automatically. If you're authenticating users against an external system that has ID numbers, such as your school's LDAP server, consider mapping the student ID number field to your server's ID numbers.

IMS Enterprise file

An IMS Enterprise file is a flat file (text file) that conforms to standards set by the IMS Global Learning Consortium. Many student information systems and human resources information systems can export an IMS-compliant file. For example, PeopleSoft and Oracle can export IMS files. These standards enable human resource systems and learning management systems to exchange data. Just like many word processors can read and write .rtf files, many human resources and learning systems can read and create IMS files. As you choose a file, you will need to ensure that it conforms to the correct configuration in Moodle. This applies to MoodleCloud as well.

If your organization uses an HR system that can produce IMS files, you can use this method to enroll and unenroll students. You can also use this method to create new courses. This will be especially useful for a school that wanted to offer teachers the option of an online work space for every course. Each semester, the school could export an IMS file from their enrollment system, read this into Moodle, and use it to create an online course for every class that your school offers.

Alternatively, let's return to an example used in the preceding flat file section. Suppose that all the nurses at your hospital need to be trained in patient privacy laws. We can assume that these nurses have records in the hospital's HR system. The HR system may also be used to track the courses and certifications that the nurses need. You can export the nurses' information from the HR system, including the courses and certifications that they need. When you import the IMS file into Moodle, it will create the courses needed and enroll the nurses in them.

You can find the IMS Enterprise Best Practice and Implementation Guide at
`http://www.imsglobal.org/enterprise/enbest03.html`. That document states:

> *"Corporations, schools, government agencies, and software vendors have a major
> investment in their systems for training administration, human resource management,
> student administration, financial management, library management, and many other
> functions. They also have the existing infrastructure and systems for managing access to
> electronic resources. To be effective and efficient, Instructional Management Systems need
> to operate as an integrated part of this Enterprise system environment."*

The objective of the IMS Enterprise specification documents is to define a standardized set
of structures that can be used to exchange data between different systems.

LDAP

Remember that authentication happens when a user logs into your site, and enrollment
happens when a user is made a student in a specific course. LDAP can be used for both
authentication and/or enrollment. If you use LDAP for one, you do not need to use it for the
other.

LDAP, external database, and IMS Enterprise File are all able to create new courses as they
enroll students. All the other methods can only enroll students in the existing courses.

External database

You can use an external database to control student enrollment. In this case, Moodle looks
in the designated database and determines whether the student is enrolled.

Moodle will not write back to the external database. All changes in the
external database are made by another program. So to enroll and unenroll
students, you will need to change the external database.

In addition to using the external database, you can also allow Moodle's normal enrollment
routine. If you enable manual enrollments in addition to the external database, Moodle
checks two databases when a student tries to enter a course: the external one and its
internal one.

External database connection

In the **External database connection** settings, you enter information that enables Moodle to connect to the external database. You should get this information from the administrator of the external database:

External database connection		
Database driver enrol_database | dbtype	[dropdown]	Default: Empty ADOdb database driver name, type of the external database engine.
Database host enrol_database | dbhost	localhost	Default: localhost Type database server IP address or host name
Database user enrol_database | dbuser		Default: Empty
Database password enrol_database | dbpass		☐Unmask
Database name enrol_database | dbname		Default: Empty
Database encoding enrol_database | dbencoding	utf-8	Default: utf-8
Database setup command enrol_database | dbsetupsql		Default: Empty

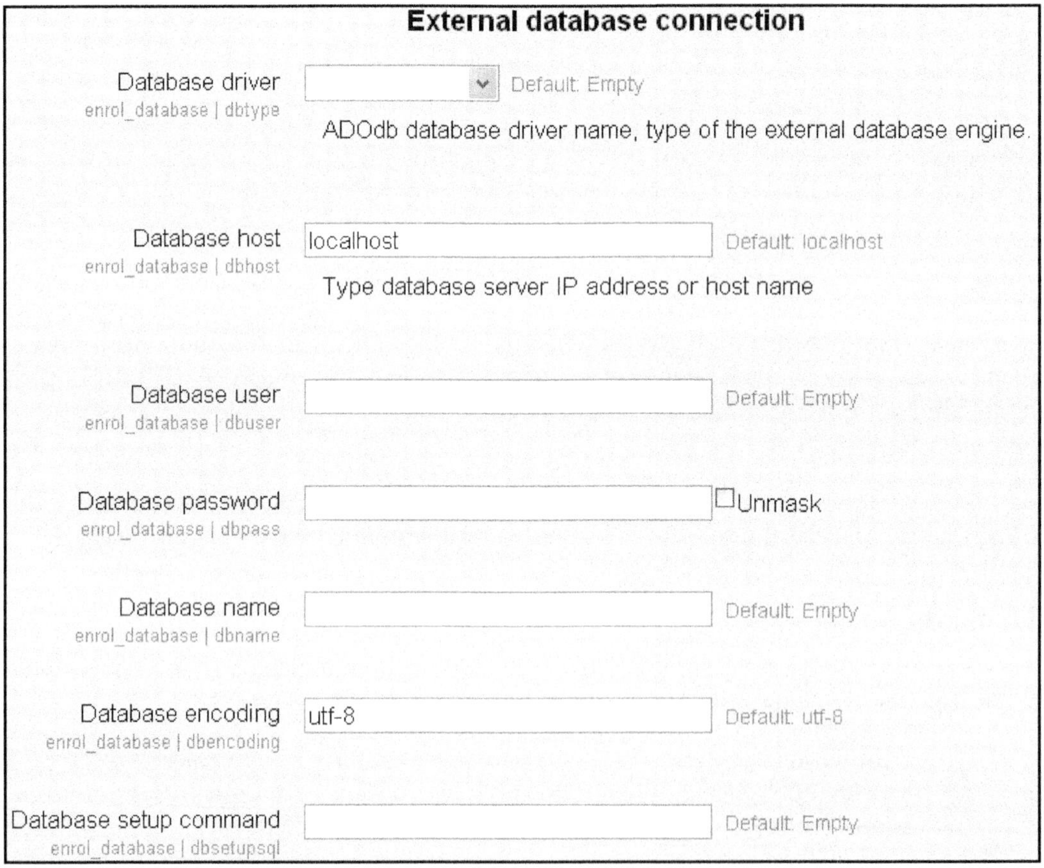

Local field mappings

In the **Local field mapping** settings, you answer the question, *what name does the external database use for the course?* In the following screenshot, you can see that you have three choices:

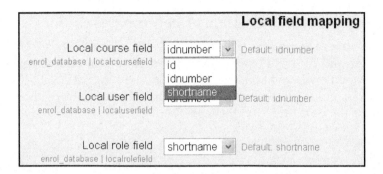

In Moodle, every course has an ID. The front page of your Moodle site is always `course number 1`. The next course that you create is `course number 2` and so on. In your external database, you can use this ID to specify your courses. However, I recommend against using the ID in an external database; let me explain why.

Suppose you install a new version of Moodle. Then, you export your courses out of your old Moodle installation. Now, suppose you import those courses into your new Moodle installation. The first course that you import will have an ID of 2. The second course that you import will have an ID of 3 and so on. These course IDs might be different from those in the external database. Therefore, when you connect your new Moodle site to the external database, the course IDs will no longer match.

Consider using the **idnumber** or **shortname** of the course in the external database. One advantage of using the **shortname** is that this is a required field for every course, so you know that every course will have one.

The **shortname** is used in the navigation bar at the top of the page. In the following screenshot, the **shortname** of the course is **Scientific Method 1**:

The **idnumber** of a course is optional. Students will not see the **idnumber**; only administrators and teachers see it.

Remote enrolment sync and creation of new courses

In the **Remote enrolment sync** settings, you tell Moodle where in the external database the student information and course identifiers are stored. In the **Creation of new courses** settings, you tell Moodle where in the external database to find information for creating new courses. In both areas, you are entering the name of tables and fields in the external database that holds the data that Moodle needs.

PayPal

The PayPal option enables you to set up paid access to the site, or to individual courses. When you select this option, you enter a value into the **Enrol Cost** field. This becomes the fee for joining the site. If you enter 0 into **enrol_cost**, students can access the site for free. If you enter a non-zero amount, students must pay to access the site.

Selecting this option also puts an **Enrol Cost** field into each of the **Course settings** pages. Again, entering zero into **Enrol Cost** for a course enables students to access it for free. Entering a non-zero amount requires students to pay in order to access the course.

The PayPal payment screen displays a notice that the course requires a payment for entry.

Mnet remote enrollments (formerly Moodle networking)

The official *Moodle documentation* describes Moodle networking as follows:

> *"The network feature allows a Moodle administrator to establish a link with another Moodle, and to share some resources with the users of that Moodle."*

The initial release of the Moodle network is bundled with a new authentication plugin, which makes single-sign-on between Moodles possible. A user with the Jody username logs in to her Moodle server as normal and clicks on a link that takes her to a page on another Moodle server. Normally, she would have only the privileges of a guest on the remote Moodle, but behind the scenes, single sign-on has established a fully authenticated session for Jody on the remote site.

If you need to authenticate users across Moodle sites that are owned by different people, then Moodle networking is an obvious choice. However, if all the sites are owned by the same person or institution, you need to weigh the advantages and disadvantages of using Moodle networking versus some kind of central login. For example, suppose several departments in your university install their own Moodle sites. If they want to authenticate students on all their sites, they can use Moodle networking to share student login information. This will make sense if the university's IT department could not, or would not, let them authenticate students against the university's LDAP server or student database. However, if all the departments could authenticate against a central database maintained by the university, it would probably be easier for them to do so.

Language

The default Moodle installation includes many language packs. A language pack is a set of translations for the Moodle interface. *Language packs translate the Moodle interface, not the course content.* The following screenshot depicts the front page of a site when the user selects Spanish from the language menu:

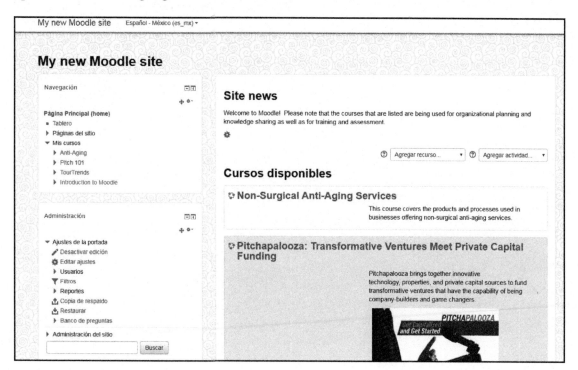

Note that the interface is being presented in Spanish: menu names, menu items, section names, buttons, and system messages. Now, let's take a look at the same front page when the user selects **Tagalog** from the language menu in the following screenshot:

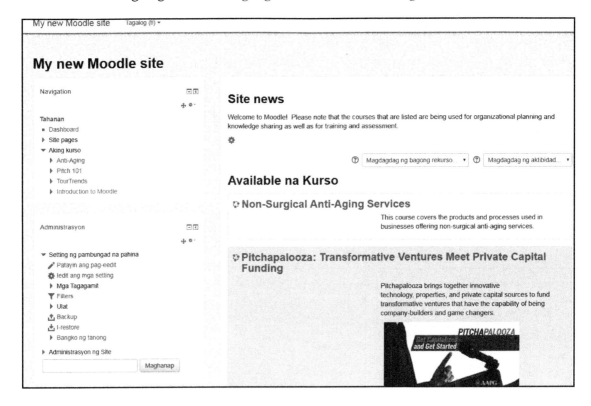

Note that some of the interface has not been translated. For example, the month name in the calendar and some of the links under **Navigation** are still in English. When a part of Moodle's interface is not translated into the selected language, Moodle uses the English version.

About language files

When you install an additional language, Moodle places the language pack in its home directory, under the /lang subdirectory. It creates a subdirectory for each language's files. The following screenshot shows the results of installing the International Spanish and Romanian languages:

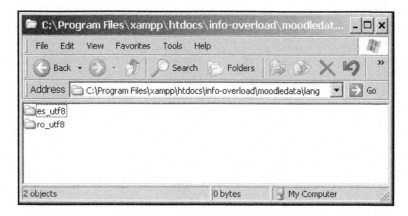

For example, the /lang/en_us subdirectory holds files for the U.S. English translation, and /lang/es_es holds the files for traditional Spanish (Espanol/Espana) translation.

The name of the subdirectory is language code. Knowing that code for translations can be useful. In the preceding example, es_utf8 tells us that the language code for International Spanish is es.

Inside the directory of a language pack, we see a list of files that contain the translations, as follows:

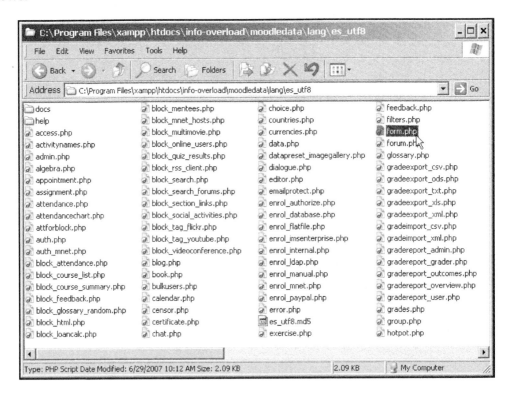

For example, the `/lang/es_utf8/forum.php` file holds text used on the forum pages. This includes text that is displayed to the course creator when creating the forum and text that is displayed to the students when they use the forum. The following are the first few lines from the English version of that file:

```
$string['addanewdiscussion'] = 'Add a new discussion topic';
$string['addanewtopic'] = 'Add a new topic';
$string['advancedsearch'] = 'Advanced search';
```

The following are the same first three lines from the Spanish version of that file:

```
$string['addanewdiscussion'] = 'Colocar un nuevo tema de discusión
  aquí';
$string['addanewtopic'] = 'Agregar un nuevo tema';
$string['advancedsearch'] = 'Búsqueda'Búsquedaavanzada';
```

The biggest task in localizing Moodle consists of translating these language files into the appropriate language. Some translations are surprisingly complete. For example, most of the interface has been translated to **Irish Gaelic**, even though this language is used daily by only about 350,000 people. This is the nature of open source software; it's not always the largest group of users who get what they want, but often the most active one.

Installing and enabling additional languages

Using the **Site administration** menu, you can install additional languages and make them available to your users. In the following subsections, we'll cover installing an additional language and configuring the language settings.

Installing additional languages

To install additional languages, your Moodle site must be connected to the internet:

1. Select **Administration** | **Site administration** | **Language** | **Language packs**. The page displays a list of all the available language packs:

2. From the list of available languages on the right, select the language that you want to install.

3. Click on the button for **Install selected language pack**. Moodle retrieves the most recent version of the language pack from the web and installs it. This is why Moodle must be connected to the web to use this feature. If Moodle is not connected, you will need to download the language pack and copy it into the /lang directory yourself.

If you don't see the language you want on the list of **Available language packs**, it's not available from the official Moodle site.

Configuring the language

The settings covered in this subsection are found under **Administration | Site administration | Language | Language settings**.

The **Default language** setting specifies the language that users will see when they first encounter your site. If you also select **Display language menu**, users can change the language. Selecting this displays a language menu on your front page:

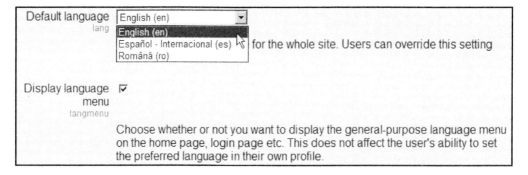

The **Languages on language menu** setting enables you to specify the languages that the users can pick from the language menu. The directions tell you to enter *language codes*. These codes are the names of the directories that hold the language packs. In the preceding subsection on language files, you saw that the es_utf8 directory holds the language files for International Spanish. If you wanted to enter that language in the list, it would look as follows:

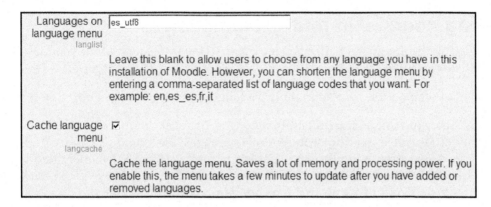

Leaving this field blank will enable your students to pick from all the available and installed languages. Entering the names of languages in this field limits the list to only those entered.

Sitewide locale

Enter a language code into this field, and the system displays dates in the format appropriate for that language:

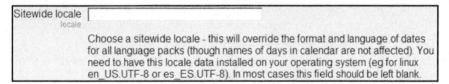

Excel encoding

Most of the reports that Moodle generates can be downloaded as Excel files. User logs and grades are two examples. This setting lets you choose the encoding for those Excel files.

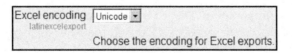

Your choices are **Unicode** and **Latin**. The default is **Unicode**, because this character set includes many more characters than **Latin**. In many cases, Latin encoding doesn't offer enough characters to completely represent a non-English language.

Offering courses in multiple languages

The settings on the **Language Settings** page apply to the translation of the Moodle interface. However, they do not apply to the translation of course content.

If you want to offer course content in multiple languages, you have several choices:

1. You could put all the different languages into each course, that is, each document would appear in a course in several languages. For example, if you offered a botany course in English and Spanish, you might have a document defining the different types of plants in both English and Spanish, side by side in the same course: **Types of Plants** or **Tipos de Plantaras**. While taking the course, students would select the documents in their language. Course names would appear in only one language.

2. You could create separate courses for each language and offer them on the same site. Course names would appear in each language. In this case, students would select the course in English or Spanish: **Basic Botany** or **BotánicaBásica**.

3. You could create a separate Moodle site for each language; for example, `http://moodle.williamrice.com/english` and `http://moodle.williamrice.com/spanish`. At the home page of your site, students would select their language and be directed to the correct Moodle installation. In this case, the entire Moodle site would appear in the student's language: the site name, menus, course names, and course content. These are things you should consider before installing Moodle.

4. You could use the **Multi-Language Content** filter, as described later in this chapter, to display the course content in the language selected by your user.

5. Lastly, you could use groupings to hide the different languages from different users.

Security settings

You will find security settings under **Site administration | Security**. This section will not cover every option under that menu. Instead, it will focus on the options that are not self-explanatory, and how they affect the user experience.

The IP blocker – Limiting access to specific locations

This page enables you to block and allow users from specific IP addresses. If you want to limit access to your Moodle to only the users who are on campus, this is especially useful.

Site policies

The site policies page contains a variety of security settings that you should either set yourself or work with your administrator to set.

Protect usernames

If you forget your password, Moodle can display a page that enables you to retrieve it. If you enter your username or email address, Moodle will send an email with your login information:

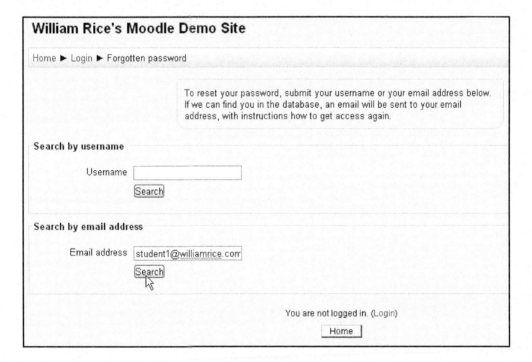

When Moodle sends this email, it confirms the sending but does not display the email address to which the message was sent:

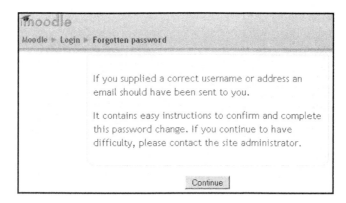

The email address is hidden to protect the user's privacy. Many countries have laws that forbid the disclosure of personal information. If someone could guess the usernames (which is often the case in large institutions), they could enter them into the lost password page and harvest email addresses for abuse.

Forcing users to log in

As stated in the directions, setting the password policy the default, which is **Yes** causes the front page to become hidden until a visitor logs in to Moodle. When visitors first hit your Moodle site, they see the Moodle login page.

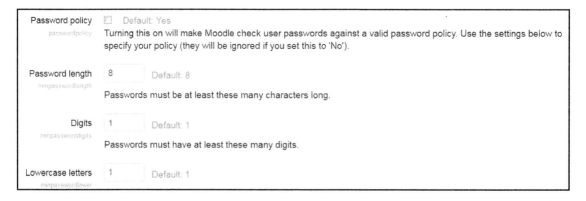

Setting this to **Yes** means that you cannot use Moodle's front page as an information and sales tool. You can customize the text on the login page, but you won't be able to add all the features available on the front page.

Forcing users to log in for profiles

What the directions don't state is that setting this to **No** enables anonymous visitors to read not only teacher profiles but also the profiles of any students enrolled in courses that have guest access. This may be a privacy issue.

The effect of enabling **Force users to login for profiles** is that anonymous visitors cannot read the profiles for the teachers in a course that accepts guest access. They must register as a student before being able to read student and user profiles. This may be a drawback if your teacher profiles are a selling point for the course.

Consider enabling this to force people to register before reading student or teacher profiles. Then, if your teacher profiles are a selling point, you can add a section to the front page for **About Our Teachers.**

Open to Google

This setting lets the Google indexing robot into courses that allow guest access. If you want to know more about the **Googlebot**, refer to `http://www.google.com/bot.html`.

It seems that everyone with a website wants their site to be ranked high in Google's search results. However, you should consider whether you really want Google to add each of your guest-enabled courses to its search engine. There are several disadvantages:

- If your course content changes frequently, Google might index out-of-date information for your courses.
- Your students and teachers might not want their names and materials to be indexed and available to the public.
- If Google indexes all your guest-enabled courses, you have less control over what information about your site appears in Google. Everything on the pages that the Googlebot searches is used in indexing your site. There might be items on those pages that don't accurately represent your site; for example, a negative forum posting or an off-topic discussion could become associated with your site. Also, if the focus or structure of your Moodle site changes, it may take a while before all the Google references to all those pages are corrected.

If you want strict control over what information appears in Google about your site, set **Open to Google** to **No**. Put only the information that you want to appear in Google on the front page of your site, and do not allow teachers or students to modify anything on the front page. This way, Google will index only your front page.

You should also request anyone who links to your site to link only to the front page (for example, link only to `http//www.williamrice.com/moodle`, and not directly to a course page). Google and other search engines use links to your site to calculate your ranking. If all those links point to the same page, you can better control your site's public image. By disabling **Open to google**, and requesting that people link only to the front page, you are trading away some of your search engine presence in exchange for greater control of your site's public.

For the ultimate in controlling what kind of indexed information is available about your site, consider this plan: disable **Open to google** and enable **Force users to login** to keep search engine robots out of Moodle completely. Under **Users | Authentication**, set **Guest login button** to **Hide** to eliminate the possibility of any other search engine robots crawling your guest courses. Now you've locked out all but the registered users.

Put Moodle into a subdirectory of your site. Link to Moodle from the index page at the root of your site. In the demo site, we would put Moodle into `moodle.williamrice.com/moodle/` and link to it from `moodle.williamrice.com/index.htm`. Then, use `index.htm` as an introduction to the site. Ensure that `index.htm` contains exactly the kind of information you want the public to know about your site and optimize it for the best search engine placement.

Maximum uploaded file size

On this page, you will also find a setting to limit the size of files that users and course creators can upload:

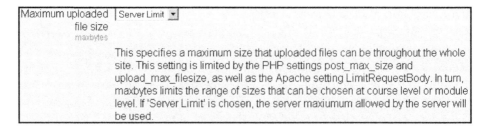

This setting affects students, teachers, and course creators. If you're creating a course that has a large file, such as a video, and Moodle forbids you from uploading the file, this setting might be the cause.

As stated in the directions on the page, there are three other settings that limit the size of a file that can be uploaded to your server. The first two are PHP settings, and the third is an Apache setting. To see the PHP settings on your server, go to **Site administration** | **Server** | **PHP info**. Scroll down until you see `post_max_size` and `upload_max_filesize`.

The `LimitRequestBody` Apache setting also sets a limit on the size of uploaded files. The official Apache 2 documentation states the following:

> *"This directive specifies the number of bytes from 0 (meaning unlimited) to 2147483647 (2 GB) that are allowed in a request body.*
> *The LimitRequestBody directive allows the user to set a limit on the allowed size of an HTTP request message body within the context in which the directive is given (server, per-directory, per-file, or per-location). If the client request exceeds that limit, the server will return an error response instead of servicing the request. The size of a normal request message body will vary greatly depending on the nature of the resource and the methods allowed on that resource. CGI scripts typically use the message body for retrieving form information. Implementations of the PUT method will require a value at least as large as any representation that the server wishes to accept for that resource."*

Changing the limit on uploaded file size in PHP

If you have your own server, you can change the values for `post_max_size` and `upload_max_filesize` in the `php.ini` file. You will usually find this file in `/apache/bin`.

If you are using someone else's server (such as a hosting service), you probably can't change anything in `php.ini`. Try creating a file called `.htaccess` in the root of your Moodle installation that contains the following lines:

```
php_valuevaluepost_max_sizesize128M
php_valuevalueupload_max_filesizefilesize128M
```

Replace `128M` with any value that you need. If the server times out while uploading large files, you might add lines like the following to `.htaccess`:

```
php_valuevaluemax_input_time 600
php_valuevaluemax_execution_time 600
```

The `max_execution_time` and `max_input_time` variables set the maximum time allowed by a page to upload and process the files to be uploaded. If you will be uploading several megabytes of data, you may want to increase this setting. The execution time is specified in milliseconds (thousandths of a second). You can check your host settings for these under **Site administration | Server | PHP info**.

Then, place `.htaccess` into the directory with the PHP scripts that you want to run. For example, the script for uploading files is in the `/files` directory.

Your hosting service can disable `.htaccess`, which will make this solution impossible. You will need to ask your hosting service to change these values for you.

Changing the limit on uploaded file size in Apache

Just like you might be able to use `.htaccess` to override the PHP settings, you also might be able to use it to override the Apache settings. For example, placing the following line in `.htaccess` changes the limit on uploaded files to 10 MB:

```
LimitRequestBody 10240000
```

Note that the limit is specified in bytes, not megabytes. Setting it to zero will make the setting unlimited. The highest number you can specify is `2147483647`, or 2 GB.

Allowing embed and object tags

By default, you cannot embed a Flash or any other media file in a Moodle page. Instead, media files are automatically embedded and played in Moodle's built-in media player. However, many course developers do not like to use Moodle's built-in media player. Instead, they prefer that their media plays on the course page, in the player designed for that media. One example of this is embedding a YouTube video in a web page.

If you allow users to embed objects in a Moodle page, users can embed objects only in pages where they have editing rights. For example, a teacher can embed a YouTube video on a page in the teacher's course, but a student cannot, because the student cannot edit course pages.

However, every user has a profile that they can edit. In the following screenshot, `Student1` has embedded a video in their profile:

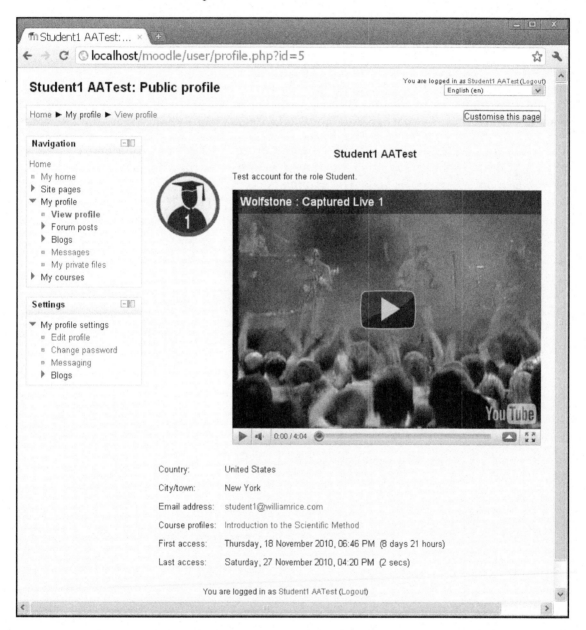

HTTP security

The HTTP security page has several options that you can use to further secure your site.

Using HTTPS for logins

This setting is found under **Security** | **HTTP security**. If you enable this setting but your server doesn't have HTTPS enabled for your site, you will be locked out of your site. Moodle will require you to use HTTPS when you log in, but you won't be able to comply. If that happens to you, you must go into the Moodle database and change this setting to **No**.

The following screenshot shows an administrator using the web-based product **phpMyAdmin** to edit this setting in Moodle's database. Note the setting for logging in via HTTPS is in the `mdl_config` table. The administrator is clicking on the edit icon. If this cell contains a 0, HTTPS login is not required. If it contains a 1, HTTPS login is required. If you're locked out because of HTTPS login, change the contents of this cell to 0 and then try logging in again.

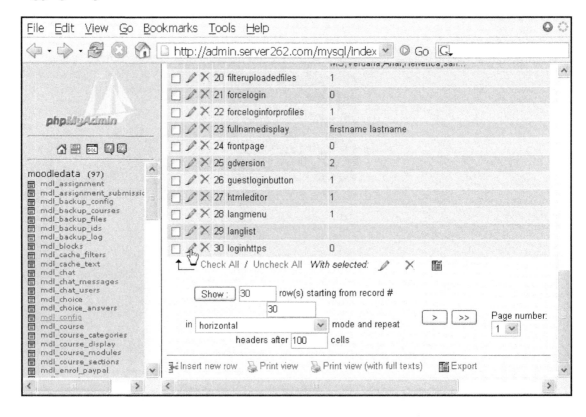

Running Moodle entirely from HTTPS

While this is not a setting on the HTTP security page, we should note at this point that you can run Moodle entirely from a secure connection. You can do this by configuring your web server to serve Moodle's address using a secure connection. You will need to speak to your web server administrator for this.

Note that this greatly increases the amount of memory and processing time that your server will use when serving Moodle. Your system administrator will need to closely monitor the performance of the server to ensure that it gives your users acceptable performance.

Filters

Moodle's filters read text and media that the users put on the site. The filters can then do three things with that material: **link**, **interpret**, and/or **restrict**.

These filters can now be enabled site-wide by the administrator, disabled site-wide, or be turned off by default with the option of the teacher enabling them in individual courses.

A filter can automatically link words and phrases to items in your site. For example, suppose you create a Glossary that contains the phrase **self-determination**. If you activate the **Glossary Auto-linking** filter, whenever that phrase appears on your site, it will be highlighted and will link to its glossary entry. When a reader clicks on the phrase, the reader is taken to the glossary entry.

Secondly, a filter can interpret what you have uploaded. For example, you could upload a document that is written in the markup language called; TeX (think HTML on steroids). The **TeX Notation** filter would interpret this document and enable Moodle to display it correctly. There's also an **Algebra Notation** filter that interprets a special markup language for writing math formulas.

Finally, a filter can restrict the kind of content that a user can place on the site. For example, the **Word Censorship** filter can filter out a list of **bad words** that you don't want to appear on your site. Every time that text is uploaded or entered, it is checked against the list of forbidden words.

You'll find the **Filters** settings under **Site administration** | **Plugins** | **Filters**. Read the following descriptions for detailed information about what each filter can do for your site.

Activity names and glossary auto-linking filters

The Auto-linking filters search the text on your site and automatically link to items when they find an item mentioned in the text. For example, **Glossary Auto-linking** looks for terms that are in any glossary, and when it finds them, it links the term to the glossary entry. The term is highlighted, and when a user clicks on it, they are taken to the glossary.

Activity Names Auto-linking searches course text for the names of course activities. When it finds the name of an activity, it links the activity. This means that whenever a student sees the name of an activity, the student can just click on the name and be taken to the activity, wherever they may be in the course. **Activity Names Auto-linking** works the same way for course activities.

Math filters

Algebra Notation and **TeX Notation** search the text for special characters used to describe mathematical formulas. For example, if you enter `@@cosh(x,2)@@` the **Algebra Notation** filter will display it as follows:

$$\boxed{\cos h^2\left(x\right)}$$

If you enter `$$\Bigsum_{i=\1}^{n-\1}$$`, the **TeX Notation** filter will display it as this:

$$\sum_{i=1}^{n-1}$$

Algebra Notation and **TeX Notation** are standard markup languages. The `http://www.moodle.org` site contains more information about **Algebra Notation**. For more information about **TeX**, refer to the **TeX Users Group** at `http://tug.org/`. TeX is more mature and complete than **Algebra Notation**. If you plan on writing more complex equations, I suggest making the **TeX Notation** filter active and leaving the **Algebra Notation** filter inactive.

The **MathJax** filter enables you to include mathematical expressions that are created using the MathJax language in your course material. MathJax is supported in the latest versions of all major browsers. The user's browser does not require any plugins or special fonts to render the mathematical expressions. It has several other advantages over the alternatives for displaying equations. Check out `http://mathjax.org` for more.

Email protection filter

Activating this filter makes email addresses on the site unreadable to search engines, while keeping them *human-readable*. If you set **Open to google** to **No**, or require users to log in, then you probably don't need to worry about search engines automatically picking up the email addresses of your students. If your site is open to search engines and anonymous users, you might want to use this filter to protect user's email addresses.

Multimedia plugins

If you leave the multimedia plugins filter inactive, multimedia content will usually play in a separate window. For example, without this filter, when a user clicks on a video, that video might open and play in a separate **Windows Media Player** or **RealPlayer** window. By activating this filter, you cause multimedia to play in Moodle's multimedia player.

Multi-language content

Earlier, you might have used the **Display language menu** setting to give your users a list of languages for the site. When a user selects one of these languages, only the Moodle interface is translated. The course content remains in whatever language you created it. If you want your site to be truly **multi-lingual**, you can also create course content in several languages. Activating the **Multi-Language Content** filter will then cause the course material to be displayed in the selected language.

To create course content in multiple languages, you must enclose the text written in each language in a `<span>` tag, as follows:

```
<span lang="en" class="multilang">Basic Botany</span>
<span lang="es" class="multilang">Botánica Básica</span>
```

This requires that you write the course material in HTML. This can be done for headings, course descriptions, course material, and any other HTML document that Moodle displays.

Word censorship

When this filter is activated, any word on the list of offensive words is blacked out. You can enter a list of banned words under the **Settings** for this filter. If you don't enter your own list, Moodle will use a default list that is found in the language pack.

HTML tidy

This filter checks the HTML that is written or uploaded to Moodle and attempts to *tidy* it by making it compliant with the XHTML standard. If your audience is using a wide variety of browsers (or browser versions), or a screen reader for the blind, making your pages compliant with this standard can make them easier to render.

Configuring the front page

Your site's front page welcomes the world to your learning site. Moodle treats your front page as a special course. This means that you can do everything on the front page that you can do in a normal course, plus make a few additional settings.

How to use this section

Early in the process of building your site, you can make some decisions about the look and functioning of your front page. This section deals with the settings that make sense to select when you're first building your site. However, some configuration settings on the front page won't make sense until you've created some courses and seen how Moodle works.

Front page settings page

The settings for the front page of your site are found under **Site administration | Front Page | Front Page Settings**.

Full site name

The **Full site name** appears at the top of the front page, in the browser's title bar, and also on the page tab when browsing with tabs.

You may create a summary of the site:

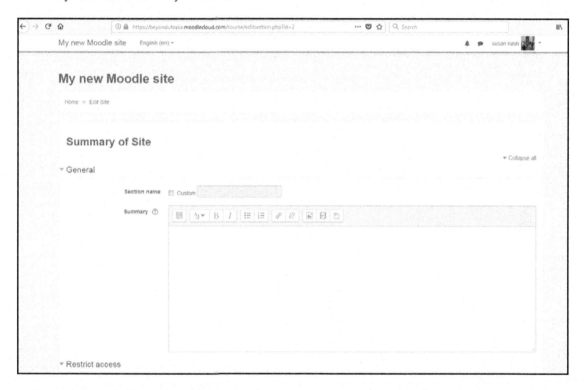

This summary appears in the left or right column of your site's front page. If you require visitors to register and log in before seeing the front page, remember that visitors will see this description *after* they have logged in. In that case, the front page summary can't be used to sell your site. Instead, it can instruct students on how to get started with your site; for example, `Take the introduction course to learn how to use this site....`

If your front page is visible to all visitors, you can use this summary to sell your site, tempt visitors to take a sample course, tell them what's inside, and so on.

Also, this summary appears in the metadata of the first page, so even if you decide to hide the box that displays the front page description, enter the description into the front page settings. It will make your site more findable on search engines.

Front page items

Two settings determine whether the center column of the front page shows news items, a list of courses, and/or a list of course categories. These settings are **Front Page** and **Front page items when logged in**:

Note that the front page settings apply to visitors who are not logged in. In the preceding example, we want to entice visitors with a list of the courses that we offer. However, since site news would probably not be of interest to anonymous visitors, we will show site news only to logged-in users. Each choice has its unique advantages.

Using a topic section on the front page

Remember that the front page description always appears in the left or right column of the front page. It does not appear in the center column. If you want your site description (for example, `Welcome to the....`) at the top and center, you'll need to include a topic section, which always appears in the center of your front page, as seen in the following screenshot:

You can make your site description the first topic. In this example, we turned the **Front Page Description** off. We are using the first topic to introduce the site instead. That puts the site description top and center, where it's most noticeable.

Show news items

This setting is useful if the content of your site changes frequently and you want to keep the visitors informed. If one of the primary purposes of your front page is serving repeat customers, showing news items on the front page is a good idea.

Backup

You'll find the backup settings under **Site administration** | **Courses** | **Backups**. Most of these settings enable you to choose the type of data that gets backed-up. You also choose which days of the week the backup will automatically run, and the hour the backup job will start. Usually, you want to choose a time when there are few users on the site. The backup is activated by the cron job routine.

Setting up the cron job

Some of Moodle's functions happen on a regular, timed schedule. The most visible example is mailing out notices to the subscribers of a forum that a new message has been posted. A script called `cron.php` checks periodically to see whether new messages have been posted to any forum. If so, the script causes the notice to be emailed to the members of that forum.

The cron job also triggers routines that clean up old data and back up your courses.

The `cron.php` script must be triggered at regular intervals. You can set this interval. The mechanism that triggers the script is called a **cron job**. Directions for setting up the cron job are in the `http://moodle.org/` installation guide.

Some web-hosting services allow you to set up cron jobs. If you're buying hosting services, look for a host that allows you to set a cron job to run every hour or even every few minutes. Some hosting services allow you to run a cron job only once a day. This means that Moodle will perform those functions that depend on `cron.php` only once a day.

If you've been given space on your school or company's web server, speak to the system administrator about setting up the cron job. Moodle's `cron.php` uses very little memory and few system resources. Most servers can run it every 15 minutes without affecting the server's performance.

If you cannot set up the cron job on your host, your only other option is to set up the cron job on a Windows machine that you control. The cron job will reach out over the internet to your Moodle site and activate the `cron.php` script. Again, directions for this are in the `http://moodle.org/` installation guide. However, if you choose this option, you must keep that Windows PC running all the time, and it must also be connected to the internet at all times. If the Windows PC goes down or offline, the Moodle functions that require periodic triggering will also go down.

Summary

This chapter told you how to make changes to your site's configuration. It covered the settings that, in our experience, you are most likely to change. Many of these settings affect the behavior of the entire site. You don't need to get these choices perfect the first time, because you can return to these settings and edit them at will. As you proceed with building your site, you will probably want to experiment with some of them. At the same time, if you are using MoodleCloud, you may wish to think about the fact that you may be building a course for individuals to find from your social media sites. In that case, you'll probably need to make the enrollment aspects the easiest and also enable PayPal and make it clear how to register and pay.

In the next chapter, we will create courses and categories for our course catalog.

4
Creating Categories and Courses

This chapter shows you how to create a new, blank course. In this chapter, you will see how to create the course, choose the best format for your course, and enroll students into the course. In addition, we will ensure that the course is well designed and that you are continuously mindful of the overall learning objectives.

You will also learn how to create course categories and to use those categories for organizing your course catalog. They will align with your institution's mission and vision so that you maintain a coherent presence. You will also be able to use the results for marketing and promoting your programs and your institution. While someone else may have installed Moodle and created categories for you, you can always go back and change them. Thus, you will be able to constantly update and refresh your content.

We will also cover some of the more advanced settings that you can use in your course completion and conditional activities. These settings will enable you to better track your students' progress through the course and will require students to complete the course material in a specific order.

Later chapters in this book will show you how to fill your course with resources and activities.

If your students enroll themselves, they will usually choose the course from a list or a catalog of courses. The list of courses is organized by category, so we will begin by learning how to use course categories to organize our courses. We will then tie together vision, mission, and course objectives.

Planning based on your institution's mission and vision

Many learning organizations offer similar courses, yet their students report remarkably different experiences and outcomes. How can that be, if the content is identical? The reality is that your course content is just a part of the learning equation. A large component has to do with how the content is framed, contextualized, and then applied. Each ties to the primary mission and vision of your organization.

As your organization decides what it wants to be in the world, and how it wants to make an impact, it must devise its primary mission, that is, the *how we will do it* component to the overarching *what our ideal world looks like* question. If you think this sounds a bit utopian, you are right. It does; it is. The best learning organizations want to create a better world, even if that utopia will never actually exist in the real world, and, to get there, they need to determine action steps, which translate to a mission implemented by strategy and tactics, and can be implemented as follows:

- **Framework**: Think of the framework as the pillars that hold up your mission and vision. Define them. Then, as you do, they will help you create structures and categories of your organization's offerings.
- **Contexts**: Who do you identify as your main student body? What is your main target? Who are your learners? Where are they? What are their main strengths, abilities, and cultural backgrounds? You will need to define your audience as well as your instructors if you want to have an effective learning organization. You'll also need to have a sense of your learners, the learning environment, and the limiting/enabling technologies in order to sequence your courses, and ensure that they are at the correct level and presented in the right order.
- **Application**: Engaged students are the ones who are actively working with the content. They are the ones who are focused on being able to do more than simply memorize facts, answer questions, and then forget it all. Application involves invoking experiential learning and connecting to real-world situations and problems. So, as you create your courses and classify them, be sure to think about how it will be possible for your learners to put learning blocks together across the curriculum and prepare themselves to be completely autonomous.

You may think that frameworks, contexts, and application is too much to think about right now. After all, aren't you just putting together a list of courses? Yes and no. The list cannot be properly categorized if you do not know its ultimate purpose, its level, and what you want your students to do with the knowledge. This is particularly the case as you start thinking about ways to build on knowledge and have your students develop knowledge that will have real-world implications.

Using course categories and the user experience

Categories are a site-wide way to organize your courses. You can also create subcategories. The categories or subcategories become an online course catalog. Organize them in the same intuitive way that you would organize a printed course catalog.

Every Moodle course must be assigned to at least one-course category. Even if you choose to hide the display of categories, each course must still belong to a category; that's how the Moodle platform is organized. For sites with one or a few courses, we often hide and ignore the categories and display just the courses. When we need to show our users an organized catalog, we display the categories and subcategories.

Displaying courses and categories on your front page

There are several ways to display categories on the front page of your Moodle site.

The list that shows both course categories and the courses is called the *combo list*. You can configure the courses block to make it visible on the left or right of the screen in *clean* theme, as shown:

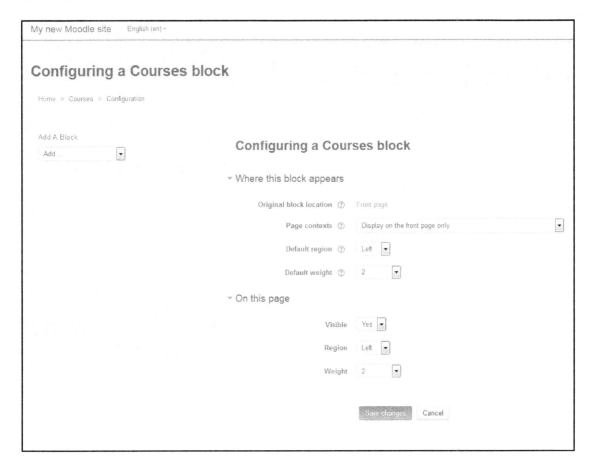

The combo list gives your front page an organized appearance. If you have a relatively modest number of courses, and the categories are self-explanatory for your users, the combo list might be a good option for your front page.

If you have a large number of categories and courses, or they are complex, a combo list might be too long for your front page. In that case, you can display just the course categories.

Then, the user would select a category and see the courses under that category, as they show up as drop-down menus or a simple list.

You have the option to create new categories and also to organize them so that they appear in the order that you would like. Keep in mind that these categories will appear in the block to the left. You can also edit the names of the courses in case they are too long for the space.

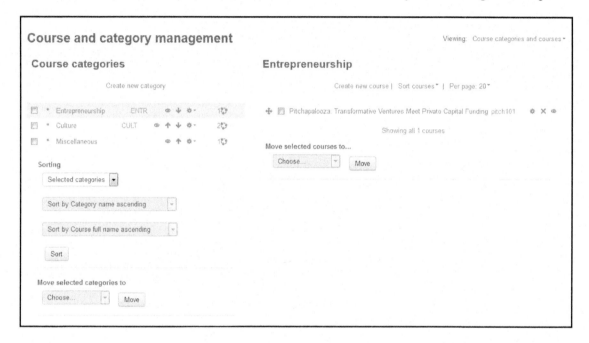

Note that when you open the **Course and category management** page, you have the opportunity to customize the category itself. You can edit the category, add a description (through **Manage this category**), assign roles, create permissions, create cohorts of students who are enrolled in Moodle, and create filters. You can also upload a **Learning plan** template and a competency framework. There are many competency frameworks available through the **Plugins** library, or you can develop your own:

 If you have too many categories to display on the front page, organize them into categories and subcategories. Then, hide the subcategories using the setting under **Site administration | Front page | Front page settings | Maximum Category Depth**.

Displaying an uncategorized list of courses on your front page

The third option for showing courses on the front page is an uncategorized list of courses. This is a good option if your site has only a few courses, or if you are trying to establish a new brand or certificate program that contains an unusual combination of courses. You want the unusual combination to appear so that you can provide explanations and launch into a vision of your approach.

You can take this to an extreme. For example, some sites start out with only one course. In that case, creating a separate category for that course and displaying a category list doesn't make sense. For example, the site shown in the following screenshot offers a demonstration course and two courses that require payment. A simple list of courses with the course descriptions makes the most sense for this site:

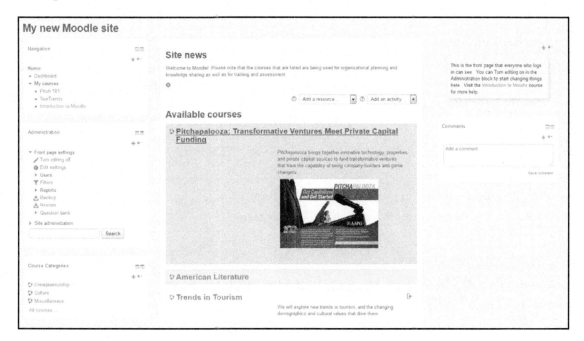

Choosing the best option for your front page

When you are deciding which option to use for your front page, try to put yourself into your student's situation:

If your students will be looking for the following	Then consider using the following
A specific course by name	An uncategorized list of courses, displayed alphabetically.
A specific type of course, but they are unsure of the name	A combo list or category list so that the student sees the types of courses offered.

If your students will be looking for the following	Then consider using the following
Either specific courses by name, or types of courses	A combo list. Add a notice to the front page that the student can search for courses by name (refer to the *Add instructions to your front page with labels* section in `Chapter 5`, *Resources, Activities and Conditional Access*).
If users are not sure what they are looking for	An uncategorized list of courses, if you have only a few courses. You can use the course description to sell each course. If your list of courses is too long for the front page, you'll need to use a category list and include information on the front page to convince visitors to explore the categories (the *Add instructions to your front page with labels* section in `Chapter 5`, *Resources, Activities, and Conditional Access*).

Now that we have discussed how each option can affect how your student sees and uses the site, let's see how to implement each of these options.

Creating course categories

You must be a site administrator to create, edit, and delete course categories. Perform the following steps to create course categories:

1. If you're not logged in as the administrative user, log in now. Use the **Login** link in the upper-right corner of the page.
2. You should be looking at the home page of your new Moodle site.
3. From the **Administration** menu on the left of the page, click on **Site administration** | **Courses** | **Manage courses and categories**. This displays the **Course categories** page. In this page, you create new categories and courses. Here, you can also arrange the order in which the categories are displayed on the front page.
4. Click on the **Create a new category** link. The **Add new category page** is displayed.
5. Select where in the hierarchy of categories this one will be. In the following example, it will be a subcategory of **Entrepreneurship**:

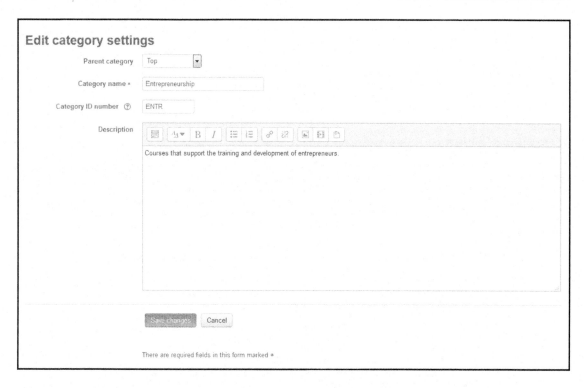

6. In the **Category name** field, enter a name for the category. Your users will see this in the category list.

7. In the **Description** field, enter a description for the category. If you configure your front page to show a list of categories, the user will see this description on selecting a particular category. Enter some information in order to help your users decide whether this is the category they need.

8. The category description can have the same features as any Moodle web page. For example, you can add a graphic to the category description, as shown in the following screenshot:

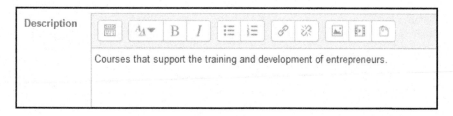

9. In `Chapter 5`, *Resources, Activities, and Conditional Access*, we show you how to use Moodle's web page editor. This is the same editor that you see in the preceding screenshot.

10. Click on the **Create category** button. Moodle creates the category and redirects you to the **Manage courses and categories** screen.

Rearranging course categories

You must be a site administrator to rearrange course categories. The order in which you put them on this page is the order in which your users will see them listed.

If you're not logged in as a site administrator, log in now. Use the **Login** button in the upper-right corner of the page. Here are the steps to follow:

1. You should be looking at the home page of your new Moodle site.

2. From the **Administration** menu on the left of the page, click on **Site administration** | **Courses** | **Manage courses and categories**. This displays the **Course categories** page.

3. To move a category up or down in the list, click on the arrow button next to the category:

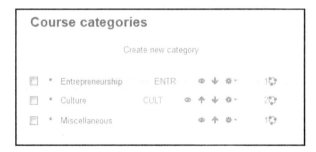

4. To convert a category into a subcategory, select the category and then use the **Move selected categories to** drop-down list:

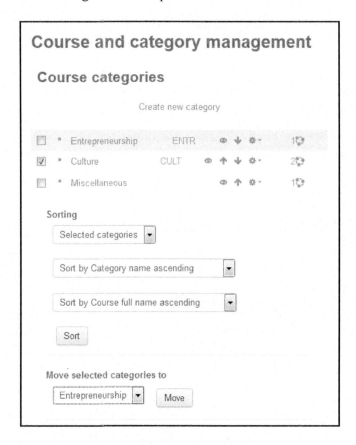

5. You do not need to save your changes. The changes you made on this page are automatically saved as you make them.

Creating courses

As stated earlier, every course belongs to a category. Don't worry if you mistakenly put a course into the wrong category. It is easy for a site administrator manager to change the category of a course.

Creating a course and filling it with content are two different functions. In this section, we talk about creating a blank course, with no content. In the later chapters, we will learn how to add material to a course.

To create a course, a user must have the site-wide role of the site administrator or manager. To add material to a course, a user must be the site administrator, course creator, manager, or teacher (usually the teacher adds material).

Creating a new and blank course

When you create a blank course, most of your choices and settings will be done on the settings page for the course. The Moodle Help icons on this page do a good job of explaining the purpose of each setting. However, the directions do not specify the implications of the choices you make on this page.

In the instructions given next, I've added some commentary to help you determine how your choices will affect the operation of your course, and how the student/teacher is affected by those choices. My goal is to help you make the right choices in order to create the teacher/student experience you want.

The result of this procedure is a new course, ready for adding course material.

To create a new, blank course, follow the given steps:

1. Log in to the site as a site administrator, manager, or course creator.
2. Select **Site Administration** I **Courses** I **Manage courses and categories**.
3. Click on the **Create new course** link. The **Edit course settings** page is displayed.
4. From the drop-down list at the top of the page, select a category for the course.
   - You can use the drop-down list to change the category at any time. The list shows both visible and hidden categories.
   - As your site grows and you add more categories, you might want to reorganize your site. However, if a student logs in while you are in the middle of creating categories and moving courses, he or she might be confused. It would be best if you can make the reorganization as quickly as possible—ideally and instantaneously.

- You can speed up the reorganization time by hiding your categories as you create them. This lets you take your time while thinking about what categories to use. Then, move the courses into the categories. Each course will disappear until you finally reveal the new categories.

5. Enter a **Full name** and a **Short name** for the course.
6. The full name of the course appears at the top of the page when viewing the course, and also in the course listings. The short name appears in the breadcrumb, or **Navigation** bar, at the top of the page. In the following example, the full name is **Non-Surgical Anti-Aging Services** in plain language and the short name is **Anti-Aging**:

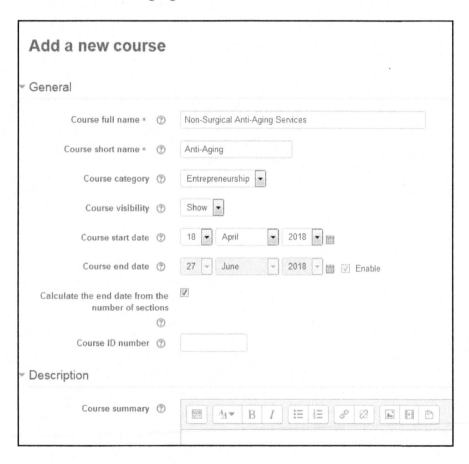

The full name also appears in the page's title and metadata, which influences how it appears in the search engines. The following is the HTML code, generated by Moodle, for the preceding example:

```
<head>
<title>Course: Non-Surgical Anti-Aging Services </title>
<link rel="shortcut icon"
href="http://localhost/moodle/theme/image.php/standard/theme/1359480837/fav
icon" />
<meta http-equiv="Content-Type" content="text/html;
charset=utf-8" />
<meta name="keywords" content="moodle, Course: Non-Surgical Anti-
Aging Services" />
```

Note the full course name in the `<title>` and `<meta>` tags. Many search engines give a lot of weight to the title tag. If your Moodle system is open to search engines, choose your course title with this in mind.

7. Enter a **Course ID Number**: `Chapter 3`, *Configuring Your Site,* talks about using an external database for enrollment information. If you are using an external database to enroll students, the ID number that you enter into this field must match the ID number of the course in the external database. If you're not using an external database for enrollment information, you can leave this field blank.

8. Enter a **Course summary**; if you choose to display a list of courses on the front page, the course summaries are displayed with the names of the courses, as seen in the following screenshot:

Course categories: Entrepreneurship ▾

Courses that support the training and development of entrepreneurs.

Search courses: [   ] Go

✿ Non-Surgical Anti-Aging Services

This course covers the products and processes used in businesses offering non-surgical anti-aging services.

✿ Pitchapalooza: Transformative Ventures Meet Private Capital Funding

Pitchapalooza brings together innovative technology, properties, and private capital sources to fund transformative ventures that have the capability of being company-builders and game changers.

Add a new course

You can add the description of the course through the **Course summary**. You can format it in many ways:

9. If you allow visitors to see your front page without logging in, they will probably read your course summaries before enrolling. Consider the summary to be a resume of the course. Your course summaries need to be informative and work as a sales tool. They should offer enough information to help your visitors decide whether they want to enroll and should describe the courses in their best light.

10. Select a format for the course. Among your choices are the following:
    - **Topics**
    - **Weekly** (unless this is changed by the site administrator, this is the default format for a new course)
    - **Social**
    - **Single Activity**

The **Topics** format is the most intuitive format to use for a course. As it displays each part of the course as a numbered topic, this format encourages most students to proceed through the course sequentially. However, by default, Moodle does not enforce this sequence, so students are free to jump ahead and behind in the course.

You can force students to complete the activities in a specific order using conditional activities. This is covered in detail later in the book. To use conditional activities, your system administrator must enable the feature **Enable conditional access** under **Site administration | Advanced Features**. If you want to force students to complete sections of your course only at designated times, consider using the **Restrict Access** setting under each topic's (or each week's) **Summary Settings**. Again, this is covered later in the book. For now, just select the **Topics** format. Later, we'll show how to force students to complete topics in a specific order or during a specific time period.

The **Weekly** format appears almost identical to the **Topics** format, except that it displays dates for each topic. As of this writing, Moodle does not automatically enforce these dates, that is, Moodle does not turn the weekly sections on and off on the appropriate dates. The site administrator or teacher must do that.

The **Social** format turns the entire course into one discussion forum. Discussion topics are displayed on the home page of the course. Replies to a topic are added and read by clicking on **Discuss this topic**.

The **Social** format is very different from a traditional, sequential course. It lacks the ability to add activities and resources in the main course area, which you find in the **Topic** and **Weekly** formats. However, because the **Social** format turns the entire course into a discussion forum, it offers you the chance to put a discussion forum right into the course listings. Then, you can have a discussion appear in the course listing on the front page of your site.

The **Shareable Content Object Reference Model (SCORM)** format enables you to upload a SCORM compliant activity. This activity then becomes the entire course.

When to use the SCORM course format?
If you want to use a SCORM package as a part of your course, use the **Topics** or **Weekly** format. Then, you can add the SCORM package as an activity in the course. If you want to use a SCORM package as your entire course, use the **Single Activity** format and upload the SCORM. That package becomes the entire course.

11. Select the **Number of weeks/topics**. If you selected the **Topics** or **Weekly** format for your course, you must specify how many topics or weeks your course will have. You can change the number of weeks or topics in a course whenever you want. If you increase the number, blank weeks/topics are added. If you decrease the number, weeks/topics are deleted, or so it seems. One of Moodle's quirks is that when you decrease the number of sections in a course, the topics that are dropped are not really deleted. They're just not displayed to the students. If you increase the number of topics, those hidden topics will again be displayed to the students with their content intact. Also, teachers who are in editing mode will see the dropped topics as grayed out, under a section called *Orphan*. The teacher can still access and edit those orphaned topics.

Note that this is different from hiding weeks/topics from students. When you hide topics or weeks, students can't see them but the teacher can. When a section disappears because the number of weeks/topics in the course was reduced, it is unseen to everyone, even the teacher. The only way to bring it back is to increase the number of weeks/topics.

If you accidentally decrease the number of weeks or topics too much and some of the sections that you created disappear, don't panic. They are still there. Just increase the number of weeks or topics and the sections will reappear, or go into the editing mode for the course and you will see the orphaned topics.

12. Set the **Course start date**:

For a **Weekly** course, this field sets the starting date shown. It has no effect on the display of **Topic** or **Social** courses. Students can enter a course as soon as you display it; the course start date does not shut off or hide a course until the start date. The only other effect of this field is that logs for the course activity begin on this date.

If you want to limit the dates on which a course is available for the students to enroll in, look under **Course administration** | **Enrolled users** | **Enrolment methods**. Enable the enrollment method for **Self enrolment**. Then, under the settings for **Self enrolment**, set the **Enrolment duration**.

If you want to test a course without creating user records, enter a date in the future into the **Enrolment duration**. As you test the course, your activity will not be included in the logs.

13. Select how the course will display **Hidden sections**. You can keep a section that you're working on hidden and then reveal it when you're finished. If you want to modify an existing section, you can create a hidden duplicate of the section, work on it, and with a few clicks in a few seconds, hide the old section and reveal the new one.

You can move resources between sections in a course. This makes a hidden section a convenient place to hold the resources that you might want to use later or that you want to archive. For example, if you find a site on the web that you might want to use in your course later but you're not sure, you can create a link to the site in a hidden section. If you eventually decide that you want to use the site, you can just move that link from the hidden section to one of the sections in the use-later pile.

14. Specify how many news items to show in the **Latest news** block.

The maximum number of news items that the block will show is 10.

15. If **Show gradebook to students** is set to **Yes**, a student can view a list of all their grades for the course by clicking on the **Grades** link in the **Course administration** block, as shown in the following screenshot:

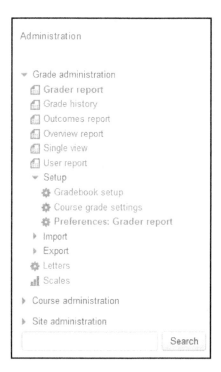

If the course allows **Guest access**, the guests will not be able to earn grades. So if your site has a free sample course, and you want people to see how Moodle displays their grades, you might want to make people register for that free sample.

16. You can see a report of your activity in each course that you take under your profile. Note that your personal activity report is in your profile, not in the courses. Whether a student's activity for a course will be kept in the student profile is determined by the **Show activity reports** setting. For a course that allows guest access, setting this to **Yes** usually doesn't make much sense. Remember that every anonymous, unregistered user enters the course under the **Guest** name, so having a report that shows the grades and activities for a **Guest** is usually not very useful. To track how many people tried a sample course and the parts of the course that they sampled, allow the users to create a free account in the fully functioning sample course. Make this especially easy by not requiring email confirmation when the student registers; instead, give instant approval. Now you can track and study individual usage in the sample course. To keep anonymous users out of the courses requiring registration or payment, use a **Login** page for such courses.

17. The setting for **Maximum upload file size** limits the size of a file that a student can upload into this course. There is also a site-wide limit set under **Site Administration** | **Security** | **Site policies**. The smaller of the two settings—site-wide or course-wide—takes precedence here.

18. The color and icons that Moodle uses are determined by its theme. Usually, you would use the same theme throughout your site. However, teachers and even students can change the theme that they use. The **Force theme** setting determines whether users can choose a different theme when they are in this course, or if they must use the selected theme.

 A theme can do more than just providing a pleasant color scheme. For example, you can assign the courses a distinctive theme for each teacher or assign the same theme to all the courses in a category, and so on. For more about themes, check out the official Moodle site at `http://moodle.org`.

19. Under **Guest** access, choose whether to allow guests to take the course. You can also set a guest password. This password applies only to guests, not to enrolled students.

20. Select the **Group mode**.

Later in the book, you will learn how to separate the students in a course into groups. This setting determines how the individual activities in the course react to the presence of groups in the course. If you do not use groups in the course, this setting has no effect.

When set to **No**, all students in the course are considered to be in one big group. When set to **Separate**, students in a group cannot see the names of any other groups, that is, the work done by different groups is kept separate. When set to **Visible**, students in different groups can see the students from other groups.

You can change this setting for individual activities. For example, suppose you want to run groups through a course separately. However, you have one project where you want all the students, in all the groups, to be able to see each other's work. You can choose **Separate** for the course, and, for that one project, override the setting with **Visible**. Now, only for that one project, each group can see the other group's work.

Running Separate groups through a course versus having separate courses:

Using **Separate** groups enables you to reuse a course for many groups, while giving the impression to each group that the course is theirs alone. However, this doesn't work well for a **Weekly** format course, where the weeks are dated. That's because the course home page displays the dates for each week. If you start each group on a different date, the weekly dates will become incorrect.

If you're running a **Topics** format course, you can easily reuse the course by separating your students into groups and running each group individually. Later, you'll see how to assign teachers to a course. You can assign a teacher to a group and remove their ability to see other groups (remove the capability *access all groups*). This will result in each teacher seeing only their students.

If you run several groups through a course and those groups are at different points in the course, be aware that the teacher cannot regulate the flow of students through the course by turning the topics off and on, that is, you cannot reveal just Topic 1 until the group has finished it, and then reveal Topic 2 until the group has worked through it, and then Topic 3, and so on. If you tried this while running several groups that were at different points in the course, you'd be turning off topics that some groups need.

If you really must enforce the order of topics, use conditional activities to reveal activities after the previous ones have been completed by a student.

21. Normally, the group mode of the course can be overridden for each activity. When the course creator adds an activity, the teacher can choose a different group mode than the default one set for the course. However, when **Force group mode** is set to **Yes**, all activities are forced to have the same group mode as the course.

22. The **Default grouping** for the course determines how groups are filtered in the grade book. This setting has no effect unless you are using groupings. A grouping is a group of groups. It can consist of one or more groups from the course that is put into a grouping. All groups can then be managed as a single group.

23. While you're working on a course, you may want to set **Availability** for **This course is not available to students**. This will completely hide your course from the students' view. Teachers and administrators can still see the course, so you can collaborate on the course content with them.

24. Select a setting for **Force language**. Selecting **Do not force** enables a student to select any language on the pull-down list of languages.

25. Remember that the languages on the pull-down list are limited by the setting you choose under **Site administration** | **Language** | **Language settings** | **Display language menu** and **Languages on language menu**. Also, you must have the language pack installed for any language that you want to use.

26. Also, remember that only the standard Moodle menus and messages are translated automatically when a student selects a different language. Course material is not translated unless the course creator entered material in another language and used the **Multi-language content** filter.

27. If you want to use different terms for the roles in your course, you can use **Role Renaming**. Moodle inserts your term for a teacher or student into its standard messages. You can substitute the term teacher with instructor, leader, or facilitator. For students, you can use terms like participant or member.

28. At the bottom of the page, click on the **Save changes** button.

Congratulations! You now have a new, blank course. You're ready to start configuring and filling it with great material.

Enrolling teachers and students

Who will teach your course? Also, how will students be enrolled? The settings that you choose for your course enrollment will determine that.

Assigning teachers

After a site administrator, manager, or a course creator has created a blank course, they can assign a teacher to build the course.

The teacher needs an account on your site. If you need to manually create the teacher's account, refer to the *Creating test accounts* section in `Chapter 3`, *Configuring Your Site*.

To assign a teacher to a course, carry out these steps:

1. Enter the course as administrator or manager.
2. From within the course, select **Course administration** | **Users** | **Enrolled users**.
3. In the upper-right corner of the page, click on the **Enrol users** button. The **Enrol users** window is displayed as in the following screenshot:

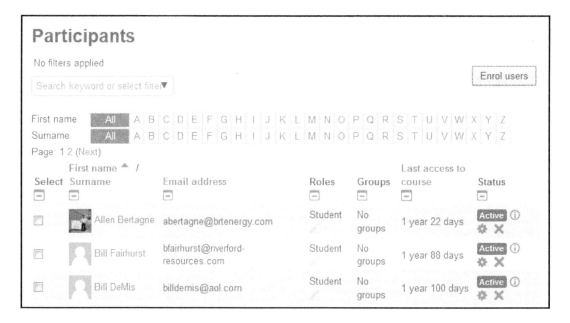

4. To find a user, enter any part of the user's name into the **Search** field and then press *Enter* or *return* on your keyboard:

5. From the **Assign roles** drop-down list, select **Teacher**.
6. Next to the user's name, click on the **Enrol** button. The display of that user's name will change to indicate that they are enrolled.
7. When you finish enrolling users, click on the close box for this window. On returning to the **Enrolled users** page, you will see the user added to the list of enrolled users.

How to set enrollment methods

The teacher can enable, disable, and arrange only the interactive enrollment methods. Interactive enrollment happens when a user tries to enroll on a course. The user must do something to be enrolled, such as select a course and confirm that they want to enroll, or pay for a course. Non-interactive enrollment methods are checked when a user tries to log in to a course, for example, an external database or LDAP server. Only a site administrator can enable or disable a login-time enrollment method. These are not managed at the course level, but at the site level.

In the *Enrolment methods* section in `Chapter 3`, *Configuring Your Site*, you enabled a list of enrolment methods for your site. For each course, you can enable or disable any or all of these enrolment methods. The following steps will guide you:

1. Enter the course as a site administrator or teacher.
2. Select **Course administration** | **Users** | **Enrolment methods**. The **Enrolment methods** page displays all the enrollment methods that are enabled for the site, as shown in the following screenshot:

3. To enable or disable an enrollment method for a course, click on the Eye icon. When the it is open, that enrollment method can be used for that particular course. When the eye is closed, that enrollment method is not available for that course.
4. Place the enrollment methods in the order in which you want this course to use them. Do this by clicking on the up and down arrows next to each enrollment method.

Many enrollment methods have a separate page for settings where you can configure that method, as follows:

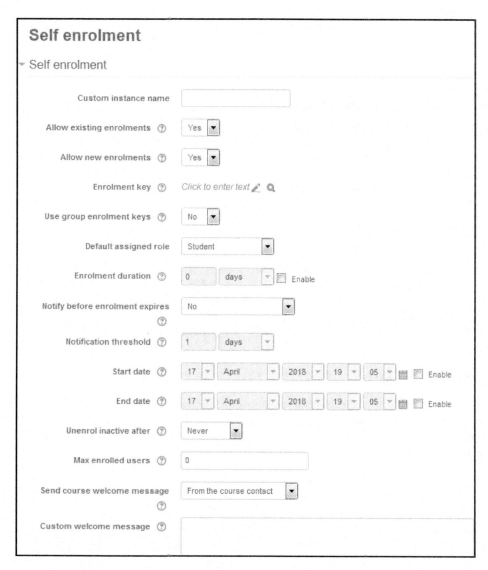

If you enable an enrollment method, you should at least look at the settings page for that method and determine whether you need to change any of the settings.

Handling course requests

The site administrator can enable course requests. When this is enabled, any logged-in user can request a course. The site administrator, manager, and course creator can then create the requested course.

Enabling course requests

The site administrator must enable course requests while logged in as a site administrator. There are a few steps, and they are very intuitive:

1. While logged in as the administrator, select **Administration** | **Site administration** | **Courses** | **Course request**.
2. Click to place a checkmark in the field labeled **Enable course** requests.
3. Other settings on this page will enable the users to select a category for the course that they select.
4. For the **Course request notification** field, select everyone you want to be notified when someone requests a course. If you want to select several users, use control-click to select them all.
5. Save your changes.

Getting notified about course requests

By default, when someone requests a new course, Moodle will send an email to the users who have the ability to create courses. It will also send an email to the course requester when the course is denied or created. How you receive these messages can be changed in your profile.

The following procedure can be used to change when you are notified about course requests that involve you, and also how you are notified:

1. After logging in, select **Home** | **Site administration** | **Courses**.
2. Select **Site administration** | **Courses** | **Course request**.
3. The page displays settings to configure notification methods for incoming messages.
4. Select if, and how, you want to be notified about the requests to create courses, as illustrated:

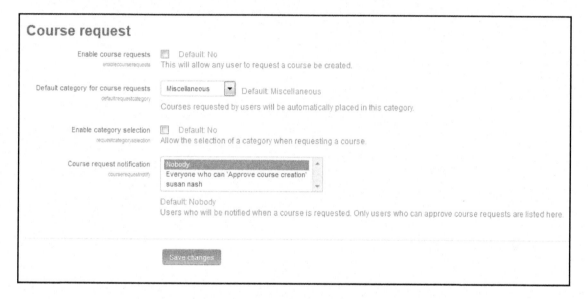

5. Click on the **Update profile** button to save your changes.

How to request a new course (teachers and students)

Any logged-in user can request a new course to be created if Enable course requests is checked:

1. Log in to the site.
2. From the **Site administration menu**, select **Courses**:

3. The **Course request** form will be displayed.
4. Fill out all the required fields and then click on the **Request a course** button.
5. The course request is sent to the users specified by the administrator.

Summary

In this chapter, we learned how to start the process of building courses. We started by identifying how to work with categories and then to configure the courses in several different ways.

In this chapter, we covered how to customize the appearance so that it matches the needs of your learners. You can select from a number of language preferences as well as layouts.

Learning how many blocks to use and where to position them will be helpful to your students because the blocks enable them to navigate through the course without getting lost. If your students are new computer users, they may assume that the presence of a block means that it requires their attention or interaction. Also, remember that you can turn blocks off and on, as needed.

In general, make your best guesses when you first create a course, and don't let uncertainties about any of these settings stop you. As you add static, interactive, and social materials in the coming chapters, you can revisit the course structure and settings in this chapter and change them, as needed.

5

Resources, Activities, and Conditional Access

As you develop your courses and curriculum in Moodle, it is important to plan well so that there is a level of consistency in the organization and presentation. Not only will you standardize your curriculum, you will also standardize your courses. At the heart of your organizing principles are the learning objectives. After that, you will include course material.

On Moodle, the course material is either a resource or an activity. A **resource** is an item that the student views, listens to, reads, or downloads. They can include web pages, links, files, videos, audio, and embedded social media.

An **activity** is an item that the student interacts with, or one that enables the student to interact with the teacher or other students. Examples include quizzes, assignments, wikis, forums, and more.

Usually, resources are ungraded, while activities are graded. Further, if you are developing a course curriculum for a certificate or degree program, you will need to ensure that they are presented in a consistent manner. You may wish to create a set of guidelines in a **Course Design Document (CDD)**, which you will share with all your instructors and instructional designers/technologists, who are involved in creating courses or materials for the course. The CDD can translate to a template, customized for all the courses and curriculum.

Mapping your approach

Mapping your course materials to your learning objectives will help you avoid creating a course that confuses students, and it will help them achieve their learning goals.

The best sequence for mapping is to follow a simple workflow, depicted as follows:

1. Identify your learning objectives
2. Create course sequence (chapters or units)
3. Write the specific learning goals for each chapter or unit, and tie them to your main learning objectives
4. For each unit or chapter, you'll have the following:
   - Chapter learning outcomes (tied to overall learning objectives)
   - Course content (directly ties to learning goals)
   - Activities (should be measurable and tie directly to your chapter outcomes)

Identifying course goals and learning objectives

The learning objectives for the course are the measurable outcomes that you would like your students to be able to accomplish at the end of the course. Course goals and learning objectives are often used interchangeably. They are measurable, and there should not be more than five or six for your entire course. Then, for each chapter or unit, you'll have unit learning goals, and they will tie to your overall course goals/learning objectives.

How do you actually frame learning objectives on the course and the unit level? How do you ensure that you frame them so that they're measurable and also at the correct cognitive level?

Bloom's Taxonomy is the standard used for writing learning objectives, particularly in the cognitive domain. Bloom's Taxonomy is used to classify educational learning objectives into levels of complexity and specificity. First developed in 1948 by Benjamin Bloom, and later modified, the tool provides a framework for selecting the verbs used in describing outcomes and then mapping them to activities.

As one can see in the following diagram, in Bloom's Taxonomy, the lowest rung of the ladder is the least in complexity, and it ascends to finally achieve the highest level:

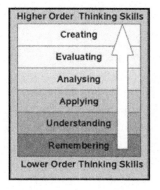

For the source of the image,
visit https://upload.wikimedia.org/wikipedia/commons/2/29/Bloom%27s_Taxonomy.png

The value of using Bloom's Taxonomy for developing a course as well as an instructional strategy is that it assures both clarity and consistency in design.

Further, by using Bloom's Taxonomy, one can ensure that they follow a sequence from less complex to more complex and properly scaffold the learning so that concepts and skills build on each other in levels of increasing complexity and difficulty.

Settings that are common to all resources and activities

Once you have mapped out your course, and you've made a list of the resources and activities that you'd like to add, you're ready to start taking a look at settings.

For all the different kinds of resources and activities, the first few clicks for adding them are the same. Also, there are some common settings that you will need to choose for all the resources and activities that you add.

Adding a resource or activity

Before you begin adding a resource or an activity, ensure that you are logged in to the course as an administrator, course creator, manager, or teacher. Also, ensure that you click on **Turn editing on**. Look in the upper-right corner or in the **Administration** menu for that button.

To begin adding a resource or activity, take the following steps:

1. In a topic or week where you want to add the resource, click on **Add an activity or resource**. If you're not sure where you want to add the resource; just make your best guess. You can move it around the course later.
2. The **Add an activity or resource** dialog box will be displayed. Click on the radio button next to the kind of resource or activity that you want to add.
3. Click on the **Add** button.
4. An editing page is displayed. Some of the settings on this page are unique for that type of resource or activity. Some of them are common to all the resources and activities. The common settings are covered in the following sections.

Entering the name and description

For every resource or activity that you add, you must enter a name and description. You will also choose if and when the description is displayed. As these fields are common to every resource or activity that you add, let's cover them under the respective sections.

To give a name and description for a resource or an activity, do the following:

1. Enter a name in the **Name** block:

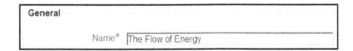

When you are done with editing and saving the resource or activity, this name will appear as a link on the course page, as seen in the following screenshot:

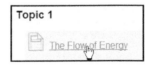

The name will also appear as a link on the navigation menu of the course. It is usually in the left or right column:

2. Enter a description in the **Description** block:

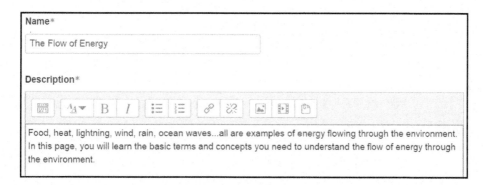

The item's description can appear on the course home page and also when the item appears in a list of resources for your course:

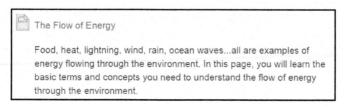

Showing and hiding a resource or an activity

When you add a resource or an activity to a course, you can make the item invisible to the students until you are ready for them to see it. For example, you might want to keep a web page hidden until you have finished writing it. Alternatively, you might want to reveal a series of activities as the class completes them, as a group.

When you hide an item, it is still visible to the teacher, course manager, and site administrator. It is hidden only from the students and visitors.

To show or hide an item, click on the Eye icon next to it to get the options as follows:

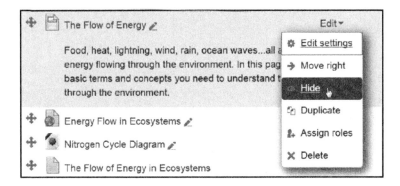

Setting the availability of a resource or an activity

Every resource or activity that you add will have **Common module settings**. If conditional access and/or completion tracking is enabled for the site, **Restrict access** settings are also added. As each item comes with these settings, we'll go through them once in the following sections.

Using the visibility setting to show or hide a resource

Under **Common module settings**, the **Visible** setting determines whether this resource or activity is visible to students, as shown:

Teachers and site administrators can *always* see the item. Setting this to **Hide** will hide the item from the students. Teachers can hide some resources and activities at the beginning of a course and reveal them as the course progresses. Alternatively, you can keep an item hidden while you're developing it and reveal it only when it's complete.

Using the ID number to include a resource in the grade book

The **ID number** field enables you to add an identifying number to a resource. Remember that we said that most resources are ungraded. By default, an activity is automatically included in the course's grade book, but a resource is not.

You may wish to include the resource in the grade book if you want to encourage and reward the action of reading or reviewing a resource.

Now suppose that you want to give the students credit (a grade, or some points) for viewing a web page. A web page is a resource. Somehow, you need to include the resource in the course's grade book. To do that, give it an ID number.

It will be the ID number of the resource, not its name, that appears in the grade book. Later on, you will learn how to add the resource to the grade book. For now, just add the ID number to the resource so that it is possible to add it to the grade book. The ID number of each course must be unique.

Restricting access

The **Restrict access** setting enables you to set conditions that control whether the student can see this resource. You can use three kinds of conditions: dates, user fields, and grades. Let's discuss each one now:

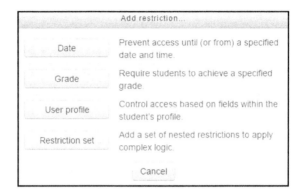

In the following screenshot, the user is adding a date restriction to a resource:

Adding a **from** restriction makes the resource available on that date and time onward. If you do not add a **from** restriction, the resource becomes available immediately.

Adding an **until** restriction sets a date and time when the resource becomes unavailable. If you do not add a **from** restriction, the resource remains available indefinitely.

If you leave **Allow access from** blank, the item is available immediately. If you leave **Allow access to** blank, the item will stay available forever.

The **Grade condition** setting enables you to specify the grade that a student must achieve in another activity in this course before being able to access this item.

In the following screenshot, you can see that the item will become available to the student only after the student scores at least 70 percent in an activity called **Terminology**. Also, the teacher is about to add another grade condition for an activity called **The Plants Around You**:

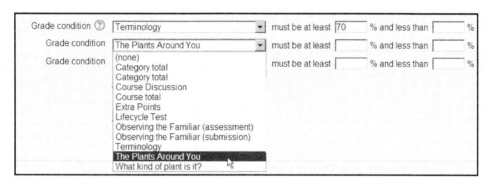

Summary of the process to use completion conditions

Using completion conditions to restrict access is not difficult. However, you do need to do some things in a specific order, explained as follows:

1. The site administrator must enable completion tracking site-wide, and the teacher must enable it in the course settings
2. Create the activities and resources that will need to be completed
3. For each item that needs to be completed, determine how it gets marked as completed (**Activity completion settings**)
4. Create the activity or resource that will be restricted
5. In the restricted activity or resource, select the activities and resources that need to be marked as complete before it can be accessed (**Activity completion conditions**)

In the following subsections, we will look at the detailed instructions for each step.

Creating the activities and resources that need to be completed

The later chapters will show you how to create resources and activities. After you've created all the resources and activities that will need to be completed, return to this section for instructions on how to set their completion conditions.

Creating the activity completion settings

The activity completion settings determine what needs to happen for an activity or resource to be marked as complete:

1. Select the activity or resource.
2. Under the **Administration** menu for the activity or resource, select **Edit settings**. In the following example, we are working with a glossary in the course:

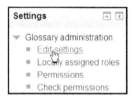

3. The **Settings** page is displayed. Scroll down to the section that is labeled as **Activity completion**.
4. The **Completion tracking** field determines how this activity or resource gets marked as complete, as seen in the following screenshot:

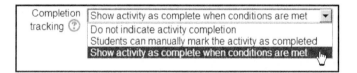

Either the student deliberately marks it as complete (**Students can manually mark the activity as completed**) or the student does something and then the activity is automatically marked as complete (**Show activity as complete when conditions are met**).

If you choose to have the student manually mark the activity or resource as complete, the student will mark it as complete from the home page of the course. For example, the following screenshot shows what the student sees on the home page when marking the glossary activity as complete:

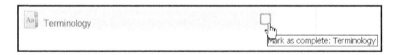

If you choose to have the activity or resource automatically marked as complete, in the next step, you will choose the conditions that cause it to be marked as complete.

5. If you selected **Show activity as complete when conditions are met**, you must select the conditions that will cause the activity or resource to be marked as complete:

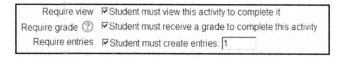

If this is a resource, the student cannot earn a grade for it. Only **Student must view this activity to complete it** will be available.

If this is an activity, both **Student must view this activity to complete it** and **Student must receive a grade to complete this activity** will be available.

In the preceding example, we are using a glossary activity. The **Student must create entries** condition is unique to glossaries. Other kinds of activities also have completion conditions that are unique to them. For example, in addition to the normal completion conditions, a forum can have the following conditions for completion:

6. At some point, you might want to run a report called the **activity completion report**. We will cover that in Chapter 14, *Features for Teachers*. If you think you will want to use that report, then enable the setting for the expected completion date, as seen in the following screenshot:

This does not display the expected completion date to the student. You are not setting a due date with this setting. Only the teacher will see this date in the activity completion report. If you want to tell the student to complete this activity or resource by a specific date, you will need to use some other method to do so.

7. You have finished setting the completion conditions. Either save the activity or resource, or continue modifying the other settings on the **Settings** page and then save.

Creating the activities or resources that will be restricted

Now that you have created the activities that need to be completed and set their completion conditions, you are ready to create the activity that will be restricted.

As stated earlier, the later chapters show you how to create resources and activities. Once you've created the resource or activity that will be restricted, proceed to the next set of instructions.

Setting the competency conditions

Finally, in the resource or activity that we are trying to restrict, let's choose when it becomes available, as follows:

1. Select the activity or resource.
2. Under the **Administration** menu for the activity or resource, select **Edit settings**
3. The **Settings** page is displayed. Scroll down to the section that is labeled as **Competencies**.
4. For the **Activity completion condition** field, select the activity or resource that must be completed. In the following example, it is a resource called **Glossary**:

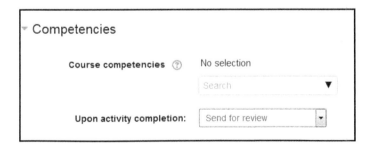

5. Select the **Send for review** condition.
6. You can add more completion conditions by clicking on the **Upon activity completion** button.
7. Either save the activity or resource or continue modifying the other settings on the **Settings** page.

Allowing students to see the activity or resource before they can access it

When an activity or resource is not yet open to a user, you can prevent users from seeing it on the course home page. The following example shows the Eye icon next to the access condition. If the Eye icon is open, then the student sees the activity/resource listed on the course home page even before the user has access. The activity/resource will be displayed in gray type. If the Eye icon is closed, the item will be hidden from the user until the user has access:

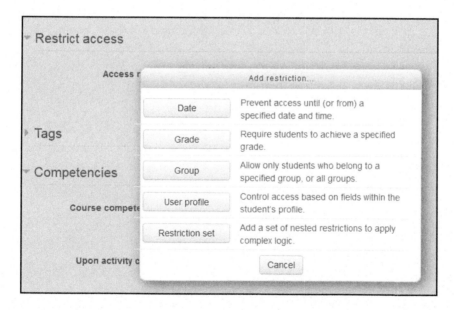

This setting is especially useful for quizzes. You can ensure that students review the material they need before taking the quiz and that they know what is required before the quiz becomes available.

Rearrange/move items on the course home page

As you build your course, you will be adding resources and activities to the course page. Moodle enables you to easily reposition these items. It's so easy to reposition them that I recommend that you don't even worry about getting them in the right place as you are creating them. Just forge ahead and create, and you can rearrange later.

Rearranging items on the course page can be done like this:

1. Log in to your course as a teacher or site administrator.
2. In the upper-right corner of the page, if you see a button that reads **Turn editing on**, click on the button. If it reads **Turn editing off**, you do not need to click on this button.
3. Next to the item that you want to move, place the mouse pointer over the crosshairs icon, as seen in the following screenshot:

✛ This Is Not Your Grandmother's Beach ✐

Edit▾

What's new in beach communities — how and why coastal communities have changed.

✛ ⊞ Attracting Passionate & Quirky Affinity Groups: Save the Sea   Edit▾ 👤
Turtles, Stand-Up Paddleboarding, ZombieNights, and more ✐

The new beach scene is all about affinity groups, who like both quirkiness and flexibility. You're likely to find sea turtle nurseries, stand-up paddleboarding (SUP), and Zombie-themed music, film, and costume-fests, all in the same community and on the same beach.

Beach tourism has evolved far, far beyond the idea of sunbathing and beach volleyball.

In this lesson, we explore some of the winners and losers in the beach community tourism game.

✛ 💬 Attracting Loyal and Passionate Tourists ✐   Edit▾ 👤

Use this chat space to get to know each other and to discuss the projects and collaborations on how to attract affinity tourists who can be loyal and passionate.

✛ 💬 My Quirky Affinity Group ✐   Edit▾ 👤

Here's where I start to pull together information about the kinds of quirky affinity groups I want to target, with the goal of using this information to identify potential groups and to develop a plan.

✛ 💬 EcoTourism Case Study: Sea Turtles ✐   Edit▾ 👤

Let's discuss EcoTourism by focusing on endangered sea turtles.

⑦ Add a resource... ▼   ⑦ Add an activity... ▼

✛ Topic 2 ✐

Edit▾

⑦ Add a resource... ▼   ⑦ Add an activity... ▼

4. Drag the item to where you want it on the course page and drop it.

 You can also drag and drop entire topics, if your browser has JavaScript enabled and Moodle has AJAX-enabled (both should be the default). You'll know that you can do this if you see a Crosshairs icon next to the topic. Just drag the Crosshairs icon and drop it where you want the topic to go.

Summary

In this chapter, you learned how to plan your courses so that you map the resources and activities to the course learning objectives. You learned about Bloom's Taxonomy and how it forms the cornerstone and cognitive foundation of the instructional strategy. The chapter also covered the difference between resources and activities and the basics of adding them to a course. You also went through settings that are common to the different kinds of resources and activities. In the next few chapters, you will learn about the specific settings for specific resources and activities and how to make the best use of them. While you're learning how to work with those items, you can refer back to this chapter for a reminder on how to use the common settings.

6
Adding Resources

Resources are course materials that students read but don't interact with, such as presentations, graphics, and PDFs. This chapter teaches you how to add those resources to a course, and how to make the best use of them. We will also discuss how to select, sequence, and deploy the resources so that they clearly contribute to the students' success in achieving outcomes.

In this chapter, we also discuss organizing your course and adding different kinds of resources, URLs, pages, and adding files.

Tying resources to course outcomes

Have you ever taken a course that has folder after folder of great articles, lots of embedded videos and audio, maps, charts, graphics, and interactive "discovery" activities, but, instead of feeling that you had all you needed at your fingertips, you felt lost, frustrated, and overwhelmed?

If you did, you were not alone. It is great to have lots of resources in the course. However, unless they are organized well, and they tie really clearly to course outcomes, you'll generate frustration instead of confidence.

Planning and organization are the keys to success in selecting, sequencing, and deploying your resources. Always tie them first to the learning outcomes, and then ensure that they are grouped in ascending order of complexity so that you're building in a strong foundation and then scaffolding on to higher levels.

So, the first step should always be to list the course outcomes and then create an outline of your course in which you start to identify the resources you'll need:

1. List course outcomes
2. Review your course outline
3. Identify the resources you'll need
4. Map the resources to your outcomes and identify any gaps that might exist

Adding different kinds of resources

The following table lists the types of resources that are available in Moodle. Resources are added from the **Add an activity or resource** drop-down menu. Using this menu, you can add these resources:

Resources	Description
Book	A **Book** is a series of web pages, organized into chapters. A **Book** can consist of one or more chapters. This is a good option for presenting a series of web pages that you want the student to read in order. It keeps things neat and clean so that your students do not have to wade around in a chaotic jumble of content.
File	Moodle can serve a single **File** to your student. If Moodle's built-in media player can play the **File**, you can configure it to automatically embed. Alternatively, you can configure the **File** so that it downloads to the student's computer and lets the student's computer determine how to open and display it. You can place **File** instances within the folder of a chapter, which makes it easy for the student to know which resources correspond to particular sections of the course.
Folder	A **Folder** is a collection of files that you have added to the course. For example, you can have a **Folder** for each topic in a course, where you give the student all the files needed to complete the exercises for that topic. Alternatively, a **Folder** can be for a specific activity, especially if there is a project that needs to be completed and the instructions, guidelines, and examples are within that set.
Label	A **Label** is a text, graphic, or a media file that you put on the home page of a course. Almost anything that you can put onto a web page, you can put onto the home page of your course. You usually use a **Label** to describe or label the content around it.

Resources	Description
Page	A Moodle **Page** is a web page that you create using Moodle's web page editor. A **Page** is effective in organizing content around a specific topic. In the **Page**, you can include links, folders, and files, and you can also create your own text content. A Page can have the appearance of a digital textbook.
URL	A **URL** is a link to another place on the web. Usually, you link to a page or file that exists outside of Moodle. However, you can link to a place inside your own Moodle site.

Each of these resources is covered in the following sections.

> Refer to Chapter 5, *Resources, Activities, and Conditional Access*, for information about the settings that are common to all resources.

Adding URLs

On your Moodle site, you can show content from anywhere on the web using a link. You add the link to your course's home page. When the student clicks on the link, the linked item is displayed.

When using the content from outside sites, you need to consider the legality and reliability of using the link. Is it legal to display the material within a window on your Moodle site? Will the material still be there when your course is running?

Display options – Embed, Open, and In pop-up

You can choose how the page is displayed; there are three options.

You can **Embed** the linked page into a Moodle page. Your students will see the **Navigation** bar; any blocks that you have added to the course and navigation links across the top of the page, just like when they view any other page in Moodle. The center of the page will be occupied by the linked page.

Open will take the student off of your site and open the linked page in the window that was occupied by Moodle.

In pop-up will launch a new window on top of the Moodle page, containing the linked page.

In the following examples, we linked to a page called **Energy Flow in Ecosystems**. That page exists on another site, `http://wikieducator.org/Main_Page`. We'll look at some thumbnail pictures of how each option looks.

Embed

When the user clicks on the link on the course home page, the outside page is displayed in a frame. The user is still on your Moodle site:

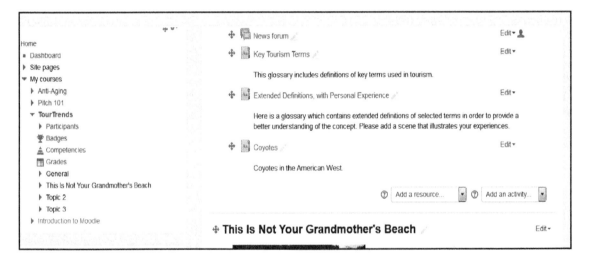

Open

When the user clicks on the link on the course home page, Moodle displays the page with the description of the link and a link to the outside page:

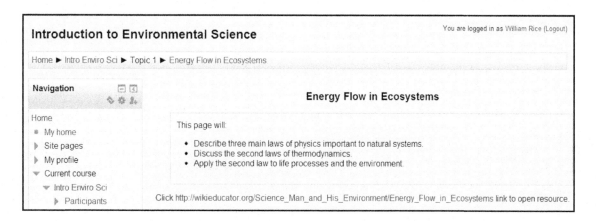

Clicking on the link brings the user to the outside page. They have left your Moodle site:

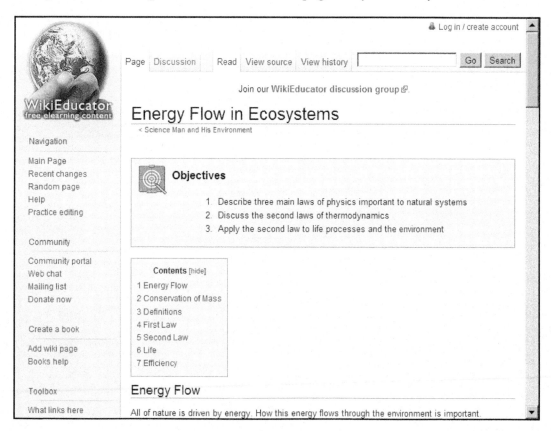

In pop-up

When the user clicks on the link on the course home page, Moodle displays the page with the description of the link and a link to the outside page:

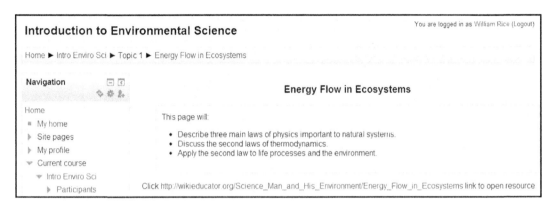

Clicking on the link opens a pop-up window with the outside page. It is displayed on top of the window with your Moodle site:

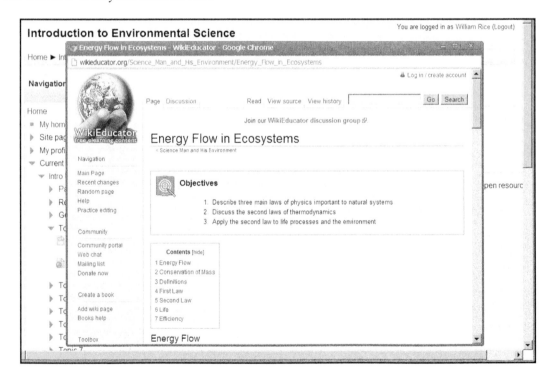

The following section contains instructions for creating a link on your course home page, and for using these options.

To add a link to a resource on the web, follow these steps:

1. In the **Topic** or the **Week**, where you want to add the resource, click **Add an activity or resource**. If you're not sure where you want to add the link, just make your best guess. You can move it around the course later.

2. The **Add an activity or resource** dialog box will be displayed. Click on the radio button next to **URL**.

3. Click on the **Add** button.

4. Moodle displays the settings page for this resource.

5. Enter a **Name** and **Description** for the link. For more about how the name and description affect the user experience, refer to `Chapter 5`, *Resources, Activities, and Conditional Access*.

6. In the **External URL** field, enter the web address for this link.

7. Under **Appearance**, from the **Display** drop-down menu, select the method that you want Moodle to use when displaying the linked page: **Embed**, **Open**, or **In pop-up**. **Automatic** will make Moodle choose the best method for displaying the linked page.

   For more about these display options, check out the *Display options – Embed, Open, and In pop-up* section, explained previously.

8. The checkbox for **Display URL description** will affect the display of the page, only if **Embed** is chosen as the display method. If selected, the **Description** will be displayed below the embedded page.

9. Under **Appearance**, you can set the size of the pop-up window. If you don't select **In pop-up** as the display method, these fields have no effect.

10. Under **Parameters**, you can add parameters to the link. In a web link, a parameter will add information about the course or a student to the link. A discussion of URL parameters is beyond the scope of this book. If you have web programming experience, you might take advantage of this feature. For more about passing parameters in URLs, refer to `http://en.wikipedia.org/wiki/Query_string`.

11. The **Common Module Settings**, **ID number** field, and **Restrict Availability** settings are covered in `Chapter 5`, *Resources, Activities, and Conditional Access*.

12. Click on one of the **Save** buttons at the bottom of the page to save your work.

Adding pages

Moodle enables you to compose a web page and add it to your course. The page that you add will be created and stored in your Moodle site. Be very strategic when adding Moodle pages. If you are not careful, you'll create confusion. Here are the best ways to use pages:

- **Content that ties to the course outline**: You may have short narratives or an entire chapter. Creating pages rather than a file allows you to also include links and for the navigation to flow very smoothly so that your students stay within Moodle at all times.
- **Portal pages with introductions, plus links, files, and books**: You may wish to have a long introduction to your content for a specific unit or chapter of your course. You can create a page, add your introduction (including graphics and text), and then have a clearly organized set of links, files, folders, and even books.

When you add a page to your course, Moodle displays a text editor. Using this editor, you can put almost anything onto the Moodle web page that a normal web page can contain.

A link to the page that you create will appear on the course's home page.

If you can use a basic word processor, you can use most of the web page editor's features. A full discussion of the editor's features is beyond the scope of this section. Instead, we will examine a few of the key features available in Moodle's HTML editor.

Adding a page to your course

To add a page to your course, follow the given steps:

1. In the topic or the week where you want to add the resource, click on **Add an activity or resource**. If you're not sure where you want to add the link, just make your best guess. You can move it around the course later.
2. The **Add an activity or resource** dialog box will be displayed. Click on the radio button next to **Page**.
3. Click on the **Add** button.
4. Moodle displays the settings page for this resource.
5. Enter a **Name** and **Description** for the page. The name will become the link to this page and will appear in the section that you added it to on the course's home page.

6. If you select the checkbox for **Display description on course page**, the description will appear on the course's home page. You can use this feature to tell the student what to expect when they view the page and tell them the purpose of the page. Here's an example of a link to a page, with its description displayed below it:

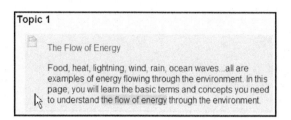

7. For more about how the name and description affect the user experience, refer to `Chapter 5`, *Resources, Activities, and Conditional Access*.

8. Even though this is the **Settings** page, this is also where you compose the web page. Scroll down to the **Content** section and you will see a test editor for composing the page:

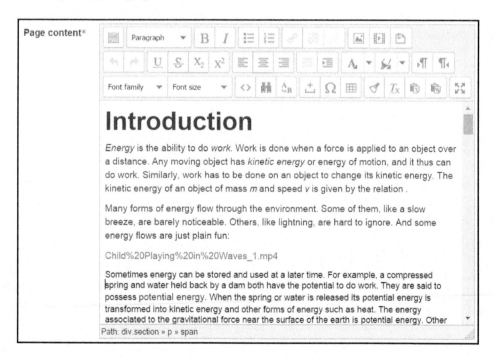

9. If you can use a basic word processor, you can use Moodle's web page editor. Most of the text-and-paragraph formatting options are the same as what you have seen in word processors and other web-based text editors. So, instead of covering those options, we will cover some of the functions that are less intuitive. Go through the following sections.

Adding images

When you select an image to add to a Moodle page, you can choose images from those that you have already uploaded in Moodle, or you can upload a new image.

A less obvious feature is the ability to link to a picture that is hosted on another website. For example, you can link to a picture hosted on a Flickr account or the one that appears on a non-profit educational website. If you are using pictures hosted in another website, you can add the link, but be aware that link addresses change often. Also, be sure to give credit.

Inserting an image file

This procedure is for inserting an image file that you have on your computer. In our example, the user has a diagram that they want to insert into the page.

To insert an image file, follow the given steps:

1. On the Moodle page, click to place the insertion point where you want the image to appear.
2. Click on the **Insert Image** icon, as shown:

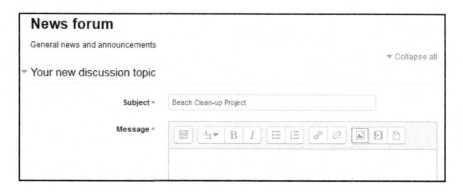

3. The **Insert/Edit image** window appears. In this window, click on the button labeled **Find or upload an image**.
4. The **File picker** window will be displayed. In this window, click on the **Upload a file** link.
5. Click on the **Choose File** button.
6. Locate the file on your computer and select it.
7. Click on the **Open** or **OK** button.
8. In the **Save as...** field, give the file a user-friendly name. You can use special characters and spaces.
9. The **Author** field is automatically filled in with your name. If someone else is the owner of this file, enter their name here.
10. From the drop-down list, choose a **License** for this file. This enables you to inform other Moodle teachers who want to use this file about what they can legally do with the file.
11. Click on the **Upload this file** button. The file is uploaded to your Moodle system and you are returned to the **Insert/edit image** window.

12. It is a good practice to fill in the **Image description** field. This is used by visually impaired users who can't see the image and by search engines to index the image.
13. If needed, fill out the fields under **Appearance**. You might want to resize the picture, since Moodle will, by default, display the picture at its original size.
14. Click on the **Insert** button. The picture is inserted into the page.

Inserting a hot-linked picture into a Moodle page

This procedure is for inserting a linked image, which appears in another location on the web. If you want to insert an image file that you have on your computer, refer to *Inserting an image file* in the previous section:

1. Find the image that you want to link to.
2. In your browser, right-click on the image. A pop-up menu will appear. One of the options on this menu will enable you to copy the URL (the web address) of the picture. For example, in **Internet Explorer**, you would select **Properties** and then copy the **Address** of the image. In **Firefox**, you would select **Copy Image Location**.
3. Switch back to Moodle, where you are editing the page.
4. Click on the page; so the insertion point is where you want the picture to appear.
5. Click on the **Insert Image** icon:

6. A pop-up window appears. In this window, paste the address of the image into the **Image URL** field. In the following screenshot, you can see the **HTML editor** window in the background. On top of that, you can see the **Insert/edit image** window. At the bottom of the screen is the original location of the image:

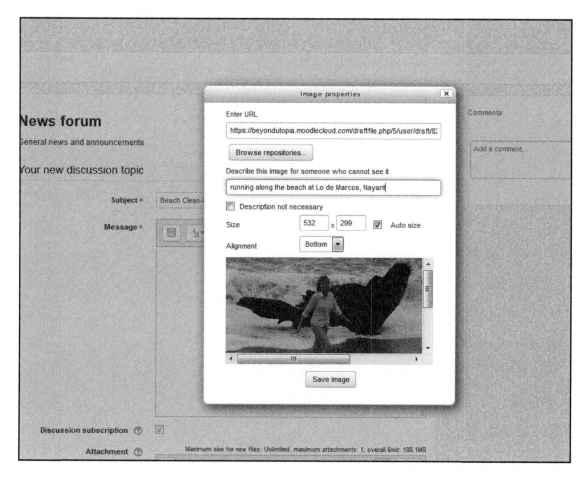

7. If needed, fill out the fields under **Describe this image....** You might want to resize the picture, since Moodle will, by default, display the picture at its original size.

Pasting text

Many times, we prefer to write text in our favorite word processor instead of writing it in Moodle, or we find text that we can legally copy and paste into Moodle. Moodle's text editor does enable you to do this. You can choose from the default editor, Atto, or you can select TinyMCE from course settings. Both work well, but you may need to do a bit of clean up.

However, ensure that you keep in mind that Microsoft Word's various versions can do strange things to formatting. You may wish to strip out all the macros that create very clean text. You can use Notepad, or even Notepad++ (`https://notepad-plus-plus.org`). After you've stripped out Microsoft's macros, you'll have to go back in and format (bold, underline), and you'll have to make your URLs live.

To paste text into a page, you can just use the keyboard shortcut. Try *Ctrl + V* for Windows PCs and *command + V* for Macintoshes. If you use this method, the format of the text will be preserved.

Stripping out the formatting – Pasting plain text

To paste plain text, without the format of the original text, click on the **Paste as Plain Text** icon:

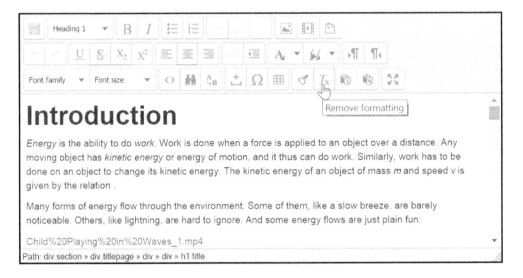

Pasting text from Microsoft Word

When you paste text from a Microsoft Word document onto a web page, it usually includes a lot of non-standard HTML code. This code doesn't work well in all the browsers and it makes it more difficult to edit the HTML code in your page. Many advanced web page editors, such as Adobe Dreamweaver, have the ability to clean up the Word HTML code. Moodle's web page editor can also clean up Word HTML code.

When pasting text that was copied from Word, use the **Paste from Word** icon. This will strip out most of Word's non-standard HTML code:

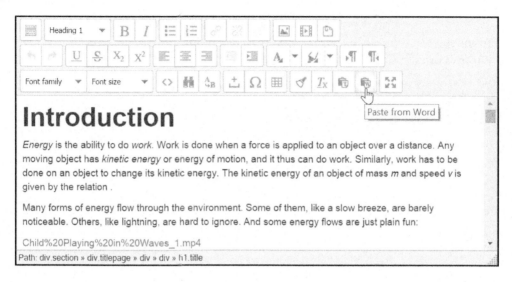

Composing in an HTML editor and uploading to Moodle

For long or complex HTML pages, or just for your own comfort, you might want to compose your web page in an HTML editor such as Dreamweaver or even the free web-based HTML editor, SeaMonkey. This is especially true if you want to take advantage of these editors' ability to insert JavaScript timing, and other advanced features into your web page. How then, do you get that page into your Moodle course? You can copy and paste the HTML code from your web page editor into the Moodle page editing window. To do this, you would do the following:

1. Select HTML view in your web page editor. For example, in Dreamweaver, you would select **View | Code**, and in the front page, you would select **View | Reveal Codes**.
2. Select the HTML code in your web page between the two body tags, that is, drag from just after the `<body>` tag near the top, to just before the `</body>` tag at the end. Copy the code with **Edit | Copy** or by pressing *Ctrl + C*.

3. Switch over to Moodle, and create the new web page.
4. Show the HTML code by clicking on the icon.
5. Paste the code by pressing *Ctrl + V*.

A second method is to publish your web page to someplace outside of Moodle and create a link to it from your course.

Learn more about HTML

To learn more about HTML code, you can start with the organization responsible for defining the standards. The World Wide Web Consortium maintains the complete standards for HTML online at `http://www.w3.org/TR/html4`. It maintains a basic tutorial at `http://www.w3.org/MarkUp/Guide/`. Everything covered in this basic guide can be done using the editor in Moodle in its normal mode. The advanced HTML guide at `http://www.w3.org/MarkUp/Guide/Advanced.html` covers some features that you would need to go into HTML view to add, such as defining clickable regions within images and using roll-overs.

Adding files for your students to download

You can add files to a course so that your students can download them onto their personal computers. Some examples of files you might want students to have are forms to fill out, readings to complete before class, and word processing files to edit.

When a student selects a file from the course

When a student selects a file from your course, the student's computer will attempt to open that file. Moodle will only pass the file to the student's computer. For example, if it's a PDF file, your student's computer will probably try to use Adobe Reader or the Preview app to open the file. If it's a word processing file, your student's computer will attempt to use Word or some other word processor to open it. If your student's computer doesn't have a program that can open that type of file, it will probably prompt the student to save the file. In the case of a graphic or a sound file, their computer will use whatever resident application is most convenient. It is usually not the ideal one.

You can override this behavior with a setting called **Force download**. When you choose that setting, your student's computer will not try to open the file. Instead, it will download the file and prompt the student to save it.

If you want the student to use the file immediately upon accessing the file, just go with the default behavior. If you want the student to save the file for future use, select the **Force download** setting.

You will see this setting in a later section, when we look at the instructions for adding files to your course.

File repositories

Every file that you upload into a Moodle course is stored in a Moodle repository. Before we add files to our course, we need to understand how repositories work and how to choose the right kind for our course.

Types of repositories

A repository is a storage area that Moodle can access. The repository doesn't need to be on your server. It just needs to be accessible to your Moodle system.

Repositories need to be enabled by the site administrator, under **Site administration** | **Plugins** | **Repository** | **Manage repositories**. Here are some examples of file repositories:

Type of repository	Use this when
Server files	You want to reuse a file that you uploaded into another course. For example, you want to reuse a graphic that you added to a page in another course, or a document that you added to another course.
Upload a file	The file that you want to add to your course resides on your computer, and you want to use it in the current course. The file must be no larger than the upload limit for your Moodle system.
Filesystem	The file that you want to use has been uploaded to the Moodle data directory. You usually do this when the file is too big to upload directly into Moodle or when you need to upload a lot of files all at once.

Type of repository	Use this when
Box.net, Dropbox, Google Docs, Amazon Web Services	You want to use a service outside of Moodle to store your files. If you're using an inexpensive, shared hosting service for Moodle, you might get more storage space and better upload/download speed using a third party to store your large course files.
Flickr, Google Photos, Picasa Web Album	You want to use photos that are part of an online album.

Using file-sharing services to collaborate

When you use a file repository such as Dropbox, Google Drive, or Box, you are storing your files outside of Moodle. This is a great way to collaborate. However, be aware that only with Google Docs, can you push files up into the cloud. If you use the Dropbox and Box.net repositories, you can only pull files down into Moodle. You will need to go outside of Moodle to push files up into those repositories. It is a good idea to use file-sharing services as well when collaborations continue beyond the time and scope of the course.

Using repositories to overcome Moodle's limit on file sizes

There is a limit to the size of a file that can be uploaded into your Moodle system. This limit changes for different Moodle sites. If you are using MoodleCloud, there are even more compelling reasons to use repositories. You will be able to create a master document with links, and such that lives outside your course.

There are three settings that limit the size of a file than can be uploaded into Moodle. Two of those settings are on your web server. The administrator for your web server will need to change them. If you are using a shared hosting service, you might not be able to change these settings. The third setting is in Moodle; it can be changed by the system administrator.

The size limit for uploaded files is the smallest of these three settings.

Your web server is probably using Apache to serve web pages. Apache can (but does not need to) have a limit set on the size of files that can be uploaded to the server through web pages. To determine whether Apache is limiting the size of uploaded files, you should ask your web server administrator.

Moodle uses the PHP programming language. The PHP language is in addition to Apache. PHP can also set a limit on the size of files that can be uploaded. In the `php.ini` file, look for the line that says `upload_max_filesize =`.

The Apache limits, and the PHP limit, are settings that you should discuss with your server administrator.

In Moodle, under **Site administration** | **Courses** | **Course default settings**, look for the setting labeled **Maximum upload size**. The maximum size available under that setting is taken from the `php.ini` file. You can set a lower limit than this but not a higher limit.

When you upload a file into Moodle, it will be placed in a file repository. By default, it will appear in the **Server Files** repository. If the **Recent Files** repository is enabled, the file might also appear there. If the file is too large, Moodle will not allow it to upload.

The most common way to get around Moodle's size limit on file uploads is by using a **File system** repository. When the site administrator creates a filesystem repository, the administrator first creates a folder, or directory, on the server where the Moodle data is stored. The administrator then creates a repository in Moodle that points to this directory. When you need to add a large file to a Moodle course, you go outside of Moodle and upload the file to this directory. Usually, you use an FTP client such as WinSCP or FileZilla to upload the file to the server. Now that the file is on the server, and in the repository's directory, you can go into Moodle and add the file to your course.

The following are the step-by-step instructions for each of these processes:

1. Enabling the filesystem repository
2. Creating the directory for the filesystem repository
3. Uploading files to the filesystem repository
4. Creating the filesystem repository in your course
5. Selecting a file from a filesystem repository

Enabling the filesystem repository

Before anyone in your Moodle site can use a filesystem repository, the site administrator needs to enable that option:

1. Log in to your site as an administrator
2. Select **Site administration** | **Plugins** | **Repositories** | **Manage repositories**

3. Next to **File system**, select **Enabled and visible**:

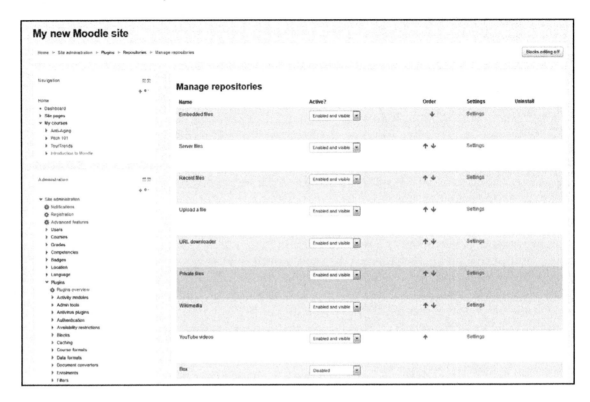

Creating the directory for the filesystem repository

We are creating a filesystem repository, which means the files will be stored on your server. Therefore, we need a directory in which to store them.

This part of the process needs to be done by someone with access to the server.

In the Moodle data directory, create a subdirectory named `repository`. In that subdirectory, create a subdirectory for each repository that your users will want:

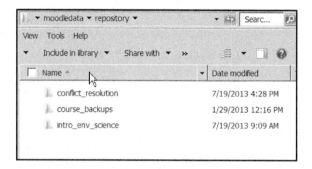

To determine the correct permissions for the repository folders, look at the permissions for the folders under `filedir`, which is also in the Moodle data directory. Duplicate those permissions for the folders that you create for your repositories.

Uploading files to the filesystem repository

Again, this part of the process needs to be done by someone with access to the server.

Now, you can upload files of any size into the directories. You would use an FTP client such as FileZilla, Fetch, or WinSCP:

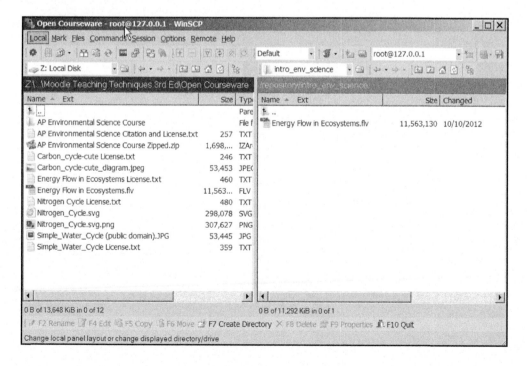

To determine the correct permissions for the repository files, look at the permissions for the files under `filedir`, which is also in the Moodle data directory. Duplicate those permissions for the files that you upload into your repositories.

Creating the filesystem repository in your course

This must be done by the site administrator:

1. Log in to the course. From the Course Administration menu, select **Repositories | Course repositories**.
2. If any repositories have already been created in this course, they will appear on this page. You can create multiple repositories for the same course.
3. Click on the link for **Create File system instance**.
4. The page will display a field where you enter the **Name** of the repository. It will also display a drop-down list of the subdirectories that are in the /repository directory.

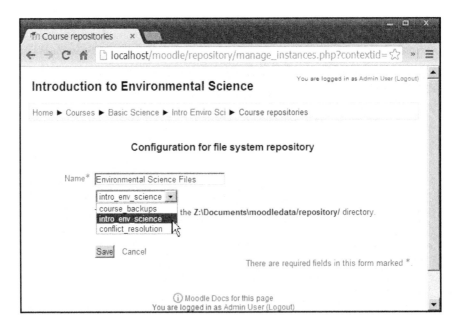

Following the steps for adding a file to your course:

1. Log in to your course as a teacher or a site administrator.

2. In the upper-right corner of the page, if you see a button that reads **Turn editing on**, click on the button. If it reads **Turn editing off**, you do not need to click on this button.

3. In the section where you want to add the file, click on the link for **Add an activity or resource**.

4. A pop-up window is displayed. It lists the types of items that you can add. Under **Resources**, select **File**.

5. Click on the **Add** button.

6. Moodle displays the **Adding a new File** page.

7. Enter a **Name** for the file. This is the name that people will see on the home page of your course:

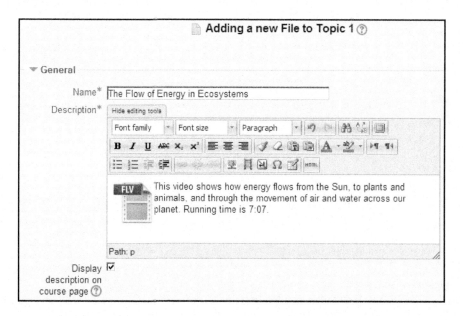

8. Enter a **Description** for the file. When the student sees the course's home page, they can see the **Description** if you select **Display description on course page**. Note that in the preceding screenshot, the user has added a graphic to the file's **Description**.

9. Under **Content**, click on the **Add...** button. The **File picker** window displays:

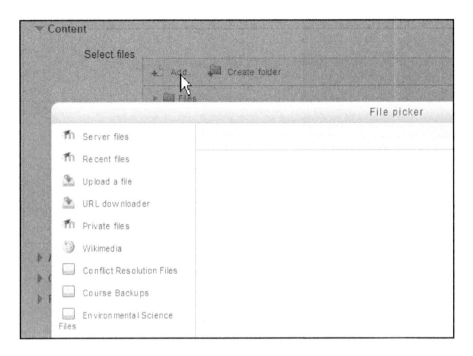

10. Select the repository that holds the file. In this example, we are using the one labeled **Environmental Science Files**.

11. Click on **Browse...** and select the file. After selecting the file, a dialog box is displayed:

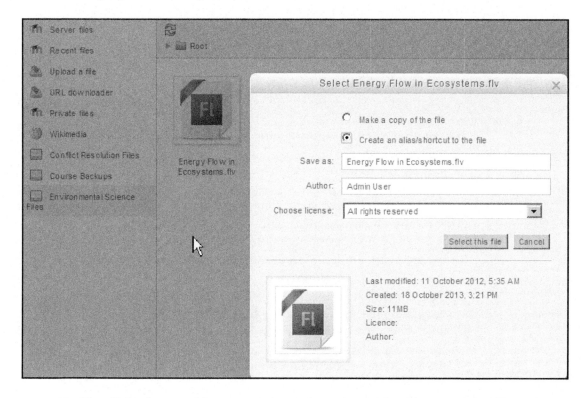

12. The dialog box enables you to choose between **Make of copy of the file** and **Create an alias/shortcut to the file**.

If you choose to make a copy of the file, your course will use its own, separate copy of the file. If the original file, the file in the repository folder, is changed, that will have no effect on your course.

If you choose to create an alias to the file, your course will use that actual file, which resides in the repository folder on the server. If the original file is changed, then your course will use the updated file. If you are using the same file in many courses and sections, it is always a good idea to keep the repository folder on the server so that you only have to change it one time.

13. In the **Save as** field, you can change the file's filename.

14. By default, the **Author** field has your name. If someone else created this file, give them proper credit by entering their name as the author.

15. The **Choose license** drop-down list enables you to select a license so that other teachers know what kind of copyright this file has.

16. Click on **Select this file**. The **File picker** window closes, and you are redirected to the page where you edit the file.

17. From the **Display** drop-down menu, select the method that you want Moodle to use when displaying the file:

    - **Automatic**: It will make Moodle guess the best method for displaying the linked page.
    - **Embed**: It will insert the file into a Moodle page. Your students will see the navigation bar, any blocks that you have added to the course, and navigation links across the top of the page, just like when they view any other page in Moodle. The center of the page will show the file. The file's **Description**: It will show below the embedded file.
    - **Force download**: It will force the file to be downloaded and saved to your student's computer.
    - **Open**: It will show the file in a plain web page. There will be no navigation bar, blocks that you have added to the course, or navigation links across the top of the page.
    - **In pop-up:** It will launch a new window, containing the file. Just like the **Open** option, the browser window will be plain, without any Moodle items.

18. The checkboxes for **Display resource name** and **Display resource description** will affect the display of the page, only if **Embed** is chosen as the display method. If selected, the **Name** of the file will be displayed above the file, and the **Description** will be displayed below the file.

19. The **Restrict access** settings enable you to set conditions that will control whether this resource is available to the student. These are discussed in detail in Chapter 5, *Resources, Activities, and Conditional Access*, in the *Restricting access* section.

20. Click on one of the **Save** buttons at the bottom of the page to save your work.

Adding media – Video and audio

If you want to add video or audio to your course, you have three choices. First, you can add it as a resource or file. If you do that, when the student selects the file, one of two things will happen: either the media file will be downloaded to the student's computer, and played by the software on the student's computer, or Moodle will try to play that file with its built-in media player. If multimedia plugins are enabled under **Site administration | Plugins**, Moodle will try to play the file in its built-in media player. If multimedia plugins are not enabled, the file will be played using whatever media player that is on the student's computer (such as Windows Media Player or QuickTime).

Second, you can embed the media on a Moodle page (refer to the *Adding pages* section explained earlier). That will cause the media to be played on the web page.

Third, you can copy embed code into the HTML of your page in Moodle. You will see a small screenshot with the URL and a Play icon. The player looks like it is in Moodle, but it's actually being played from the host (YouTube, Vimeo, and so on).

Adding video or audio to a page

This procedure will add video, audio, or an applet to a Moodle page. You must be in possession of the file that you are adding, that is, the file is on your computer and not on another website. If the file that you want to appear is on another website, see the procedure for embedding media from another website on a page:

1. On the Moodle page, click to place the insertion point where you want the media to appear.
2. Click on the **Insert Moodle media** icon:

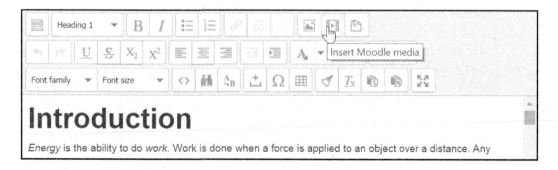

3. A pop-up window appears. In this window, click on the button labeled **Find or upload a sound, video, or applet**.

4. The **File picker** window displays. In the *File repositories* section, you saw how to add a file from a repository. In this example, let's upload the file from your computer. Click on the **Upload a file** link:

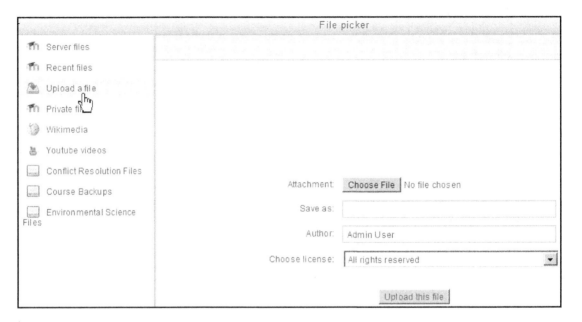

5. Click on the **Choose File** button.

6. Locate the file on your computer and select it.

7. Click on the **Open** or **OK** button.

8. Optionally, give the file a name that you want it to have in Moodle. This is in the **Save as** field.

9. By default, the **Author** field has your name. If someone else created this file, give them proper credit by entering their name as the author.

10. The **Choose license** drop-down list enables you to select a license so that other teachers know what kind of copyright this file has.

11. Click on the **Upload this file** button; the file is uploaded to your Moodle system.

12. If needed, fill out the fields under **Appearance**. You might want to resize the picture, since Moodle will by default display the media at its original size.

13. Click on the **Insert** button. The media is inserted into the page.

While you are editing the page, the media might not display in the editor. Instead of seeing the media, you might just see a link, like this:

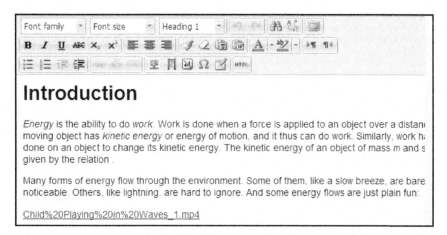

When the user views the page, the media will display. It can be played with Moodle's built-in media player:

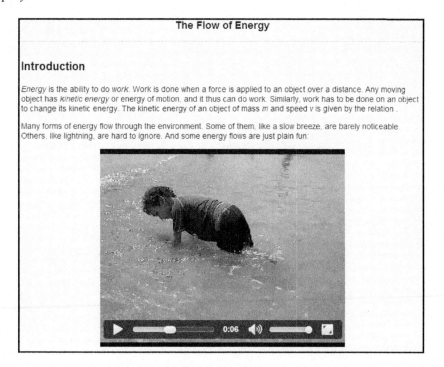

To embed a video on a page, do this:

1. Find the media that you want to link to. For example, you might find a video on https://vimeo.com/ or https://www.flickr.com/ that you can use.

2. Check the license for the material to ensure that you have the right to use it as you intend.

3. Somewhere on the page, you will see a button or link that will give you the HTML code to embed the video:

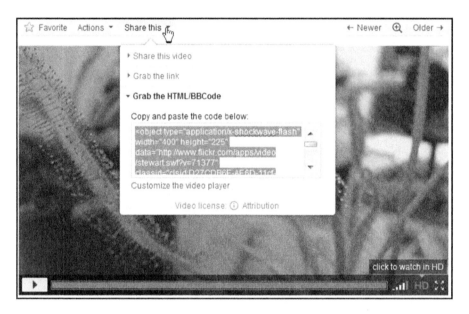

4. Copy the code for embedding the video.

5. Switch back to Moodle, where you are editing the page.

6. On the Moodle page, click to place the insertion point where you want the media to appear.

7. Click on the **Edit HTML source** icon:

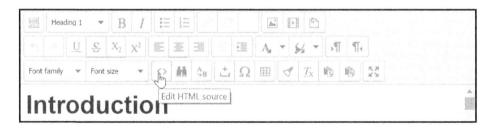

8. The **HTML Source Editor** displays. In this window, paste the code that you have copied from the video sharing site. Note that I'm using the TinyMCE text editor (which I've selected using **Course Settings**). The default text editor for Moodle 3.4 and later is Atto. I like TinyMCE because it gives me flexibility. Here's the **HTML Source Editor**:

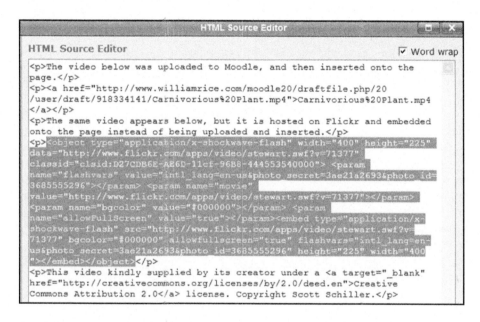

9. At the bottom of the editor window, click on the **Update** button.
10. You are redirected to the editing page. Continue editing and then save your work.

Organizing your course

The main tools for organizing a course in Moodle are sections and labels. In this section, we'll look at how to use them and how to move material around on the course page.

Name your topics

In a course that uses the topics format, your topics are automatically named and numbered, like this:

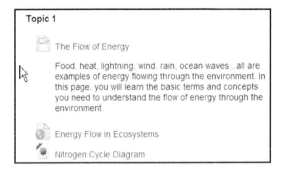

This works well if you want your topics to be automatically numbered. If you rearrange the topics, the numbering will automatically be updated.

Instead of using the default topic numbering, you might want to name your topics and add a description to them, as follows:

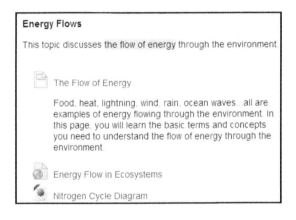

To add a name and description to a **Topic**, do as follows:

1. Log in to your course as a teacher or a site administrator.
2. In the upper-right corner of the page, if you see a button that reads **Turn editing on**, click on the button. If it reads **Turn editing off**, you do not need to click on this button.
3. Next to the topic's number, click on the **Edit summary** button:

4. The **Summary** page for your **Topic** is displayed. You must uncheck the checkbox for **Use default section name**. If there is a checkbox in this field, you cannot edit the name or description of the **Topic**.
5. In the **Section name** field, enter the name for your **Topic**.
6. In the **Summary** field, enter a description. This is a full-featured web page editor, so you can enter text, graphics, and media.
7. Save your work. You will be returned to the course home page. The name and summary of the **Topic** are displayed.

Rearrange/move items on the course home page

As you build your course, you will be adding resources and activities to the course page. Moodle enables you to easily reposition these items. It's so easy to reposition them that I recommend that you don't even worry about getting them in the right place as you are creating them. Just forge ahead and create, and you can rearrange later.

Rearranging items on the course page can be done like this:

1. Log in to your course as a teacher or a site administrator.
2. In the upper-right corner of the page, if you see a button that reads **Turn editing on**, click on the button. If it reads **Turn editing off**, you do not need to click on this button.

3. Next to the item that you want to move, place the mouse pointer over the Crosshairs icon:

4. Drag the item to where you want it on the course page and drop it.

You can also drag and drop entire topics, if your browser has Ajax enabled. You'll know you can do this if you see a Crosshairs icon next to the topic. Just drag the Crosshairs icon and drop it where you want the topic to go.

Giving directions and organization with labels

In our example, the course creators used text labels to organize the course content. A label can also hold a graphic. Adding a graphic to the beginning of each topic is a good way to add visual interest to a course. Also, a label can consist of a large amount of text. You can introduce activities with a paragraph-long label. In the screenshot shown, perhaps a sentence explaining each activity will help the student understand the course flow. This can be added with a label. Make creative use of labels for organization, interest, and information.

To add a label to the course's home page, perform the following steps:

1. Log in to your course as a teacher or a site administrator.
2. In the upper-right corner of the page, if you see a button that reads **Turn editing on**, click on the button. If it reads **Turn editing off**, you do not need to click on this button.
3. From the **Add an activity or resource** drop-down menu, select **Label**.
4. The **Adding a new label** page appears. In the **Label** text field, you can enter anything that can appear on a web page: text, graphics, media, and so on.
5. Save your work and return to the course home page.

Summary

In this chapter, we took a look at resources in Moodle. They are the static course materials (books, pages, URLs, files, and labels) that form the core of most online courses. Most student/teacher interaction will be about something the student has read or viewed. Adding static material first gives you a chance to think about how the material will be discussed and used.

What we emphasized on in this chapter was the importance of selecting, sequencing, and deploying resources so that they always advance the goals of the course and help students meet learning objectives.

Further, the clear organization of your resources for students to know which chapter or unit they correspond to and help instill a sense of confidence and an "I can do it!" attitude in them.

In the next chapter, you will see how to add some interactive material. Instead of just reading and viewing material that you post, the student will produce work and interact with their teacher and peers online.

7
Adding Assignments, Lessons, Feedback, and Choices

Course activities enable students to interact with the instructor, the learning system, or each other. They also allow students to develop confidence by being rewarded with a badge or certificate when they complete the activities. Above all, course activities should connect to the learning objectives of the course and correspond to the appropriate level of knowledge in the cognitive domain, as indicated in Bloom's Taxonomy, which we reviewed in an earlier chapter. Your instructional strategy will be very effective if you ensure that every step of your course planning integrates the learning objectives with the appropriate level of content and activities and that each step has measurable outcomes.

In this chapter, you will learn about Moodle's assignments and how to select them appropriately to achieve optimal outcomes. Note that Moodle doesn't categorize activities into *static*, *interactive*, and *social* as we do in this book. We use the terms *static*, *interactive*, and *social* as a convenient way to categorize the activities that Moodle offers. In addition, we will review Bloom's Taxonomy and discuss how to apply it.

In the previous chapter, we saw how to add resources, or static course material, such as web pages, links, and media. We saw that all activities are added from the **Add an activity or resource** menu, after we select the **Turn editing on** option.

In this chapter, we will see how to add several kinds of interactive course material: assignments, lessons, choices, and feedback. We will also discuss how to organize the content to build micro-competencies, and then to affirm micro-learning milestones, and generate certificates and badges.

Instructional strategy

You should develop your instructional strategy by linking your activities to your learning objectives. Remember that your instructional strategy is the way that you map your learning objectives to your course materials, your activities, and your assessments.

As you start to organize the course, follow these steps:

1. Review the overall goals of your course
2. Review the learning objectives
3. Describe how you will measure the outcomes
4. Review the activities that connect to the learning outcomes and the course content
5. Review the activities that are most appropriate for your learners
6. Determine how you would like to best motivate your learners by developing badges
7. Determine whether or not your institution requires you to align with competency frameworks

Following these steps will help you organize your assignments and also create a template that you can use for your other courses.

Learning objectives

The learning objectives you select should clearly and concisely express the performative outcomes of your course. Keep in mind that effective learning objectives use action verbs that tie to Bloom's Taxonomy, and they result in actions that are measurable and tie directly to the course unit or the entire course.

Here's a process for writing learning objectives:

1. Identify what you want the student to be able to do
2. Identify the level of knowledge on Bloom's Taxonomy
3. Select a verb that ties to a measurable, observable action
4. Add criteria to refine the outcome so that it has qualitative or quantitative specifics

Keep in mind that some authors have critiqued the over-adherence to Bloom's Taxonomy, especially the levels of learning. Even if you have issues with Bloom's Taxonomy, it's a useful tool because it helps you ensure that you are focusing on clear, measurable outcomes and the activities that help provide evidence of learning.

Let's review Bloom's Taxonomy. As you may remember, Bloom's Taxonomy is a hierarchy that helps you describe, map, and measure knowledge in the cognitive domain.

We start with learning objectives. Bloom's Taxonomy is a pyramid, and the base is the most foundational, and it has to do with remembering. So, we can start with learning objectives that have to do with remembering. For example, we can say, "List the ingredients in Rattlesnake Chili".

As you can see in the following diagram, we move up from the base of the pyramid to tasks of increasing complexity. Each task has affiliated verbs, which will make the assessment and the determination of whether or not an individual achieved the learning objective much easier.

The top of the pyramid is **CREATING**. It is at the top of the pyramid, and at the pinnacle of the hierarchy because it brings together the lower-domain cognitive activities and requires both synthesis and analysis. The learning objective for a course that will ascend as high as the sixth level will be easier than it may seem at first. The key is to consider an activity that will allow you as the instructor to properly evaluate or assess. For example, creating the corresponding activity could be to "develop a project" or "invent a new type of magazine".

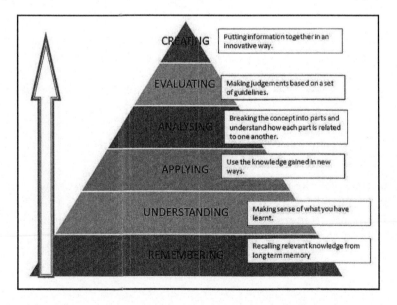

Competency learning definitions

Competency learning is an approach to learning that sets out a set of criteria that are learning outcomes corresponding to a course, and also to the outcomes of a program.

Competency learning is often required by regulatory agencies or governing bodies to assure consistency in schools and learning organizations.

Thus, it is often necessary to tie a course outcome to one of the competencies, and to make it clear that when the learning outcome is achieved in the course, the competency has been satisfied.

External affirmation of the competency having been achieved can appear in the form of badges that are generated upon successful completion of an activity. They can also be achieved by a report that is generated directly in Moodle within a competency framework.

Definitions

An **assignment** consists of something that a student creates and then uploads into the course for the teacher to grade. For example, the student could do any of these:

- Write a paragraph
- Take a photograph
- Create a piece of music
- Build something and then take pictures and write about the experience
- Visit a museum and then upload pictures and a report of the visit

Sometimes, an assignment is an activity completed outside of the course. The last two items in the preceding list—building something and visiting a place—are examples of that. An assignment can also be done entirely inside the assignment activity. For example, you could have the student write a paragraph in the assignment activity and then submit it to the teacher.

Assignments are very flexible. You can allow the student to resubmit their work until they achieve a passing grade, allow the student to leave comments, give the student comments or even a file in response to their work, and even have students submit their work in a group.

A **lesson** is a series of web pages displayed in a specific order. Most lessons consist of several pages. The next page that the student sees might depend upon the student's answer to a question. Usually, the jump question is used to test a student's understanding of the material. Get it right, and you proceed to the next page. Get it wrong, you then either stay on the page or jump to a remedial page.

A lesson gives Moodle some of the branching capability found in commercial **computer-based training (CBT)** products. You can make a course consisting of just a summary, one large lesson, and a quiz.

A **choice** is a single, multiple-choice question that the instructor asks the class. The result can be displayed to the class or it can be kept private, known only to the student and the instructor. Choices are a quick way to get feedback from the students about the class. You can plant these choices in your course ahead of time and keep them hidden until you need the students' feedback. You can also create them quickly, whenever you need them.

The **feedback** activity enables you to create surveys for your students. Do not confuse this with the survey. In survey, you must choose from several pre-made surveys; you cannot build your own surveys. In the feedback activity, you can build your own poll using several kinds of questions.

The **competency framework** allows you to connect your activities to lists of competencies that your school or institution has developed.

The **badge** activity allows you to automatically generate a badge when students complete activities. They can be used to motivate students and also to publicize your course when students put their badges on their social media sites.

Selecting assignments

Assignments should align directly with your learning objectives. As you review your learning objectives, ensure that they are arranged in ascending order of difficulty. Start with the most basic, and end with the most complex. Using Bloom's Taxonomy, that means starting with remembering, and then moving to higher-order skills, namely understanding, applying, analyzing, evaluating, and, finally, creating.

If you want the student to do or create something and then grade the results, you want an assignment.

Understanding assignments

If you would like your student to demonstrate that they have achieved mastery of a skill set or a body of knowledge, you will need to develop a way of assessing it. One good approach is to develop an assignment. An assignment in Moodle gives you space to check the student's knowledge, allow the student to have a *sandbox* experience, requires the student to complete an assessment of competency, which can involve high-pressure "winner takes all" kinds of assessments.

What you can do with an assignment

The options in the assignment activity give you many choices in how to run the assignment. Before we look at how to create an assignment, let's look at what you can do with it and what features you want to use in the assignment.

As we start, take a look at the icon that indicates that you've created an assignment:

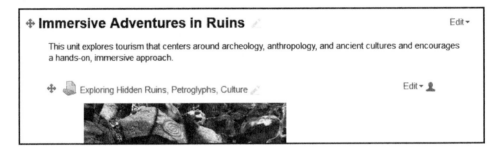

Types of work students can submit

All the following options can be combined. For an assignment, you can require the students to do these:

- Submit one or more digital files
- Write something
- Do something outside of Moodle

Each of these is covered in the following subsections.

Submitting a digital file

Anything that can be uploaded on a computer can be uploaded into an assignment. However, Moodle will enforce its limit on the size of uploaded files. For example, if you require your students to create a digital photograph, this option might work well.

Remember that a Moodle site is configured with a limit on the size of files that can be uploaded into Moodle. If you require your students to create a video, you might need to find another way for them to send you their large video files.

When an assignment requires the student to upload a file, the student sees something like this:

When the student clicks on the **Add submission** button, the student is prompted to upload a file into the submission:

Later in this chapter, you will see several ways to provide feedback to the student.

Requiring students to submit online text

In an online text assignment, you will require the student to enter text into an online text editor. This text editor is part of the assignment activity.

If students are more comfortable writing the text in a word processor, they can copy and paste it into the text editor.

You cannot paste graphics into Moodle's online text editor. Each graphic must be uploaded and placed into the document using the text editor's Insert Graphic icon. Alternatively, enable the option for adding text and file submissions so that the graphics can be uploaded as separate files.

Submitting work done in the real world

You can use an assignment to require the students to tell you that they have completed an activity outside of Moodle. For example, you can instruct your Art students to build an outdoor sculpture. Then, their submission will consist of notifying you, **It's built and ready for you to review**.

Even when you don't require students to upload or submit anything, you can give a grade for the assignment. This is a good way to get work done outside of class, into the grade book. In the following screenshot, you see an assignment that the student will do offline:

Go play in the ocean

In class today (November 7), you received a box from the teacher. If you were not in class, you must get the box as soon as possible.

Inside the box are parts and instructions for building a simple machine that uses the power of waves to turn a crank. Assemble it, and place the machine at the water's edge on the beach behind school. At the beginning and end of each school day the teacher will check for your machine.

This is due by the beginning of the school day, November 25.

Submission status

Attempt number	This is attempt 1.
Submission status	This assignment does not require you to submit anything online
Grading status	Not graded
Due date	Monday, 25 November 2013, 8:00 AM
Time remaining	16 days 8 hours

Submitting an assignment from the student's perspective

Let's look at the assignment from a student's perspective. When a student selects an assignment, they will see the assignment's description. When you write the description, include instructions for what the student must do:

Go play in the ocean

With your lab partner, go to the beach behind the school. Play in the waves. Feel the flow of energy in the ocean.

Have your lab partner take a picture of you playing in the waves.

Return to the this assignment and do two things:

1. In the online text editor, write how you played. Did you float, swim, sway, jump, etc?
2. Upload the picture of you playing in the waves.

We will talk about your experiences in class on November 25.

This is due by the beginning of the school day, November 25.

Submission status

Attempt number	This is attempt 1.
Submission status	No attempt
Grading status	Not graded
Due date	Monday, 25 November 2013, 8:00 AM
Time remaining	9 days 16 hours

Add submission

The student clicks on the **Add submission** button. The system responds by displaying a page where the student will enter the online text, upload the files, or both. What the student sees here is determined by the requirements that you selected when creating the assignment.

After the student enters the material to be graded, they click on the **Save changes** button. The system responds with a confirmation page. At this point, the student can go back and edit the submission or submit it.

The student may edit their submission while there is time remaining before the due date/time:

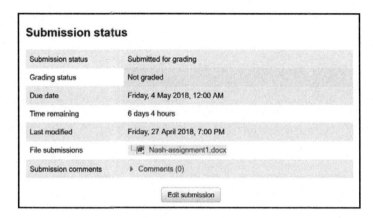

On the **Settings** page for the assignment, you can require the student to agree that they are submitting their own work.

On the **Settings** page for the assignment, you can allow the student to submit comments with the submission. If you enable this, the student can add one or more comments to the assignment any time after submitting.

Grading an assignment

In the previous section, you saw how a student submits an assignment. When assignments need to be graded, Moodle will notify the teacher by displaying a message on the teacher's **Dashboard** page:

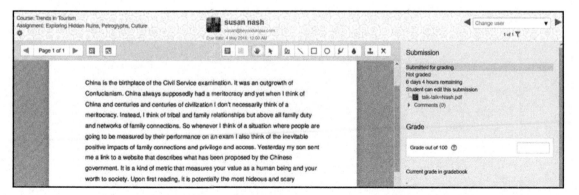

The assignment can also be configured to send an automated email to each teacher to alert them of the submitted assignments.

Moodle does not supply a link directly to the assignments that need grading, but does supply a link to the course. If you click on the icon, it will list the incomplete assignments in that course and provide a link to each of those assignments.

> **TIP**
>
> The system administrator can configure Moodle so that when a user logs in, they are automatically taken to the user's **Dashboard** page. This is done in **Administration** | **Site administration** | **Appearance** | **Navigation**, and by selecting **My home** as the default home page.

The teacher enters the course and opens the assignment. Moodle displays how many assignments have been submitted and the number of assignments that still need to be graded:

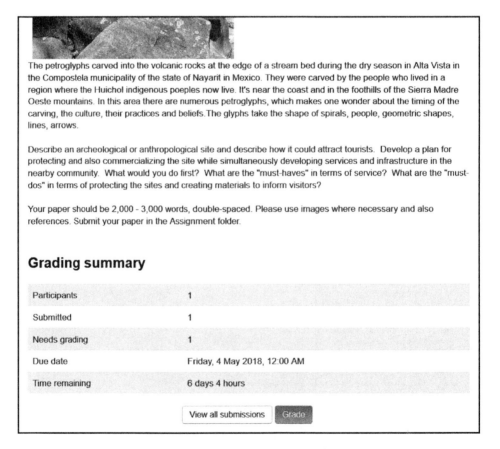

The petroglyphs carved into the volcanic rocks at the edge of a stream bed during the dry season in Alta Vista in the Compostela municipality of the state of Nayarit in Mexico. They were carved by the people who lived in a region where the Huichol indigenous poeples now live. It's near the coast and in the foothills of the Sierra Madre Oeste mountains. In this area there are numerous petroglyphs, which makes one wonder about the timing of the carving, the culture, their practices and beliefs. The glyphs take the shape of spirals, people, geometric shapes, lines, arrows.

Describe an archeological or anthropological site and describe how it could attract tourists. Develop a plan for protecting and also commercializing the site while simultaneously developing services and infrastructure in the nearby community. What would you do first? What are the "must-haves" in terms of service? What are the "must-dos" in terms of protecting the sites and creating materials to inform visitors?

Your paper should be 2,000 - 3,000 words, double-spaced. Please use images where necessary and also references. Submit your paper in the Assignment folder.

Grading summary

Participants	1
Submitted	1
Needs grading	1
Due date	Friday, 4 May 2018, 12:00 AM
Time remaining	6 days 4 hours

View all submissions   Grade

The grading page for the assignment enables the teacher to open all the submissions and enter a grade for each submission:

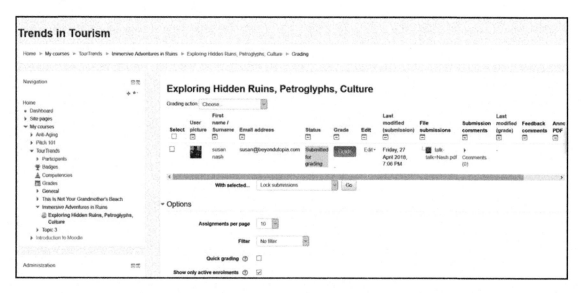

When you create the assignment, you can enable feedback comments and feedback files. If you do that, the teacher will be able to enter the comments and files while grading the assignment, shown as follows:

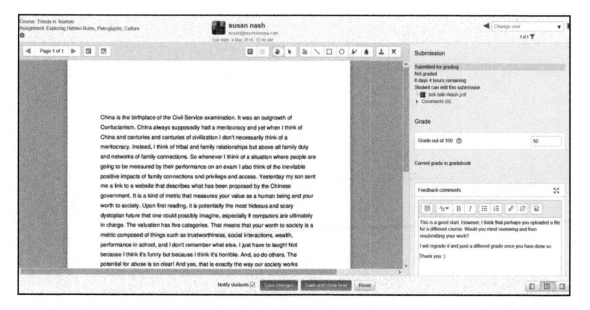

Receiving a grade for an assignment

After the teacher submits a grade for the student's assignment, the student will see a notice on the student's **Dashboard** page:

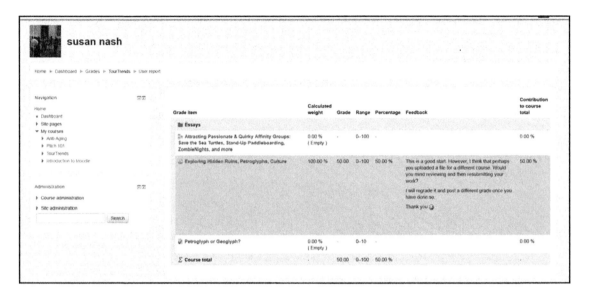

When the student enters the assignment, they will see the grade, any feedback comments, and any feedback files that the teacher has sent:

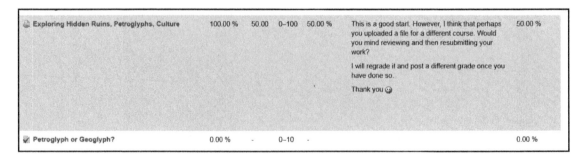

Allowing a student to resubmit an assignment

You can allow a student to resubmit an assignment. You might do this if you think the student was confused about the instructions, or if the student did not submit their best work. From the student's point of view, a reopened assignment looks like this:

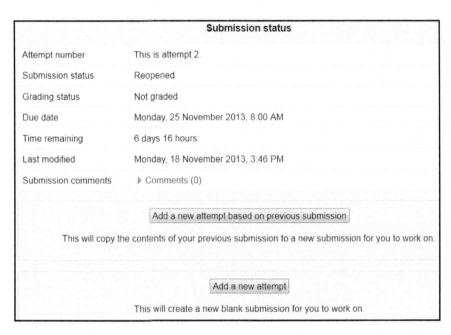

Submission status

Attempt number	This is attempt 2.
Submission status	Reopened
Grading status	Not graded
Due date	Monday, 25 November 2013, 8:00 AM
Time remaining	6 days 16 hours
Last modified	Monday, 18 November 2013, 3:46 PM
Submission comments	▶ Comments (0)

Add a new attempt based on previous submission

This will copy the contents of your previous submission to a new submission for you to work on.

Add a new attempt

This will create a new blank submission for you to work on.

There are two ways the teacher can reopen an assignment: the teacher can manually reopen the assignment for the student, or the teacher can use a combination of settings in the assignment and the grade book to make Moodle automatically reopen the assignment, if the student gets less than a passing grade. We will look at these settings in the following section.

Adding an assignment

After logging in as a teacher and turning on editing, you can add an assignment from the **Add an activity or resource** menu:

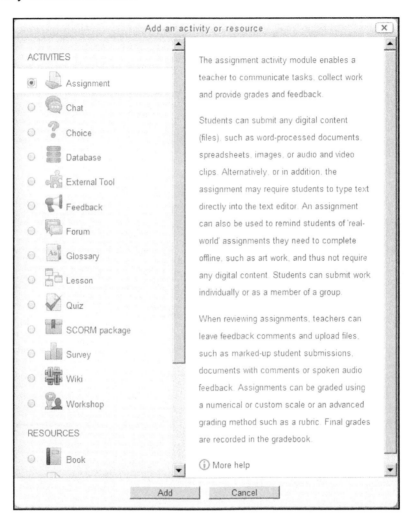

After clicking through this dialog box, you are taken to the **Edit Assignment** page. The **Edit Assignment** page will contain the same settings as all activities, including the following:

- **General** settings, such as name and description
- **Grade** settings, which are covered in the section on the gradebook
- **Common module settings**, such as visibility and ID number, which are covered in another chapter
- **Restrict access**, such as dates when access will be allowed

These common settings are covered in Chapter 5, *Resources, Activities, and Conditional Access*. The following subsections discuss the settings that are unique to the assignment activity.

Some of the settings for an activity are affected by other settings in your course and in the system. If you're unsure about some of these other settings, try speaking with your system administrator or search the forums on https://moodle.org/.

Availability

The **Availability** setting determines when the student can submit work:

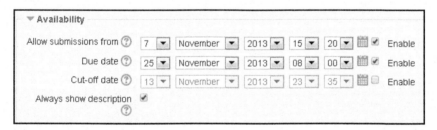

Do not confuse this with the **Allow access** settings under **Restrict access**. The **Allow access** settings determine whether the student can see the assignment on the course page, or whether the assignment is completely hidden from the student. After the student sees and selects the assignment, the **Availability** setting determines whether the student can submit work to the teacher.

Note that there is a **Due date** and a **Cut-off date**. If you do not enable a **Cut-off date**, the assignment will stop accepting work on the **Due date**. If you enable and enter a **Cut-off date**, the assignment will accept work between the **Due date** and the **Cut-off date**. That work will be marked late.

When a student clicks on an assignment, Moodle displays the assignment's description. You usually use the description to tell the student how to complete the assignment. If you enable the setting for **Always show description**, then if a student enters the assignment at any time, the student will see the description. If you want a student to be able to prepare and work ahead, this is fine. If you disable the setting for **Always show description**, then if a student enters the assignment before the **Allow submissions from** date, Moodle will hide the description for the assignment. You might use this feature to prevent students from working ahead.

Assignments that are due soon will appear in the **Upcoming events** block. If you do not set a **Due date**, by default, it will be set to today (the day you created the assignment). This will make the assignment show up in the **Upcoming events** block as if it's overdue. Ensure that you set an appropriate **Due date** for the assignment.

Submission types

The **Submission types** setting determines what kind of material, if any, the student will submit to the teacher:

In the *Types of work students can submit* section, we discussed three kinds of assignments that you can give the students:

- Submit a digital file
- Write something
- Do something outside of Moodle

This setting is where you do that.

If you want the student to write, or copy and paste some writing, select **Online text**, if you want the student to upload something, select **File submissions**, and if you want the student to be able to submit comments on their work, select **Submission comments**. In the preceding screenshot, we have selected all of these options.

You can also select none of them. In that case, the student doesn't submit anything online. However, you can still give a student a grade for some work that they did offline. If you do not require the student to submit anything online, the assignment will display a message to the student, like this:

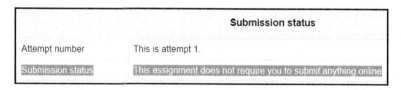

Feedback types

In the preceding example, the student received not only a grade but also feedback from the teacher. The feedback was in the form of comments that the teacher wrote, and also a file that the teacher uploaded. This is enabled under the **Feedback types** setting:

The option for **Offline grading worksheet** enables the teacher to download a **comma-separated file** (a .csv file), that has a list of all the assignments and a place for the teacher to enter grades. However, downloading the grading worksheet does not download the material that the students submitted. If the teacher wants to see the submissions offline, they must download them separately.

If offline grading is enabled, the teacher will see the **Download grading worksheet** option in the grading page for the assignment:

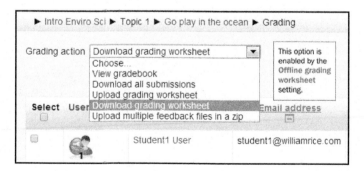

Submission settings

The submission settings determine how Moodle behaves while the student is submitting their work:

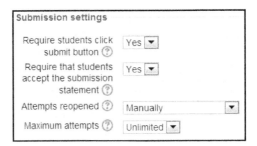

The setting for **Require students click submit button** determines whether the student must submit the assignment all at once or if the student can save their submission as a draft and submit it later. If you select **Yes** for this setting, when the student is creating a submission, Moodle will display a **Save** button. After the student saves the submission, when the student enters the assignment, they will have the option to either edit what was saved or submit it.

The setting for **Require that students accept the submission statement** determines whether Moodle displays a statement that the work belongs to the student. The submission statement looks like this:

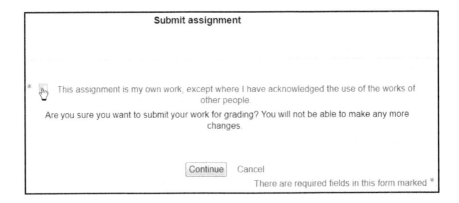

In the *Allowing a student to resubmit an assignment* section, we saw what it looks like for the student when the teacher reopens an assignment. The setting for **Attempts reopened** determines if, and how, the teacher can allow a student to resubmit the assignment. Note that a resubmission replaces the original submission.

Selecting **Never** means the teacher cannot reopen the assignment to allow the student to resubmit their work. **Manually** means the teacher can reopen the assignment. **Automatically until pass** means the assignment will remain open until the student achieves a passing grade, that is, if the teacher gives the student less than a passing grade for the student's submission, Moodle will automatically enable the student to resubmit.

To use **Automatically until pass**, you must set a passing grade for the assignment. This is done in the grade book. First, select **Course administration | Grades**, and from the drop-down list, select **Simple view**:

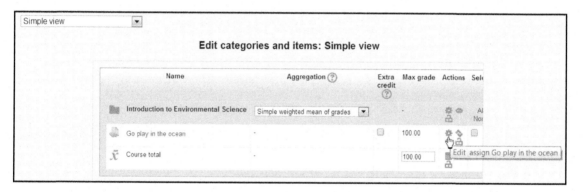

Then, select the edit icon (the one shaped like a gear) for the assignment. That brings you to a page where you can enter a passing grade for the assignment:

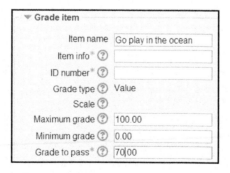

Group submission settings

Moodle enables you to assign the students and teachers in a class to different groups.

Groups are created under **Course administration** | **Users** | **Groups**. For each activity in a course, the teacher decides whether the groups will be used. In other types of activities, groups are used to prevent students in one group from seeing the work done by students in another group. In an assignment, groups work a little differently. In an assignment, groups enable students to submit their work together as a group. They can also be used to assign students to specific teachers, while they are all using the same course. For more about groups, refer to `Chapter 12`, *Groups and Cohorts*.

In an assignment, setting **Students submit in groups** to **Yes** means that each group, the teacher created, will submit their work together as a group, and that all members of a group will receive the same grade.

If you set **Require all group members submit** to **Yes**, every member of a group will need to click on the **Submit** button to finalize a submission. If you set this to **No**, any member of a group can submit the assignment for the whole group. However, even though only one member of the group may have submitted the assignment, the feedback and grade are applied to all members of the group.

Notifications

The **Notifications** settings determine whether the graders will receive messages when a student (or group) submits an assignment.

Each user in Moodle can choose how they want to receive messages. This is done under **My profile settings** | **Messaging**:

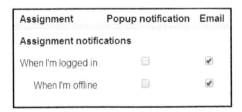

If your email application enables you to filter emails based on their subject line and sender, you can use that feature to automatically put all the notices about assignment submissions into a specific folder.

 Email alerts are especially useful in courses where you allow students to proceed at their own pace, since you will not know what activities they have completed unless you check the course and look at the grade book.

Printer-friendly directions

As assignments might be completed offline, you may want the directions to be printer-friendly so that students can take the directions with them. Ensure that any graphics you've embedded into the **Description** field are less than the width of the printed page. Alternatively, you can upload the directions as an **Adobe Acrobat** (.pdf) file and use the **Description** field to instruct students to print the directions and take the directions with them.

Indicating that assignments are mandatory

On the course's home page, an assignment link appears with its own icon, like this: . It is not immediately apparent to a new student that this icon means *do this assignment*. You might want to use a label to indicate that the assignment is something the student should do. In this example, a label instructs the student to complete the assignment and a multiple-choice survey question.

You can also label the individual activities with an imperative, such as "Read about the plants around you" or "Answer a survey question about your experience with edible plants."

Assignments are always added to the **UPCOMING EVENTS** block. Even if you have no other events planned for the course (such as a field trip, discussion, chat, and more), if you have an assignment, consider adding the **UPCOMING EVENTS** block. This will serve as an additional reminder for the students:

Lesson

A lesson is a complex and powerful type of activity. Essentially, a lesson is a series of web pages that presents information and questions.

A Moodle lesson can be a powerful combination of instruction and assessment. Lesson activities offer the flexibility of a web page, the interactivity of a quiz, and branching capabilities.

Definition of a lesson

A lesson consists of a series of web pages. Usually, a lesson page contains some instructional material and a jump question about the material the student just viewed. The jump question is used to test a student's understanding of the material. Get it right, and you then proceed to the next item. Get it wrong, and you're taken back either to the instructional page or jump to a remedial page. However, the jump question can just as easily ask a student what they are interested in learning next, or who their favorite candidate is, or be labeled **Continue** and take the student to the next page.

Example of a simple lesson with remedial page jump

The following is a screenshot of a lesson page. Its purpose is instructional, and it appears like any normal web page. Indeed, you can put anything on a lesson page that you can put on any other Moodle web page:

Relationship Between Distance and Perspective

In some photographs, space can appear compressed, so that objects appear closer together than they really are. In another photograph of the same scene, space can appear expanded so that objects appear farther apart than they are.

Distance from Camera Determines Perspective

Distortions in perspective are actually caused by the distance of the subject from the camera. The farther a scene is from the camera, the closer the objects in that scene appear. The closer a scene is to the camera, the farther apart objects in that scene appear. Distance compresses the space in a picture, and closeness expands the space.

In the photo below, look at the distance between the columns. The columns closer to the camera appear to be further apart, while those farther from the camera appear closer together.

Photo by Smiles for the world / Alex Lapuerta

Focal Length Does Not Determine Perspective

Many people think these distortions in perspective are caused the focal length of the lens being used. For example, they think that a long lens--a telephoto lens--compresses space, and a short lens--a wide angle lens--expands space. This isn't true.

A telephoto lens enables you to shoot a scene that is farther from the camera. Because the scene is far from the camera, it perspective is compressed. But it is the distance from the camera, not the telephoto lens, that is causing the compression.

A wide angle lens enables you to shoot a scene that is closer to the camera. Because the scene is close to the camera, it perspective is opened. But it is the closeness to the camera, not the wide angle lens, that is causing the opening of the space.

Click the Continue button below to go to the next page in this lesson.

Continue

At the bottom of the lesson page is a **Continue** button. In this lesson, when the student clicks on this button, they are taken to the question page, shown as follows:

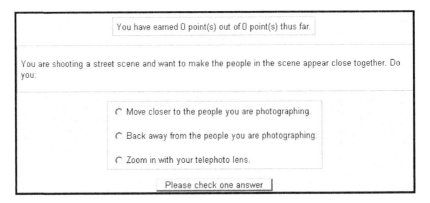

Each answer displays different feedback, just like a quiz:

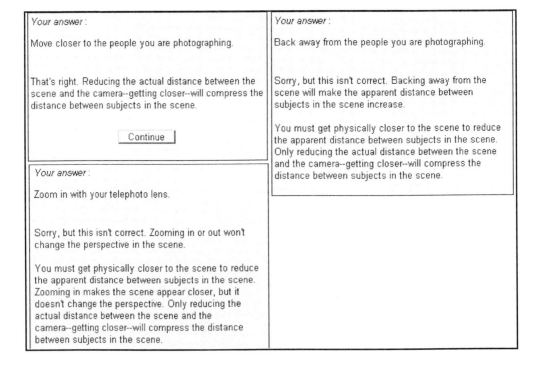

If the student answers correctly, they are taken to the next instructional page. An incorrect answer takes the student to a remedial page. The following is an example of a remedial page:

Remedial: Compressing Perspective

In the photo below, the space between each of the marchers in the front row is the same:

Photo by Celeste Hutchins.

Look at the two men closest to you. You can see that the space between them is over four feet. If one of them reached out his arm, he could not touch the other:

This is the simplest sequence for a lesson in Moodle. You can also add a few more advanced features. We'll discuss those later.

Types of lesson pages

In a lesson, different kinds of pages perform different functions. The following screenshot shows you a lesson that is built from several kinds of pages:

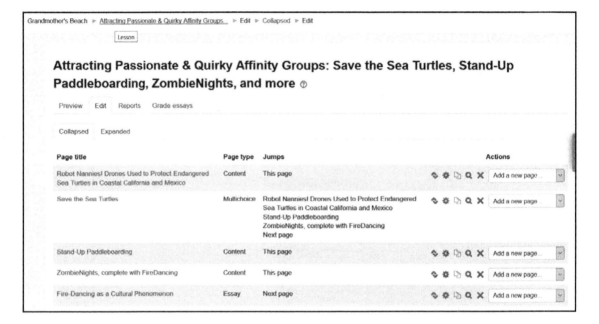

Let's look at each type of page in the following sections.

Content pages

The first three and last two pages in the preceding lesson are content pages. A content page displays some information and then offers one or more buttons for the student to click on in order to navigate to a different content page or question page.

Here's the second page from the preceding lesson:

The buttons at the bottom of this page are added by the course creator. Note that one of the buttons takes the student to the next page. However, what if, when you are creating this page, the next page hasn't been created yet? That's not a problem. After you have created all the pages in your lesson, you can go back to the content pages and add all the Jump buttons. Using the relative jumps (previous page, next page, and so on) is a big time-saver.

Cluster with questions

A cluster page, end-of-cluster page, and the pages in between them act as a single unit. In our example, we have a cluster with two question pages:

Page title	Page type	Jumps	Actions
The Carbon Cycle, Step by Step ⑦			
Preview **Edit** Reports Grade essays			
Collapsed Expanded			
About this Lesson	Content	Next page	⬦ ⚙ ⊕ ✕ Add a new page... ▾
Introduction: The Cycling of Matter	Content	Previous page Next page	⬦ ⚙ ⊕ ✕ Add a new page... ▾
About the Carbon Cycle	Content	Previous page Next page	⬦ ⚙ ⊕ ✕ Add a new page... ▾
Check Your Understanding 1	Cluster	Unseen question within a cluster	⬦ ⚙ ⊕ ✕ Add a new page... ▾
Check Your Understanding 1: Question A	Multichoice	Remedial 1: Let's Review Respiration and Photosynthesis Remedial 1: Let's Review	⬦ ⚙ ⊕ ✕ Add a new page... ▾
Check Your Understanding 1: Question B	Multichoice	Remedial 1: Let's Review Remedial 1: Let's Review Respiration and Photosynthesis	⬦ ⚙ ⊕ ✕ Add a new page... ▾
Check Your Understanding 1: End of Questions	End of cluster	Next page	⬦ ⚙ ⊕ ✕ Add a new page... ▾
Remedial 1: Let's Review	Content	Respiration and Photosynthesis	⬦ ⚙ ⊕ ✕ Add a new page... ▾
Respiration and Photosynthesis	Content	Next page	⬦ ⚙ ⊕ ✕ Add a new page... ▾

On the first cluster page, a setting directs Moodle to display an unseen question page in this cluster. You can select other options for a cluster page:

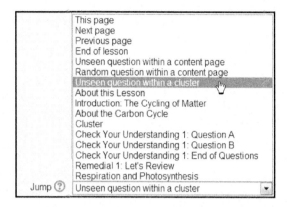

Using the option to show an unseen question within the cluster turns the cluster into a random question test.

Between the cluster and the end of the cluster are two question pages. These question pages will jump the student out of the cluster if they answer correctly, and to a remedial page if they answer incorrectly. You can see that in the three responses to the question:

The Carbon Cycle, Step by Step ⑦

Preview | **Edit** | Reports | Grade essays
Collapsed | Expanded

Page title	Page type	Jumps	Actions
About this Lesson	Content	Next page	♻ ⚙ ⚲ ✕ Add a new page... ▼
Introduction: The Cycling of Matter	Content	Previous page Next page	♻ ⚙ ⚲ ✕ Add a new page... ▼
About the Carbon Cycle	Content	Previous page Next page	♻ ⚙ ⚲ ✕ Add a new page... ▼
Check Your Understanding 1	Cluster	Unseen question within a cluster	♻ ⚙ ⚲ ✕ Add a new page... ▼
Check Your Understanding 1: Question A	Multichoice	Remedial 1: Let's Review Respiration and Photosynthesis Remedial 1: Let's Review	♻ ⚙ ⚲ ✕ Add a new page... ▼
Check Your Understanding 1: Question B	Multichoice	Remedial 1: Let's Review Remedial 1: Let's Review Respiration and Photosynthesis	♻ ⚙ ⚲ ✕ Add a new page... ▼
Check Your Understanding 1 End of Questions	End of cluster	Next page	♻ ⚙ ⚲ ✕ Add a new page... ▼
Remedial 1: Let's Review	Content	Respiration and Photosynthesis	♻ ⚙ ⚲ ✕ Add a new page... ▼
Respiration and Photosynthesis	Content	Next page	♻ ⚙ ⚲ ✕ Add a new page... ▼

If you use a cluster like the preceding one, be careful that you do not create an impossible situation. In this case, if the remedial page sent the student back into the cluster, and the student had seen both questions, then there is no way the cluster could display an *unseen question page*. Moodle would give the student an error message.

Instead of sending the student back into the same cluster, create several clusters in a row. If a student gets a question correct, you can skip over all the unseen clusters and move on to the next topic. If the student gets a question incorrect, you can send the student straight to the next cluster.

End of branch

An end-of-branch page automatically jumps to a page that is specified by the lesson creator. Just as students will never see the cluster and end of cluster pages, students will never see an end of branch page. It is, literally, just an automatic jump page.

Planning, creating pages, and adding content

If you intend to create a lesson that has jumps, clusters, and branches, draw a diagram of the lesson. A flowchart can tell you what kind of pages you will need to create.

Then, gather and organize your material in a word processor.

Then, create the pages in the lesson.

After the pages are in the Moodle lesson, create the jumps. After you have the pages and jumps, go to the **Edit Lesson** page and look at the list of all the pages in the lesson. You can compare that list to the diagram that you created when planning the lesson.

Finally, test the lesson from the student's point of view.

Configuring lesson settings

When you first create a lesson, you are presented with a window where you choose settings for the entire lesson. Before you can add even a single page to a lesson, you must select the lesson settings. If you're not sure about any of these settings, just take your best guess. You can always return to this page and change the settings.

Remember that one of the advantages of Moodle is the ease with which you can experiment with and change your course material. Get accustomed to taking a bolder, more experimental approach to using Moodle, and you will enjoy it a lot more.

This window is broken into eight areas:

- General
- Appearance
- Availability
- Prerequisite lesson
- Flow control
- Grade
- Common module settings
- Restrict access

In this section, I'll go through the **Editing Lesson** page from top to bottom. I'll focus on the settings that are unique to the lesson activity. So, by the end of this section, you will understand how most of the settings on the **Editing Lesson** page affect the student's experience.

General settings

This section consists of only the name of the lesson, which students will see on the course's home page. If you want the students to see a description for the lesson before they enter the lesson, you will need to add a label to the course home page to describe the lesson.

Appearance

This section contains settings that affect how the lesson is presented.

File popup

You can upload a file into this field. When the student enters the lesson, the file will be displayed in a pop-up window. This enables the student to refer to the file as they proceed through the lesson.

The pop-up window might be blocked by the student's browser. To ensure that the student knows that there is a file they should see, consider adding a message to the first page of the lesson that tells the student to open the file if it has not opened automatically. For example, you can use a message like this:

While you are reading this lesson, you will need to refer to a diagram. To show that diagram, on the left menu bar, under Linked Media, click on the Click here to view link.

After you display the diagram, proceed to the next page.

Display ongoing score

When this is set to **Yes**, each page of the lesson displays the student's score and the number of possible points so far.

This displays the number of points that the student could have earned for the pages that they have viewed so far.

If a lesson is not linear and if it branches, the path that each student takes through the lesson can change. This means that each student can have the chance to earn a different number of points. So, in a branching lesson, the total number of points possible for the entire lesson is not meaningful because the lesson can be different for different students. For example, you may create a lesson with many branches and pages and then require the student to earn at least 200 points on that lesson. This will encourage the student to explore the lesson and try different branches until they have earned the required points.

Display left menu and minimum grade to display menu

Display left menu displays a navigation bar on the left of the slide-show window. The navigation bar enables the student to navigate to any slide. Without that navigation bar, the student must proceed through the slide show in the order that Moodle displays the lesson pages and must complete the lesson to exit (or the student can force the window to close).

Sometimes, you may want a student to complete the entire lesson, in order, before allowing them to move around the lesson freely. The setting for **Minimum grade to display menu** accomplishes this. Only if the student achieved the specified grade they will see the navigation menu. You can use this setting to ensure that the student goes completely through the lesson the first time, before allowing the student to freely move around the lesson.

Maximum number of answers

At the bottom of each question page in a lesson, **Maximum number of answers** determines the maximum number of choices that each question can have. For example, if this were set to 4, each question could have at most four choices: **a**, **b**, **c**, and **d**.

If each answer sends the student to a different page, the number of answers is also the number of branches possible. Set this to the highest number of answers that any of your questions will have. After creating question pages, you can increase or decrease this setting without affecting the questions that you have already created.

Use default feedback

If this is set to **Yes**, Moodle does not see any custom feedback that you created for a question; it will display a default message, such as **That's correct** or **That's incorrect**. The default feedback is set in Moodle's language file, so it will be translated into whatever language the course is using. If you set this to **No**, and Moodle does not see any custom feedback that you created for a question, Moodle will not display any feedback when the student answers.

Link to next activity

This setting enables you to put a link to another activity in the course at the end of the lesson.

Prerequisite lesson

The settings in this section enable you to require the student to view another lesson before this lesson is open to the student. One of the settings enables you to specify how many minutes the student must spend on a previous lesson. You can use that setting to ensure that the student spends a certain amount of time watching a video before moving on to the next lesson. You would do this by embedding the video in the prerequisite lesson.

The prerequisite lesson settings are in addition to the **Restrict access** settings that are available for all activities. On the **Restrict access** settings, you do not have the option to specify the amount of time spent on another activity as a condition for access.

The flow control

This section contains settings that affect how a student moves through the lesson.

Allow student review

Allow student review enables a student to go backward in a lesson and retry questions that they got wrong. This differs from just using the **Back** button on the browser, in that the setting enables the student to retry questions, while using the **Back** button does not.

Provide option to try a question again

Provide option to try a question again displays a message after the student incorrectly answers a question. The message invites the student to try the question again, but for no points.

When you create a question in a lesson, you can create feedback for each of the answers to that question. However, if you set **Provide option to try a question again** to **Yes**, Moodle will override the feedback that you created for the answers. Instead, it will display a message asking you to try a question again.

 If you created custom feedback for the answers in your lesson but Moodle is not displaying the feedback that you created, check the **Provide option to try a question again** setting. It might be set to **Yes**. Set it to **No**.

Maximum number of attempts

Maximum number of attempts determines how many times a student can attempt any question. It applies to all questions in the lesson.

Number of pages to show

Number of pages to show determines how many pages are shown. If the lesson contains more than this number, the lesson ends after reaching the number set here. If the lesson contains fewer than this number, the lesson ends after every page has been shown. If you set this to zero, the lesson ends when all pages have been shown.

Grade

A lesson can be graded or ungraded. It can also allow students to retake the lesson. While Moodle allows you to grade a lesson, remember that a lesson's primary purpose is to teach, not test.

Don't use a lesson to do the work of a quiz or assignment.

The lesson's score is there to give you a feedback on the effectiveness of each page and to enable the students to judge their progress.

The Practice lesson

If you set **Practice lesson** to **Yes**, this lesson will not show up in the grade book. In a practice lesson, students see a grade after completing the activity, but this grade is only for them. It is not recorded or displayed in the grade book, and teachers cannot see it. It's a pure self-studying option.

Custom scoring

Normally, a correct answer in a question is worth the entire point value for the question, and each wrong answer is worth zero. Enabling custom scoring allows you to set a point value for each individual answer in a question. Use this if some answers are *more right* or *more wrong* than others. You can also use this to set the point value for a question. If a question is more important, use custom scoring to give it more points.

Handling of retakes

This setting is relevant only if the student is allowed to repeat the lesson (the setting is set to **Yes**). When the students are allowed to retake the lesson, the grades shown in the **Grades** page are either the average of the retakes or the student's best grade.

Minimum number of questions

Minimum number of questions sets the lower limit for the number of questions used to calculate a student's grade on the lesson. It is relevant only when the lesson will be graded. If the student doesn't answer this minimum number of questions, the lesson is not graded.

If you don't see this setting, it is probably because you have **Practice lesson** set to **Yes**. Set **Practice lesson** to **No**, save the page, and then you should see this setting appear.

Adding the first lesson page

Immediately after you save your lesson settings, Moodle presents you with the following page:

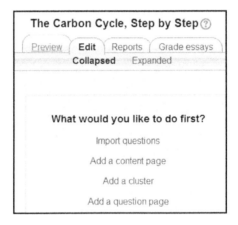

At this point, it's time to create the first question page or import question pages from another system. Let's take a look at each of your options.

Importing questions

If you choose to **Import questions**, you can import questions created by Moodle and other online learning systems. Some of the formats that you can import are as follows:

Format	Description
GIFT	GIFT is text only.
Moodle XML	These are Moodle's proprietary format. XML can include graphics and special characters.
Aiken	This format is for multiple-choice questions.

Missing word	This format is for missing-word multiple-choice questions.
Blackboard	If you're converting from Blackboard to Moodle, you can export questions from Blackboard and import them into Moodle.
WebCT	This format supports multiple-choice and short-answer questions from WebCT.
Embedded answers (Cloze)	This format is a multiple-question, multiple-answer question with embedded answers.

Each question that you import will create a question page. Each answer will create a jump button on the question page.

Adding a content page

A content page consists of a page of links to the other pages in your lesson. At this point, immediately after you've finished the lesson settings page, your lesson doesn't have any pages. However, if you want to begin your lesson with a page of instructions, you can add a content page and make it jump to the next page. Creating a content page will look like this:

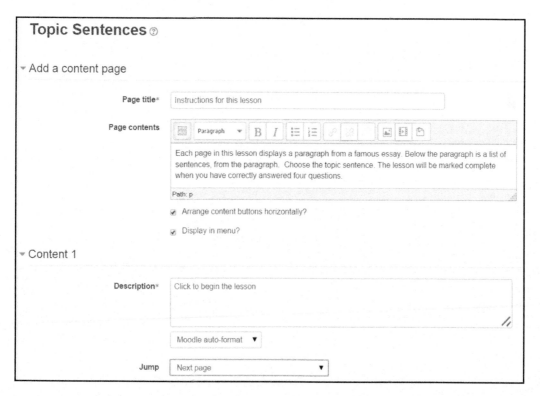

When the student runs the lesson, that content page will look like this:

Instructions for this lesson

Each page in this lesson displays a paragraph from a famous essay. Below the paragraph is a list of sentences, from the paragraph. Choose the topic sentence. The lesson will be marked complete when you have correctly answered four questions.

Click to begin the lesson

Adding a cluster

A **cluster** is a group of question pages. Within this cluster, you can require that the student correctly answers a number of questions before being allowed to proceed out of the cluster. This enables you to test that a student understands a concept before moving on.

Alternatively, you can display a random page from the cluster, and from that page, proceed to any other page in the lesson. This enables you to send each student down a different random pathway in the lesson so that not all students have the same experience.

A cluster consists of a beginning cluster page, an end of cluster page, and pages in between them.

Adding a question page

This option enables you to add a question page to your lesson using Moodle's built-in editor. The process for creating a question page is covered in the next section.

Try adding your question pages first. Then, put a content page with instructions at the beginning of the lesson. If needed, organize your question pages into branches or clusters. Finally, end the lesson with a content page to say goodbye to the student.

Creating a question page

After you fill out and save the **Settings** page, it's time to create the first question page. Even though it's called a *question page*, the page can contain more than just a question. It's a web page, so you can add any content to it. Usually, it contains information and a question to test the student's understanding. You can choose different types of questions:

- Multiple choice
- True/false
- Short answer

- Numeric
- Matching
- Essay

You can also create feedback for each answer to the question, similar to creating feedback for the answers in a quiz question. In addition, you can make the lesson jump to a new page, based upon the answer the student selects.

In the following example, you can see that the question page contains a question and several answers to the question. Note that for each answer, there is a **Response** field that the student sees immediately after submitting the answer. Also, there is a **Jump** field for each answer. For the incorrect answer that you see, **Jump** can take the student to a remedial page or redisplay the current page so that the students can try again. For the correct answer, **Jump** can display the next page in the lesson, as shown in the following screenshot:

Page Title

The **Page Title** will be displayed at the top of the page when it is shown in the lesson.

Page Contents

As was said before, a lesson page is really a web page. It can contain anything that you can put on any other Moodle web page. Usually, it will contain information and then a question to test the student's understanding.

Answers

The **Answers** will be displayed at the bottom of the lesson page, after the **Page Contents**. The student selects an answer in response to the question posed in the **Page Contents**.

Responses

For each **Answer** that the student selects, its **Response** is shown before the student is taken to a new page.

Jumps

Each **Answer** that a student selects results in a **Jump** to a page.

This Page

If the **Jump** is **This page**, the student stays on the same page. The student can then try to answer the question again.

Next or Previous Page

If **Jump** is **Next page** or **Previous page**, the student is taken to the next or previous page. After you rearrange the pages in a lesson, this jump might give you different results. Just be aware that this is a **relative** jump.

Specific Pages

You can also select a specific page to jump to. The pull-down list displays all the lesson page's titles. If you select a specific page to jump to, the jump will remain the same even if you rearrange the pages in your lesson.

Unseen question within a cluster

Recall that a branch table is a table of contents listing the pages in a lesson. When you insert a branch table into a lesson, you can also insert an end of branch later in the lesson. The pages between the branch table and end of branch become a branch. For example, a lesson with two branches might look like this:

```
Cluster 1
Question Page
Question Page
Question Page
End of Cluster
Cluster 2
Question Page
Question Page
Question Page
End of Cluster
```

For a **Jump**, if you select **Unseen question with a branch**, the student will be taken to a question page that they have not yet answered correctly in this session. That question page will be in the same cluster as the current page.

Unseen question with a branch takes the student to a question page that they haven't answered correctly. The student might have seen the page before and answered incorrectly.

Random question within a content page

For a **Jump**, if you select **Random** question within a content page, the student will be taken to a random question page in the same cluster as the current page.

In the **Lesson Settings** page, if **Maximum number of attempts** is set to something greater than **1**, the student might see a page that they have seen before. However, a page will be repeated only if **Maximum number of attempts** is greater than **1**. If it's set to **1**, a random question page that the student has not seen before will be displayed, which has the same effect as choosing **Unseen question within a cluster**.

To restate this, when in **Lesson Settings,** the **Maximum number of attempts** is set to **1**, **Random** question within a content page acts exactly like unseen question within a cluster. When **Maximum number of attempts** is set to greater than **1**, random question within a content page displays a truly random question.

One strategy for using this setting is to forgo the use of unseen question within a cluster. Whenever you want to use unseen question within a cluster, instead use random question within a content page and set the **Maximum number of attempts** to **1**. Then, you have the option of converting all of your lesson to random jumps just by setting **Maximum number of attempts** to **2** or greater.

Creating pages and assigning jumps

When filling out a question page, **Answer1** is automatically assumed to be the correct answer, so **Jump1** automatically reads next page. This is because in most cases, you want a correct response to result in the next page in the lesson being displayed. However, you can select any existing page in the lesson for the jump. Note that when you are filling out the first question page, there are no other pages to jump to, so the jumps on the first page will all read this page. After creating more pages, you can go back and change the jumps.

 It is usually most efficient to create all of your content and question pages first and then go back and assign the jumps.

The jumps that you create will determine the order in which the pages are presented to the student. For any answer, you can select a jump to the last page of the lesson. The last page displays an end-of-lesson message and, if you choose, the grade for the lesson. It also displays a link that takes the student back to the course's home page.

The flow of pages

The most obvious usage of question pages and jumps is to enforce a straight-through lesson structure. A correct answer results in a positive response such as "That's correct!" and then jumps to the next page. An incorrect answer results in a negative response or a correction. An incorrect answer can then redisplay the page so that the student can try again, as in the previous example (**Jump1: This page**), or an incorrect answer can jump to a remedial page.

The order of pages the student would follow if he/she answered every question correctly is called the **logical order**. This is what the teacher sees when editing the lesson, and displaying all of the pages in the same window.

Editing the lesson

After you've created several lesson pages, you might want to see and edit the flow of the lesson. You can do this under the **Edit** tab.

Collapsed and expanded

The **Edit** tab is where you edit the content of your lesson. From here, you add, delete, rearrange, and edit individual lesson pages.

Under the **Edit** tab, when you select **Collapsed**, you see a list of the pages in your lesson, such as the one shown in the following screenshot:

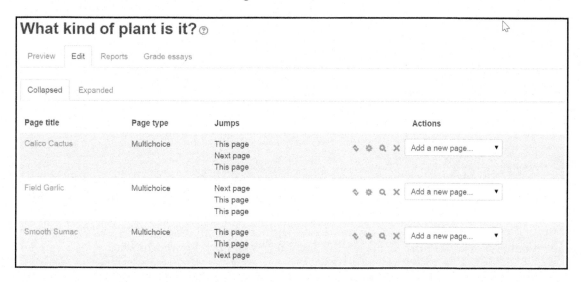

The pages display in their logical order, which would be the shortest path through the lesson if a student got all of the questions correct. Note that the content of the pages does not display. The purpose of this screen is not to edit individual questions but to help you see the flow of the lesson.

Rearranging pages

To rearrange the pages, click on the up/down arrow for the page that you want to move. Note that it is the jumps that determine the order in which Moodle presents the pages. If a question is set to jump to the next page, rearranging the pages can change the jumps. A question can also be set to jump to a specific, named page. In that case, the order in which the pages appear doesn't determine the landing point for the jump, so rearranging the pages here won't affect that jump.

Editing pages

From the **Edit** tab, to edit a page, click on the edit icon, which usually looks like this: . Clicking on this takes you to the editing page for that page. The previous section gave detailed instructions for editing a lesson page.

Adding pages

The **Add a page here** drop-down list enables you to insert a new page into the lesson. You can choose from several different kinds of pages.

Feedback

The feedback module enables you to create surveys for your students. Do not confuse this with the survey activity. In survey, you must choose from several pre-made surveys; you cannot build your own surveys. Also, do not confuse this with the questionnaire module. A questionnaire is an add-on, while feedback comes as standard with Moodle.

The feedback module needs to be enabled by the site administrator under **Site administration** | **Plugins** | **Activity modules** | **Manage activities**.

Feedback isn't just for students

Of course, you can use a Feedback activity to survey your students. You can also use it for the following:

- Conducting a survey of the employees in your workplace
- Collecting data from people who have agreed to be research subjects
- Conducting public opinion surveys of the visitors to your site

The feedback activity enables you to create different kinds of questions: multiple choice, dropdown, short answer, and more. You can share the results of a feedback with the students or keep them confidential.

Creating a feedback activity

Creating a feedback activity is similar to adding a quiz. First, you add the activity, and then you add the questions. We'll cover each in the following sections separately.

To add a feedback activity, do the following:

1. From the **Add an activity...** menu, select **Feedback**.
2. Moodle displays the **Settings** page for the activity.
3. In the **Name**, enter the name of the feedback. Your students will see this on the course home page.
4. Text and graphics that are entered into the **Description** field are displayed to students before they begin the activity. Use this to explain the activity. Remember that this is a full-featured HTML editor, so you can put text, graphics, and media into the description.
5. Under **Availability**, you can enter a time to open and close the activity. If you don't enter a time to open the activity, it is available immediately. If you don't enter a time to close the activity, it will remain open indefinitely.
6. The option to **Record user names** affects only what the teacher sees. Students do not see each others' responses. If **Record user names** is set to **User's names will be logged and shown with answers**, the teacher will be able to see a list of users who completed the feedback and their answers.
7. The setting for **Allow multiple submissions** affects the activity, only if you have allowed anonymous responses. If so, any user can submit the feedback survey as many times as they want.
8. If **Enable notification of submissions** is set to **Yes**, course administrators are emailed whenever someone submits this feedback. This includes teachers and course managers.
9. If you want Moodle to number the questions in your feedback activity, select **Yes** for **Autonumber questions**.

10. If **Show analysis page after submit** is set to **Yes**, a summary of the results so far is shown to the user after they submit their feedback.

Get this setting right the first time

Moodle doesn't allow you to change the multiple submissions setting after someone has answered the feedback activity, without losing the previous responses. So get this setting right before people start answering. If you do need to change this setting, you must first **Reset** feedback responses under the **Course administration** menu.

11. If you enter a **Link to next activity**, that page is displayed immediately after the users submit their answers. You can use this page to explain what happens after the activity. If you leave this blank, Moodle displays a simple message telling the user that their answers have been saved. At the bottom of this page, Moodle displays a **Continue** button.

Careful with the URL for link to next activity

You might be tempted to use the URL to send the user to another page in your site. Remember that if you move this activity to another course, or another Moodle site, that URL might change.

12. Common module settings and restrict availability work as they do for other activities. These are covered in a separate section of the book.

13. Click on the **Save and display** button to save the settings. It is time to start adding questions.

To add questions to a feedback activity, carry out these steps:

1. Select the feedback activity.
2. From the left menu, select **Settings** I **Feedback administration** I **Questions** I **Edit questions**. If you just created and saved the activity, click on the **Edit questions** tab.
3. From the drop-down list that is labeled **Content**, select the type of question to add.

Specific types of questions are described in the next section. The rest of this procedure covers settings that are common to almost all question types. For settings that are specific to a question type, refer to the next section.

4. If you mark a question as **Required**, the user must answer it to submit the feedback. The question will have a red asterisk next to it.

5. The **Question** field contains the text of the question. Unlike a quiz question, a feedback question can only consist of text.

6. The **Label** field contains a label that only teachers will see, when viewing the results of the feedback. The most important reason for the **Label** field is when you plan to export the results of the feedback to an Excel worksheet. The label is exported with the results. This enables you to match the feedback results with a short label in your database.

7. The **Position** field determines the order of the question, when you first add it to the feedback page. After the question has been added, you can override this number and move the question to any position on the page.

8. **Depend item** and **Depend value** can be used to make the appearance of a question dependent on the answer to a previous question. For example, you might first ask someone, **Do you have a Twitter account?** If they answer with a **Yes**, you might display a question like **How often do you tweet?** If they answer with a **No**, you would hide that question. From the **Dependence item** drop-down list, select the question whose answer will determine whether this question appears. Then, in the **Dependence value** field, enter the answer that is needed to make this question appear.

9. For a discussion of the fields that apply only to one type of question, check out the following section.

10. Save the question.

Question types

The feedback activity enables you to add several types of questions. Some of these are not actually questions, but you still add them from the same drop-down menu:

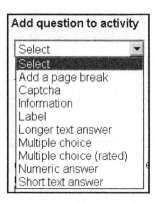

Adding a page break

Add a page break inserts a page break into the feedback activity.

Avoiding bots with captcha

A **CAPTCHA** is a test to ensure that a human is filling out an online form. It displays a picture of some text, and the user must read and type in that text. If the user doesn't correctly type the text, the feedback form is rejected. This prevents software robots from automatically filling in your feedback and spamming your results.

Inserting information

You can use this option to insert information about the feedback into the form. That information is added by Moodle and submitted with the user's answers. At this time, the options are the following:

- **Response time**: The date and time at which the user submitted the feedback
- **Course**: The short name of the course in which this feedback appears
- **Course category**: The short name of the category in which this feedback appears

Adding a label

This is the same as adding a label to a course home page. The label can be anything that you can put on a web page. This is a good way to insert an explanation, instructions, and encouragement into the activity.

Creating a textbox for a longer text answer

Use this question type to create a textbox where the user can type in an answer. You specify how many characters wide and how many lines high the textbox is. If the user runs out of space, Moodle adds a scroll bar to the box so that the user can keep on typing.

Displaying multiple-choice questions

A multiple-choice question displays a list of responses. There are three subtypes of multiple-choice questions:

- **Multiple choice - multiple answers**: In this question, Moodle displays a checkbox next to each response. The user can select as many as they want.
- **Multiple choice - single answer**: In this question, Moodle displays a radio button next to each response. The user must select only one response.
- **Multiple choice - single answer allowed (dropdownlist)**: In this question, Moodle displays a drop-down list of the responses. The user must select only one response.

You create the responses for a multiple choice question by entering one response on each line in the **Multiple choice values** field. For example, consider the following settings:

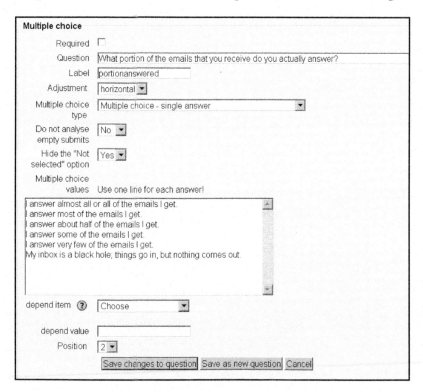

Create this question:

> What portion of the emails that you receive do you actually answer?
>
> C I answer almost all or all of the emails I get.   C I answer most of the emails I get.   C I answer about half of the emails I get.   C I answer some of the emails I get.   C I answer very few of the emails I get.   C My inbox is a black hole; things go in, but nothing comes out.

 Note that the **Adjustment** setting for this question is set to **horizontal**. This causes the responses to be listed horizontally, across the page, instead of in a vertical list.

Also, note the setting for **Hide "not selected"** option. If that is set to **No**, Moodle adds a **Not selected** response to the list of responses that you create. When set to **Yes**, Moodle displays only the responses that you create.

Creating multiple-choice questions

To the user, this type of question appears identical to a multiple-choice single-answer question. However, when you review the results, you see a number that is associated with each answer. This enables you to calculate averages and perform other calculations with the data that you collect.

In this example, the answers are rated 4 through 0:

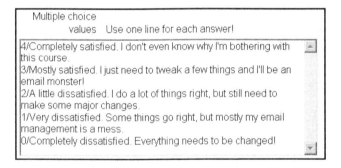

The user doesn't see these numbers when they select an answer, but when the teacher looks at the analysis for this question, the average is displayed:

(howsatisfiedworkflow) How satisfied are you with your current email workflow?	
- Completely satisfied. I don't even know why I'm bothering with this course. (4):	0
- Mostly satisfied. I just need to tweak a few things and I'll be an email monster! (3):	0
- A little dissatisfied. I do a lot of things right, but still need to make some major changes. (2):	1 (50.00 %)
- Very dissatisfied. Some things go right, but mostly my email management is a mess. (1):	1 (50.00 %)
- Completely dissatisfied. Everything needs to be changed! (0):	0
Average: 1.50	

Also, when the results of the feedback are exported to Excel, the rating numbers are exported. This enables you to do advance analysis on your results using a spreadsheet.

The numeric answer

Use this question to ask the user to enter a number. You can specify a range that you will accept.

The short-text answer

A short-text answer-question lets you limit the amount of text that the user enters. You specify the size of the text entry box and the amount of text that the box will accept.

Viewing feedback

Teachers and administrators can view the responses to a feedback activity. You can view the responses one at a time or a summary of all responses.

Seeing individual responses

If **Record User Names** is set to **User's Names Will Be Logged and Shown With Answers**, the teacher will be able to see a list of users who completed the feedback and their answers. To see this list of responses, do as follows:

1. Select the feedback activity
2. From the left menu, select **Settings | Feedback administration | Show responses**
3. For the student whose responses you want to see, click on the date:

The responses for that session will be displayed:

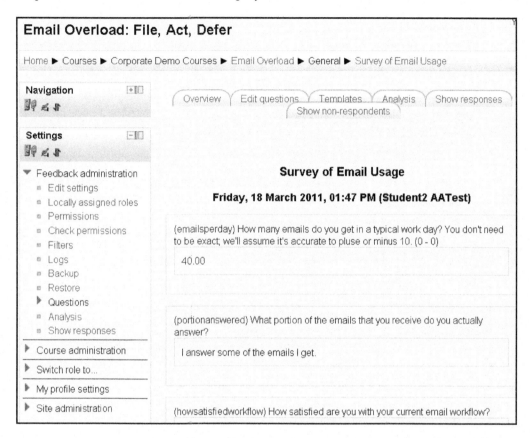

Note that if a student answers the feedback several times, there will be a date for each time that the student answered.

For anonymous responses, you will see a number instead of a name.

Analyzing responses with the Analysis tab

Under the **Analysis** tab, you can see a summary of all the responses. On this page, you also have an export to Excel button that will download all the data to an Excel spreadsheet.

Choice

Moodle's **Choice** is the simplest type of activity. In a choice activity, you create one question and specify a choice of responses. You can use **Choice** to do any of these:

- Take a quick poll
- Ask students to choose sides in a debate
- Confirm the students' understanding of an agreement
- Gather consent
- Allow students to choose a subject for an essay or project

Before we look at how to accomplish this, let's look at the **Choice** activity from the student's point of view and then explore the settings available to the teacher while creating a **Choice**.

The student's point of view

From the student's point of view, a choice activity looks like this:

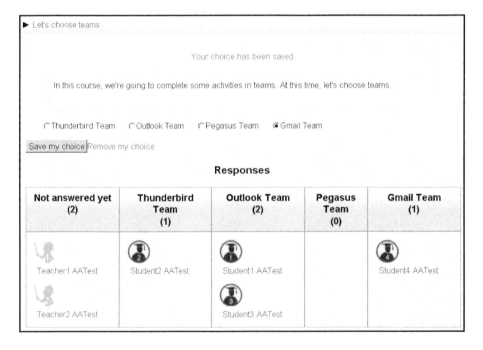

Note a few things about this choice activity:

- The student can see how many other students have chosen a response
- There is a limit on the number of students who can choose each response
- The student can remove their choice and submit again

These are options that you can set for the activity. The teacher also could have hidden other students' responses, had no limit for the number who can choose each response, and prevented the student from changing their response.

The teacher's point of view

Before we discuss some of the uses for a choice activity, let's look at the settings available on the **Editing choice** page. Then, we'll see how we can make creative use of these capabilities.

Limit

The **Limit** option next to each choice enables you to limit how many students can select that choice. In the preceding example, no more than four students can select each choice, so after four students have selected a team, that choice becomes unavailable.

For limits to take effect, **Limit the number of responses allowed** must be set to **Enable**.

Display Mode

In the preceding example, **Display Mode** is set to **Horizontal**. You can also arrange the choices vertically.

Publish results

You can choose whether to reveal the results of the choice to the students, and if so, when.

In the example at the beginning of this section, **Publish results** was set to **Always show results to students**; this is why the student could see how many students had chosen each response. If it had been set to **Do not publish results to students**, the activity would not have shown how many students had selected each response.

If you limit the number of students who can choose a response, consider using **Always show results to students**. That way, the student can see how many others have chosen the response and how many slots are left for each response.

Privacy of results

If you publish the results of the choice, you can choose whether to publish the names of the students who have selected each response. In the example, at the beginning of this section, **Privacy of results** was set to **Publish full result**, so the student could see who had selected each response.

Allowing students to change their minds

The **Allow choice to be updated** setting determines whether a student can change their answer after submitting it. If this is set to **Yes**, a student can retake the choice activity until the activity is closed.

Summary

Activities are very important in the Moodle framework because they allow students to demonstrate competency as well as stay engaged and motivated. They also allow course designers to connect learning outcomes to overall competency frameworks that may be required by governing bodies.

Moodle's assignments and lessons enable you to create course material that students interact with. This interaction is more engaging, and usually more effective, than courses consisting of static material that the students view. While you will probably begin creating your course by adding static material, the next step should usually be to ask "How can I add interactivity to this course?"

There are many ways to build engaging assignments and Moodle provides many different activities to help you do so. You can customize your own solutions, so as you work through this unit, please take a moment to experiment. Remember, you can always delete and modify your work. So, play in the sandbox!

Lessons can take the place of many static web pages, since they consist of web pages with a question at the end of each page. A lesson enables you to present information to a student, test the student on the information, and then present either remedial information or continue to the next topic.

Feedback and **Choice** activities give teachers the opportunity to assess students, their attitudes, and their satisfaction with a course. Feedback is especially useful for assessing the class's attitude and experience at the beginning of the course. You can also use feedback to create surveys for people who are not even taking a course, such as an employee survey or research data.

The **Choice** activity is especially useful for having a structured, ongoing conversation between the students and teacher. You can create several of these, keep them hidden, and reveal them when you want to measure the students' attitude.

In the next chapter, we will see how to evaluate students using the **Quiz** activity.

8
Evaluating Students with Quizzes

A foundational part of any assessment strategy in an online course often relies heavily on different types of automatically scoring quizzes. However, quizzes can often be the Achilles heel of a course or educational program if they are not designed well, and do not tie in well with overall course learning objectives.

Moodle offers a powerful solution that allows well-designed and well-placed quizzes, and the ability to tie the quizzes in with mastery learning, competency frameworks, certificates, and badges. In this chapter, we cover developing graded assignments, create quizzes, and integrate certificates and badges.

Developing graded assignments using quizzes

As you put together your lessons and assignments, you will need an assessment strategy. In online courses, it is very useful to be able to incorporate self-grading quizzes. Moodle offers a flexible quiz builder. Each question can include any valid HTML code, such as graphics, formatted text, and media. A question can include anything that you can put on a Moodle resource page.

In most instructor-led courses, a quiz or test is a major event. Handing out the quizzes, taking them in the middle of a class, and grading them can take up a lot of the teacher's time. In Moodle, creating, taking, and grading quizzes can be much faster. This means that you can use quizzes liberally throughout your courses. Here are some instances where you can use quizzes:

- You can use a short quiz after each reading assignment to ensure that the students complete the reading. You can shuffle the questions and answers to prevent sharing among the students. You can also make the quiz available only for the week/month in which the students are supposed to complete the reading.
- You can use a quiz as a practice test. You can allow several attempts and/or use the adaptive mode to allow students to attempt a question until they get it right. Then, the quiz functions both as a practice and as learning material.
- You can use a quiz as a pretest. You can ask the students to complete a quiz even before they come to the course. The students can complete this pretest at a time and place that is convenient for them. Then, you can compare their scores on the pretest and final test to show that learning has occurred.
- You can use a quiz in conjunction with mastery learning to help students achieve the minimum score to demonstrate mastery.
- You can tie quiz scores/performance to competency frameworks to help satisfy institutional or accreditation requirements.
- You can automatically generate badges and certificates based on the achievement of certain scores.

Question banks

The question bank is Moodle's collection of questions, which can be used within a quiz. In a quiz, you just choose questions from the question bank and display them all together. A quiz can be deleted from a course, but the questions remain in the question bank.

In this chapter, you will see how to create a quiz and add questions to it. While completing this process, keep in mind that when you create a question, you are adding that question to Moodle's question bank.

The questions in the question bank can be categorized and shared. The real asset in your learning site is not the quizzes, but the question bank that you and your fellow teachers build over time.

Configuring quiz settings

When you first create a quiz, you need to go to the **Settings** page. The settings that you select affect only that particular quiz. The settings affect things such as the number of questions displayed on each page of the quiz, whether a student can retry the quiz, whether the quiz has a time limit, and more. The settings affect the look and behavior of the quiz.

After the settings are chosen, you add questions to the quiz; the questions are the content of the quiz.

In Moodle, think of a quiz as a combination of the settings (display and behavior), the container (the quiz pages), and the questions (content).

The **Settings** page is divided into nine areas. Let's look at the settings under each area, top to bottom.

General

The **General** settings include the name and description for the quiz:

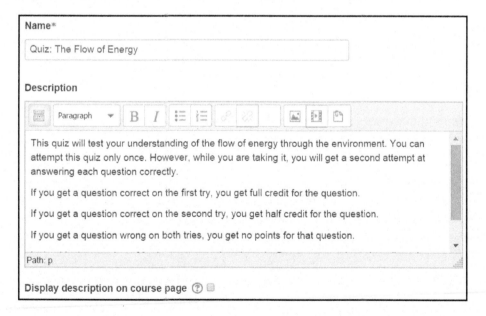

The **Name** of the quiz is displayed on course's home page, and **Description** is displayed when a student selects the quiz.

The **Description** should explain why the student is taking the quiz. It should also inform the student of any unusual features of the quiz, for example, whether it uses an animation that requires the Flash plugin or whether it uses a pop-up window. Remember that once the student clicks on the **Attempt quiz now** button, they are into the quiz, so give the student everything they need to understand why and how to take the quiz before clicking on the **Attempt quiz now** button.

Optionally, you can display **Description** on the course's home page. If you do this, it will continue to display when the student selects the quiz.

Timing

The **Open** and **Close** dates determine when the quiz is available. If you do not select the **Enable** checkbox for **Open the quiz**, the quiz will be permanently open, instead of becoming available on a given date. If you do not select the **Enable** checkbox for **Close the quiz**, then once the quiz is open and will stay open permanently instead of becoming unavailable on a given date.

 Even if the quiz is closed, it will still show on the course's home page, and students might still try to select it. When they select a closed quiz, the students see a message saying that it is closed.

If you want to hide a quiz, further down on this page, under **Common module settings**, you will see the **Visible** setting; change this setting to **Hide**.

By default, a quiz does not have a time limit. If you want to set a time limit, use the **Time limit** setting. When time runs out, the quiz is automatically submitted with the answers that have been filled out. A time limit can help prevent the use of reference materials while taking the quiz. For example, if you want students to answer the questions from memory but all the answers are in the course textbook, setting a timer might discourage students from taking the time to look up the answer to each question.

When students are taking a timed quiz, they see a countdown timer on the quiz page.

If you set a time limit for the quiz, in the quiz's description, inform the students about what happens when the time limit is reached. For example, if you configure the quiz to discard the student's answers if the student has not submitted the quiz in time, inform the student about this.

Grade

If you created categories in the courses' grade books, you can assign this quiz to one of the categories using the **Grade category** setting. If you have not created categories in the grade book, the quiz is uncategorized. You can move a quiz into a category at any time.

If you allow several attempts, the **Grading method** option determines which grade is recorded in the course's grade book: **Highest**, **Average**, **First**, or **Last**. If you do not allow multiple attempts, **Grading method** will have no effect.

Attempts allowed can be used to limit the number of times a student takes the quiz. Further down the page, you can choose settings that require the student to wait between attempts. The time delay settings will take effect only if you enable multiple attempts.

Layout

The settings under **Layout** control the order of questions on the quiz and the number of questions that appear on a page.

Question order determines whether the questions appear in the order that you place them in while editing or in a random order. The random order will change each time the quiz is displayed. This does not allow students to share quiz answers with each other and encourages them to focus on the wording when they retake a quiz.

New page determines where page breaks will fall. It determines whether you will have a page break after every question, every two questions, and so on.

The **New page** setting determines where Moodle automatically puts the page breaks. While you create the quiz, you can move these page breaks on the page where you edit the questions for the quiz.

By default, all questions in a quiz are displayed on separate pages. **New page** breaks up the quiz into smaller pages. Moodle inserts the page breaks for you. On the **Editing quiz** page, you can move these page breaks. If you want to break up your quiz into pages that each hold the same number of questions, this setting will work for you. If you want each page in the quiz to hold a different number of questions, use this setting anyway and edit the page breaks that Moodle creates for you.

The **Navigation method** setting determines whether the student can go back and forth between questions. If this setting is set to **Sequential**, the student must answer the questions in order. If questions near the end of the test give clues to the answers for questions at the beginning, you might want to change this setting to **Sequential**. This will prevent the student from going back to early questions and using those clues at the end of the test to answer the early questions.

The question behavior

The **Shuffle within questions** setting enables you to present the parts of a question in a random order. This only works if three conditions are true. First, this setting must be set to **Yes**. Second, the question must have several parts, such as a multiple choice or matching question. This setting has no effect on a fill-in-the-blank question. Third, each question also has a shuffle setting of its own. For any question, the shuffle setting must also be set to **Yes**.

For questions that have an option such as **All of the above** or **Answers A and B**, you will probably want to set this setting to **No**.

The settings for **How questions behave** determine how the quiz will present the questions to the student. Here's what each setting means.

Adaptive mode

The **Adaptive mode** setting allows multiple attempts *for each question*. This is different than **Attempts allowed**, which allows multiple attempts at *the whole quiz*.

In an adaptive quiz, when a student answers a question incorrectly, the quiz redisplays that question and gives the student another chance to answer it correctly. How many attempts the student gets is determined by how much you penalize the student for each wrong attempt.

For example, let's assume that you penalize the student 50 percent for a wrong answer. If the student gets a question wrong, they can try once more for half points. If the student gets the second attempt correct, they get half credit. If they get it wrong, the system subtracts another 50 percent from the score. Now, the question is worth zero points. The system will not redisplay the question for a third attempt, because it's now worth zero points.

If you penalize the student 33.33 percent for a wrong answer, the student will get three attempts to answer the question. The first attempt is worth 100 percent, the second is worth 66.66 percent, and the third is worth 33.33 percent. There will be no fourth attempt, because after the third wrong answer, the question is worth zero points.

The **Adaptive mode (no penalties)** setting also gives the student multiple attempts at answering a question. However, the student gets an unlimited number of tries, because there are no penalties for wrong answers.

Interactive with multiple tries

When you make a quiz interactive with multiple tries, you allow the student to try each question multiple times. After each wrong attempt, Moodle will display a message. You create these messages for each question.

This differs from **Adaptive mode**, where the student gets multiple attempts but no feedback.

Immediate feedback

When you select **Immediate feedback**, the student submits each question as they answer it. The quiz immediately displays a message based on the student's answer. You can create separate feedback messages for each answer, for any wrong answer, for any right answer, and for the question, regardless of the answer.

At this point, let's look at a comparison between the options we discussed:

	Adaptive mode	Adaptive mode (no penalties)	Interactive with multiple tries	Immediate feedback
Multiple attempts at the same question?	Yes	Yes	Yes	No
Feedback after each attempt?	No	No	Yes	Yes
Reduced score for wrong answers?	Yes	No	Yes	Yes

Deferred feedback

If a quiz uses **Deferred feedback**, the student submits the entire quiz after answering all the questions. Then, the quiz displays the student's score and any feedback that you have created for the questions.

Each attempt builds on the last

Each attempt builds on the last only has an effect if multiple attempts are allowed. When this setting is enabled, each attempt that a student makes will display the results of the student's previous attempt. The student can see how they answered and scored on the previous attempt.

The setting for **Each attempt builds on the last** is especially useful when you are using a quiz as a teaching tool, instead of an evaluation tool. The **Attempts allowed** option allows the student to keep trying the quiz. **Each attempt builds on the last** retains the answers from one attempt to another. Taken together, these two settings can be used to create a quiz that the student can keep trying until they get it right. This transforms the quiz from a test into a learning tool.

Review options

Review options determine what information a student can see when they review a quiz. These options also determine when they can see this information.

The information that the student can see is as follows:

Setting	Type of information displayed to the student
Responses	These are the answers that the student had to choose from for a question.
Answers	These are the answers that the student chose.
Feedback	Each response for a question can have its own feedback. This setting refers to the feedback for each response that the student selected (that is, the feedback for each of the student's answers).
General feedback	Each question can have its own feedback. This feedback is displayed regardless of how the student answered the question. This setting displays a general feedback for each question.
Scores	These are the student's scores, or points earned, for each question.
Overall feedback	Overall feedback is given for the student's score on the quiz.

When the information is revealed, the settings have the following meanings:

Time period	Meaning
During the attempt	With this setting, the information appears while the student is attempting the quiz. This setting has meaning only if immediate feedback is enabled.
Immediately after the attempt	With this setting, the information appears within two minutes of finishing the quiz.
Later, while the quiz is still open	With this setting, the information appears two minutes after the quiz is finished.
After the quiz is closed	With this setting, the information appears after the date and time set in **Close the quiz** has passed. If you never close the quiz, this setting has no effect.

Appearance

The settings under **Display** affect information that is displayed while the student is taking the quiz.

If **Show the user's picture** is set to **Yes**, while the student is taking the quiz, the student's picture and name will be displayed in the quiz window. This makes it easier for an exam proctor to confirm that the students have logged in themselves. The proctor can just look over the student's shoulder and see the student's picture and name on screen.

The settings for **Decimal places in grades** and **Decimal places in question grades** affect the display of grades that are shown to the student. The first setting affects the display of the overall grade for the quiz. The second setting affects the display of the grade for each individual question.

No matter how many decimal places you display, Moodle's database calculates the grades with full accuracy. When you create a course, you can add blocks to the left and right sidebars. The setting for **Show blocks during quiz attempts** determines whether these blocks are displayed while the student is taking the quiz. Normally, this is set to **No** so that the student is not distracted while taking the quiz.

Extra restrictions on attempts

If you enter anything into the **Require password** field, the student must enter that password to access the quiz.

With **Require network address**, you can restrict access to the quiz to particular IP address/addresses. For example, you can restrict the quiz's access to the following IP addresses:

- `146.203.59.235`: This is a single IP address. It will permit a single computer to access the quiz. If this computer is acting as a proxy server, the other computers *behind* it can also access the quiz.
- `146.203`: This is a range of IP addresses. It will permit any IP address starting with those numbers. If those numbers belong to your company, you effectively limit access to the quiz to your company's campus.
- `146.203.59.235/20`: This is a subnet. It will permit the computers on that subnet to access the quiz.

The **Enforced delay** settings prevent students from attempting the quiz without waiting between attempts. If you show the students the correct answers after they submit the quiz, you might want to set a delay between attempts. This prevents students from attempting the quiz, seeing the correct answers, and then immediately trying the quiz again while those answers are fresh in their memory.

If **Browser security** is set to **Full-screen popup...**, it launches the quiz in a new browser window. It uses JavaScript to disable copying, saving, and printing. This security is not foolproof.

Techniques for greater security

You should understand that the only way to make a test secure is to give the test on paper, separate the students far enough apart so that they can't see each other's papers, place a proctor in the room to observe the students, and use different questions for each group that takes the test. There is no way to make a web-based test completely cheat proof.

If you must absolutely give a web-based test that is resistant to cheating, consider these strategies:

- Create a very large number of questions, but have the quiz show only a small set of them; this makes sharing of questions less useful.
- Shuffle the questions and answers. This also makes sharing of questions more difficult.
- Apply a time limit. This makes using reference material more difficult.
- Open the quiz for only a few hours. Have your students schedule the time to take the quiz. Make yourself available during this time to help with technical issues.
- Place one question on each page of the quiz; this discourages students from taking screenshots of the entire quiz.

The overall feedback

Moodle enables you to create several different kinds of feedback for a quiz:

- You can create feedback for the entire quiz, which changes with the student's score. This is called **Overall feedback** and uses a feature called **Grade boundary**.
- You can create feedback for a question, no matter what the student's score on that question is. All students receive the same feedback. This is called **General feedback**. Each individual question can have its own **General feedback**. The exact type of feedback that you can create for a question varies with the type of question.
- You can create feedback for a response. This is the feedback that the student receives when they select that response to a question.

The following screenshot shows **Overall feedback** with **Grade boundary**. Students who score 90 to 100 percent on the quiz receive the first feedback, **You're a wizard...**, and students who score 80 to 89.99 percent receive the second feedback, **Very good!...**:

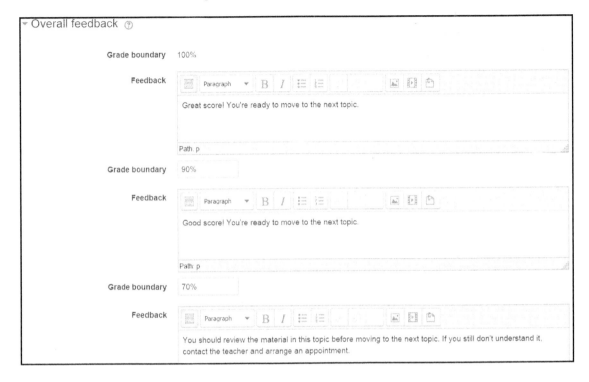

Common module settings

Group mode works in the same way as it does for any other resource. However, since students take the quiz themselves, the only real use for the group setting in a quiz is to display the high score for a group in the **Quiz Results** block.

Visible shows and hides the quiz from students. However, a teacher or course creator can still see the quiz.

Adding questions to a quiz

After you've selected the quiz from your course home page, you can add questions to the quiz. First, go to **Administration** | **Quiz administration** | **Edit quiz**. On the **Editing quiz** page, you can see the **Add a question...** button:

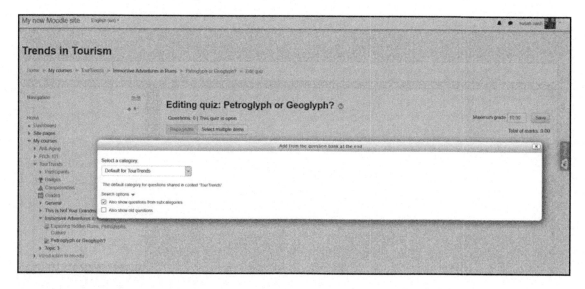

Before we look at the detailed instructions to create new questions, look at the **Question bank contents** button. Also, on the **Quiz administration** menu, you can see the options for **Question bank**; these options enable you to work with the question bank.

Adding questions to the Question bank

The question bank is a collection of quiz questions for your Moodle site. You will have access to different questions in the bank, depending on your location in your site.

In the following screenshot, the user is in the **Outlining** course. The user selected the **Question bank** and is now selecting the group of questions to work with:

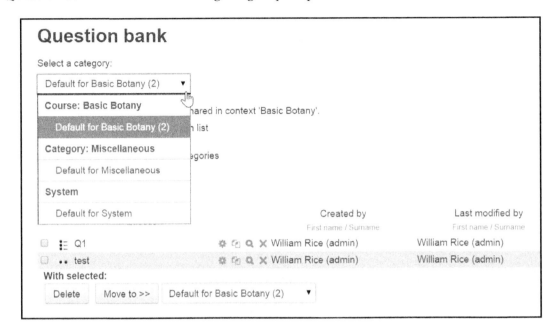

Note that the user can select questions that are stored for just this course (**Course: Basic Botany**), the category in which the course resides (**Category: Miscellaneous**), or the entire site (**System**). If the user switched to another course, the questions for this quiz and course would be unavailable. However, questions for the new course would be available. Questions for the system are always available.

Sharing questions

If you want the questions that you create for this quiz to be available to other users of the site, create the questions under **Question bank** and move them to the **Category** level or the **System** level. Note that your role determines your access to a question category.

As shown in the *Add questions to a quiz* section, you can create questions and add them directly to a quiz. As shown in the *Adding questions to the question bank* section, you can also create questions in the question bank and add them to the quiz later. If you're in a hurry to create questions for a quiz, select **Edit quiz** and start creating them. You can rearrange them in the question bank later.

You can display questions from one category at a time. To select that category, use the **Category** drop-down list.

If a question is deleted when it is still being used by a quiz, it is not removed from the question bank; instead, the question is hidden. The **Also show old questions** setting enables you to see questions that were deleted from the category. These deleted (or hidden or old) questions appear in the list with blue boxes next to them.

To keep your question bank clean and to prevent teachers from using deleted questions, you can move all the deleted questions into a category called `Deleted questions`. **Create the** `Deleted questions` category and then use **Also show old questions** to show the deleted questions. Select these questions and move them into `Deleted questions`.

Moving questions between categories

Every question in the question bank belongs to a category. If a question belongs to a category for the course, only teachers with access to that course can see and reuse the question. If a question belongs to a category for the system, the question can be seen and reused by all teachers in the system. To let your questions be used by other teachers, you might want to move them to a category that is accessible by other teachers.

Select the question(s) to move, select the category, and then click on the **Move to** button.

Managing the proliferation of questions and categories

As the site administrator, you might want to monitor the creation of new question categories to ensure that they are logically named, don't have a lot of overlap, and are appropriate for the purpose of your site. As these question categories and the questions in them are shared among course creators, they can be a powerful tool for collaboration.

Creating and editing question categories

Every question belongs to a category. You manage question categories under the **Categories** tab. There will always be a **Default** category. However, before you create new questions, you might want to check to ensure that you have an appropriate category to put them in.

To add a new category, perform the following steps:

1. To add a new question category, go to **Course administration** | **Question bank** | **Categories**.
2. Scroll to the bottom of the page to the **Add category** section.
3. Select **Parent** for the category. If you select **Top**, the category will be a top-level category. Alternatively, you can select any other category to which you have access. Then, the new category will be a child of the selected category.
4. In the **Name** field, enter the name for the new category.
5. In the **Category Info** field, enter a description of the new category.
6. Click on the **Add category** button.

To edit a category, perform the following steps:

1. Go to **Quiz administration** | **Question bank** | **Categories**.
2. Next to the category, click on the icon. The **Edit categories** page is displayed.
3. You can edit the **Parent**, **Category**, and **Category Info** settings.
4. When you are finished, click on the **Update** button. Your changes are saved, and you are returned to the **Edit categories** page.

Creating a question

To create a quiz question, follow these steps:

1. First, go to **Quiz administration** | **Edit Quiz**. Then, click on the **Add** link:

2. A pop-up window will be displayed. Select **a new question**:

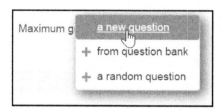

This will be a two-step process. First, you will create a question, and then you will add it to your quiz.

To create a question, perform the following steps:

1. From the pop-up window, select the type of question that you want to create:

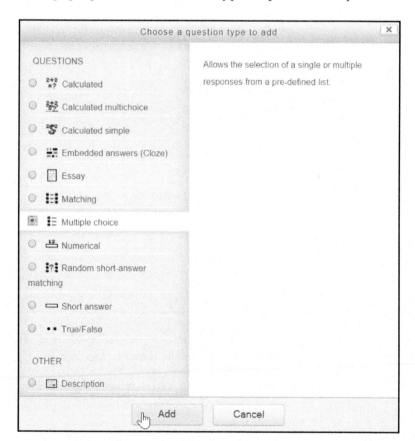

> For an explanation of the different types of questions, refer to the *Question types* section.

2. Click on the **Add** button. This will bring you to the editing page for that question. The editing page will be different for each type of question, but some features will be the same for all types of questions. This is shown in the following screenshot:

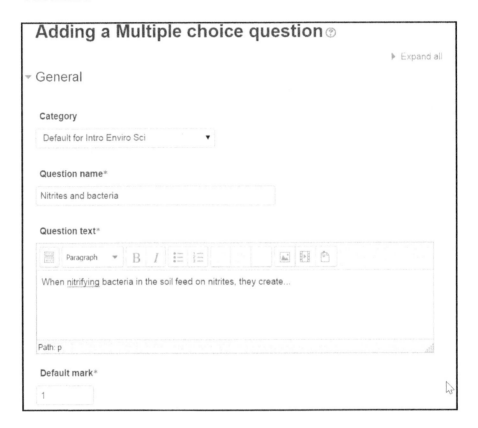

3. The question name is what the teacher will see when building and reviewing the quiz. Students don't see this field. Make the name meaningful to the teacher. For example, *Leaf Question 1* will not be a very descriptive name, but *Principles of Bio-Chap8-Pg3* will tell you the source of the question. If you forget what a question says, you can always click on the 🔍button next to the question to preview it.

4. **Question text** is the actual question that the students will see.

5. **General feedback** (not shown in the preceding screenshot to save space) is the feedback that students will see for this question, no matter what answer they gave. For more information on question feedback, refer to the *Adding feedback to a question* section.

6. Enter the choices (answers) for the question. You can enter feedback for each choice:

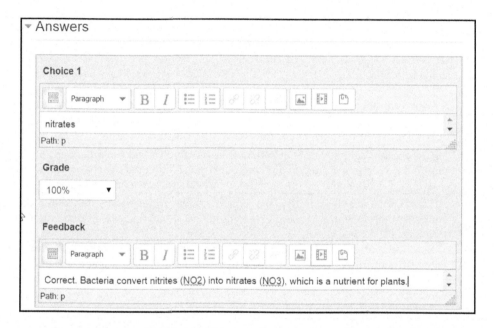

7. After you save the question, it is added to the list of questions in that category. It is also automatically added to the quiz, as shown in the following screenshot:

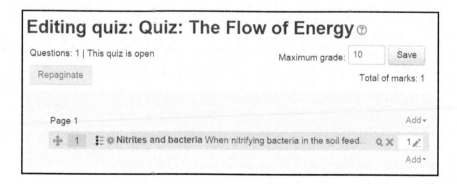

Question types

The following table explains the types of questions you can create and gives some tips on using them. These question types are included in the default installation of Moodle. You can obtain plugins from `https://moodle.org`. These plugins add more question types to your system:

Type of question	Description and tips for using them
Calculated simple	When you create a calculated question, you enter a formula that gets displayed in the text of the question. The formula can contain one or more wildcards. These wildcards are replaced with numbers when the quiz is run. Wildcards are enclosed in curly brackets. For example, if you type the question `What is 3 * {a}?`, Moodle will replace `{a}` with a random number. You can also enter wildcards into the answer field so that the correct answer is `3 * {a}`. When the quiz is run, the question will display **What is 3 * {a}?**, and the correct answer will be the calculated value of **3 * {a}.**
Calculated multichoice	Like the calculated simple question, this question consists of an equation that gets populated with a value(s) when the question is delivered. Then, the question displays several choices for the student, like a multiple choice question.
Description	This is not a question. It displays whatever web content you enter. When you add a description question, Moodle gives you the same editing screen that you get when you create a web page. Recall that under the **Quiz** tab, you can set page breaks in a quiz. If you want to break your quiz into sections and fully explain each section before the student completes it, consider adding a description on the first page of the section. For example, the description can say, *The following three questions are based on this chart* and show the chart just once.
Essay	When the student is given an essay question, they use Moodle's online rich-text editor to answer the question. Also, you might want to instruct your students to save their essay every few minutes.
Matching	After you create a matching question, you create a list of subquestions and enter the correct answer for each subquestion. The student must match the correct answer with each subquestion. Each subquestion receives equal weight for scoring the question.

Type of question	Description and tips for using them
Embedded answers (Cloze)	An embedded answers question consists of a passage of text, with answers inserted into the text. Multiple choice, fill in the blank, and numeric answers can be inserted into the question. Moodle's help file gives the following example: Question 1 Marks: --/13.00 This question consists of some text with an answer embedded right here [⌄] and right after that you will have to deal with this short answer [ ] and finally we have a floating point number [ ] . The multichoice question can also be shown in the vertical display of the standard moodle multiple choice ○ 1. Wrong answer ○ 2. Another wrong answer ○ 3. Correct answer ○ 4. Answer that gives half the credit Or in an horizontal display that is included here in a table ○ a. Wrong answer ○ b. Another wrong answer ○ c. Correct answer ○ d. Answer that gives half the credit A shortanswer question where case must match. Write moodle in upper case letters [ ] Note that addresses like www.moodle.org and smileys ☺ all work as normal: a) How good is this? [⌄] b) What grade would you give it? [ ]

Note that the question presents a drop-down list first, which is essentially a multiple choice question. Then, it presents a short answer (fill in the blank) question, followed by a numeric question. Finally, there's another multiple choice question (the **Yes/No** dropdown) and another numeric question.

There is no graphical interface to create embedded answers' questions. You need to use a special format that is explained in the help files at
`https://docs.moodle.org/29/en/Embedded_Answers_%28Cloze%29_question_type.`

Type of question	Description and tips for using them
Multiple-choice	Multiple choice questions can allow a student to select a single answer or multiple answers. Each answer can be a percentage of the question's total point value. When you allow a student to select only a single answer, you usually assign a positive score to the correct answer and zero or negative points to all the other incorrect answers. When you allow the student to select multiple answers, you usually assign partial positive points to each correct answer. That's because you want all the correct answers to have a total of 100 percent. You also usually assign negative points to each incorrect answer. If you don't bring down the question's score for each wrong answer, the student can score 100 percent on the question just by selecting all the answers. The negative points should be equal to or greater than the positive points so that if a student just selects all the answers, they won't get a positive score for the question. Don't worry about the student getting a negative score for the question, because Moodle doesn't allow this to happen. On the **Editing quiz** page, if you have chosen to shuffle answers, check all the multiple choice questions that you use in the quiz. If any of them have answers such as **All of the above** or **Both A and C**, shuffling answers will ruin these questions. Instead, change them to multiple answer questions and give partial credit for each correct answer; for example, instead of **Both A and C**, you would say **Select all that apply** and then give partial credit for A and for C.
Short answer	The student types a word or phrase into the answer field. This is checked against the correct answer or answers. There may be several correct answers with different grades. Your answers can use the asterisk as a wildcard. Also, they can be case sensitive. Moreover, accents are counted as characters, so resume and resumé are two separate answers.
Numerical	Just as in a short answer question, the student enters an answer into the answer field. However, the answer to a numerical question can have an acceptable error, which you set when creating the question. For example, you can designate that the correct answer is 5, plus or minus 1. Then, any number from 4 to 6 will be marked correct.
True/False	The student selects from two options: **True** or **False**.

Adding feedback to a question

Moodle enables you to create several different kinds of feedback for a quiz.

You can create feedback for the entire quiz or for a question.

Feedback for the *entire quiz* changes with the student's score. This is called **overall feedback** and uses a feature called **grade boundary**.

The exact type of feedback that you can create for a question varies with the type of question. In this section, we'll look at feedback for a multiple choice question.

Feedback for the entire quiz, or overall feedback, can be accessed by going to **Administration** I **Quiz administration** I **Settings**. Feedback for a question can be accessed under the editing screen for that question.

Types of feedback for a question

In a multiple choice question, you can create three kinds of feedback, which are described here:

Type of feedback	Explanation and when to use it
General feedback	If you create general feedback for a question, no matter what answer the student chooses, they will receive that feedback. Every student who answers the question gets the general feedback. If you think the student might get the correct answer by guessing, you can use general feedback to explain the method of arriving at the correct answer. Also, consider using general feedback to explain the importance of the question.
For any correct response	A multiple choice question can have two or more answers that are 100 percent correct. For example, *From the list of people below, select one person who signed the Declaration of Independence*. This list could include several people who signed, and each of them would be 100 percent correct. If the student selects any of those correct answers, they will see the feedback for **Any correct response**. This is useful when you want to teach the student which answers are 100 percent correct and why they are correct.
For any partially correct response	You can create a multiple choice question that requires the student to select several choices to get full credit. For example, *From the list of people below, select the two people who signed the Declaration of Independence*. In this case, you could give each response a value of 50 percent. The student needs to choose both responses to receive the full point value for the question. If the student selects one of the correct choices, they will see the feedback for **Any partially correct response**. This is useful when you want to teach the student the relationship between the correct responses.
For any incorrect response	Any response with a percentage value of zero or less is considered an incorrect response. If a student selects any incorrect response, they will see the feedback for **Any incorrect response**. This is useful when all incorrect responses have something in common and you want to give the feedback about this commonality.

Remember that these types of feedback are not activated because the student chose a specific response, they are activated because the student chose any correct, partially correct, or incorrect response.

We will discuss the process of creating feedback for individual responses in the *Feedback for individual responses* section.

Feedback for individual responses

You can create feedback for any individual response to a question. A response is an answer that the student chooses or types. Each response can display its own feedback.

In the following example, note how each response has its own feedback. In this example, if a student selects an incorrect response, they will see feedback for that specific response and also the feedback for the other incorrect response.

The following screenshot shows a multiple choice question that uses several kinds of feedback. You're seeing this question from the course creator's point of view and not from the student's. First, you can see general feedback—The truth is, most New Yorkers have never even thought about the "missing Fourth Avenue" issue. After the question is scored, every student sees this feedback, no matter what the student's score is.

Below that, you can see that **Choice 1** through **Choice 4** contain feedback for each response. This feedback is customized to the response. For example, if a student selects **Sixth Avenue** the feedback is Nope, that name is taken. Sixth is also known as the "Avenue of the Americas.".

For this question, we don't need any feedback such as **Any correct answer** or **Partially correct answer**. These options are useful when you have multiple responses that are correct or responses that are partially correct. In this case, only one response is correct and all other responses are incorrect. The following screenshot shows the question and its general feedback:

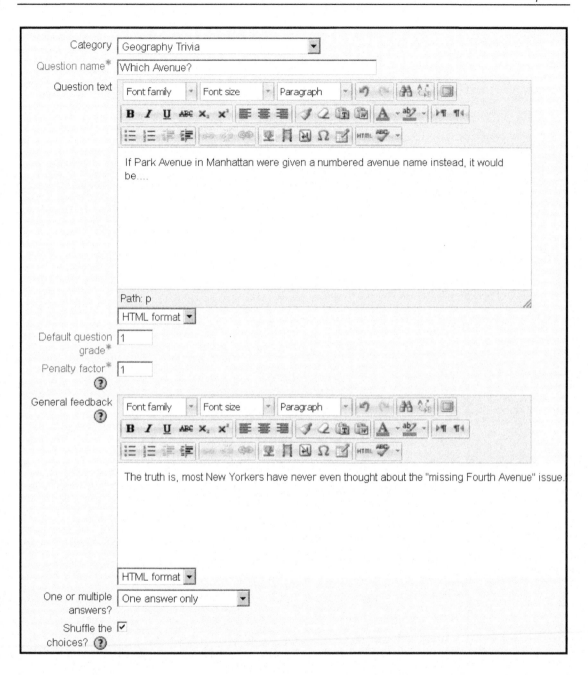

The following screenshot shows the choices and feedback for each individual answer that the student can choose:

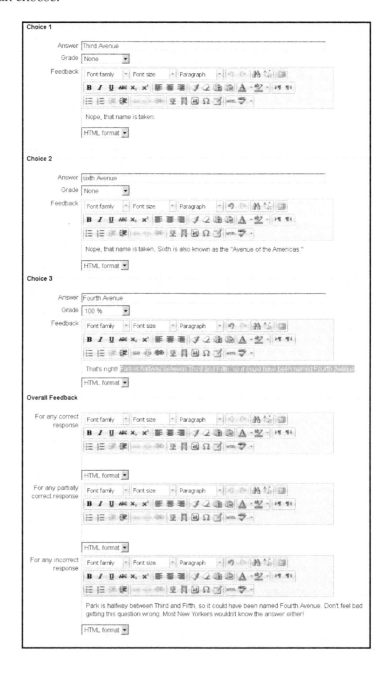

Feedback for a numeric question

The next screenshot shows feedback for a numeric answer question:

```
General    The key to this question is substituting 6 for "a" and 2
feedback:  for "b." If you make these substitutions, you can solve the
           question using simple algebra.
           a @ b = 3ab - b(3)
General       becomes
feedback ⑦  6 @ 2 = 3*6*2 - 2(3)
              which becomes
           6 @ 2 = 36-8
              which solves to
           6 @ 2 = 28
```

Note that **General feedback** explains how the question is solved. This feedback is displayed to everyone after they answer the question, even those who answered correctly. You might think that if the student answered correctly, they don't need this explanation. However, if the student guessed or used a method different from the one given in **General feedback**, explaining the solution can help the student learn from the question.

In a numeric answer question, the student types in a number for the answer; this means the student can enter literally any number. It will be impossible to create customized feedback for every possible answer, because the possibilities are infinite. However, you can create customized feedback for a reasonable number of answers. In the following question, I've created responses for the most likely incorrect answers. After I've given this test to the first group of students, I'll need to review their responses for the most frequent incorrect answers. If there are any that I haven't covered, I would need to add them to the feedback for this question.

In the following screenshot, note that each response has customized feedback. **Answer 1** is correct, and **Answer 2** would be the result of switching the two numbers while trying to solve the problem. As this is a likely error, I've included feedback just for that answer, explaining the error the student made. **Answer 3** is the result of interpreting b^3 as **b times 3** instead of **b cubed**. This is also a likely error, so I've included feedback for that answer.

Answer 4 is a wildcard and will apply if the student submitted any answer other than the three mentioned earlier:

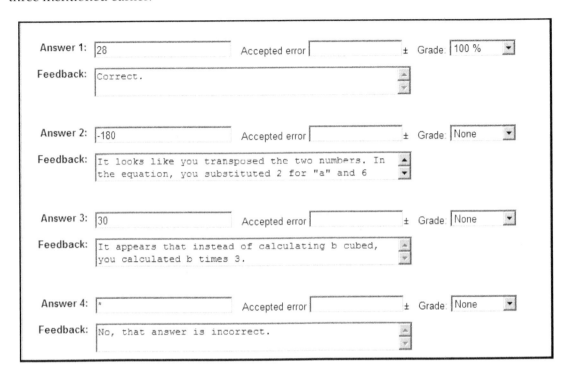

Adding the existing questions from the question bank

As you saw earlier, you can create a new question and add it to the quiz. You can also add the existing questions to the quiz. These questions come from the question bank. To add a question from the question bank, follow these steps:

1. With the quiz selected, go to **Administration** I **Quiz administration** I **Edit quiz**.
2. A pop-up window is displayed. Select **from question bank**, as shown in the following screenshot:

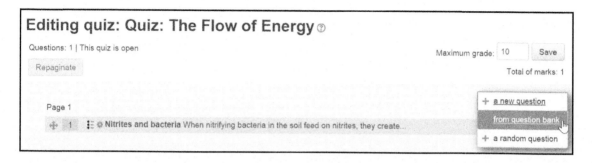

The question bank is displayed. The questions in the bank are categorized. They can belong to this quiz, to this course, to the category that this course is in, or to the system overall. In the following screenshot, the user is selecting the course's category:

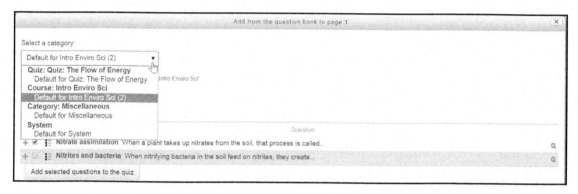

3. Select the category and question, and then select **Add selected questions to the quiz**, shown as follows:

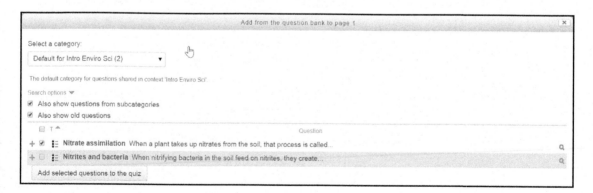

Adding random questions to a quiz

You can add a number of random questions to your quiz. In the following screenshot, note that there are three questions in the selected category. The maximum number of questions that can be added depends on the number of questions in the category:

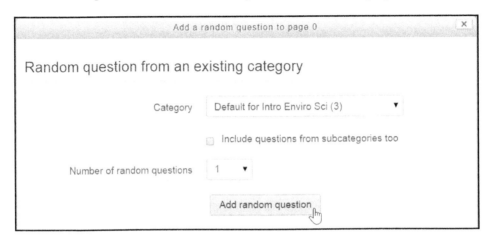

You can add random questions from several categories to the same quiz.

In the same attempt, students will never see the same random question twice. The questions are reset between attempts, so students can see the same question twice if they attempt the same quiz twice.

To add a random question(s), follow these steps:

1. With the quiz selected, go to **Administration** I **Quiz administration** I **Edit Quiz**.
2. A pop-up window is displayed; select **a random question**.
3. A dialog box is displayed. Select the category from which you want to draw the random question(s).
4. Select the number of questions to add, and then select the **Add random question** button.

Let's look at some other functions available under the **Editing quiz** tab.

Maximum grade

The quiz's maximum grade is the quiz's point contribution toward the course. In this example, the quiz is worth 10 points toward the student's total for the course.

The grade for each question will be scaled to the quiz's maximum grade. For example, if this quiz had two questions worth **1** point each but **Maximum grade** is **10**, each question will contribute **5** points to the student's total grade for the course.

Grade for each question

Each question has a point value, which is shown in this screenshot:

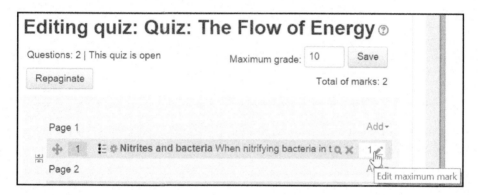

The question's point value is scaled to the quiz's **Maximum grade**. For example, if a question has a grade of **2** and the quiz has a maximum value of **10**, that question is worth one-fifth of the quiz's grade.

Changing the order of questions

You have several ways to rearrange questions. First, you can use the **Repaginate** button to specify how many questions to display on each page:

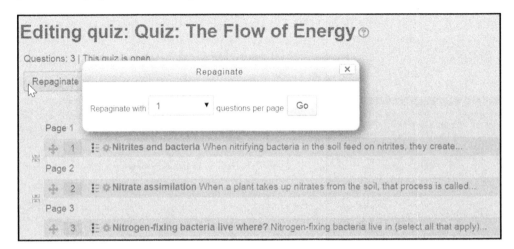

Another way to rearrange questions is to drag and drop the questions using the handle provided to the left of each question:

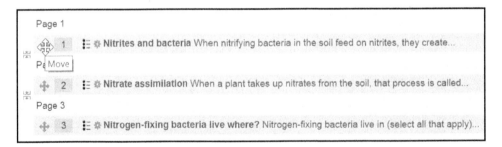

Finally, you can add and remove page breaks between questions using the icon to the left of the break between questions:

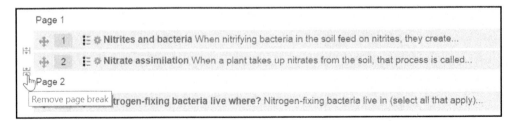

Preventing glossary auto-linking in quiz questions

If you have a glossary in your course, glossary words that are used in quiz questions will link to their glossary entries. If you don't want students to have this resource when they take the quiz, go to **Quiz administration** | **Filters** and turn off the glossary auto-linking.

Preventing an open book quiz

In most Moodle courses, quizzes are *open book* affairs. This is because when the student is taking an online course, there is nothing to prevent the student from looking things up. If you want to prevent this, you can do so with some manual intervention.

The easiest way to prevent a quiz from becoming *open book* is to put that quiz into a separate course topic, by itself. Then, hide all the other course topics. This can be done by clicking on each topic. This prevents students from seeing any of the course material while they take the quiz. Administer the quiz and redisplay the topics afterward.

Mastery learning

Many organizations require the learners to show that they have achieved mastery, which means they have achieved the minimum passing score (usually 80 percent) in knowledge and skills associated with the course outcomes. This is particularly important in the case of training and regulatory compliance.

Moodle allows you to develop a question bank that is specific to the statutes, standards, or codes for regulatory compliance. The following steps are important to follow when tying to mastery learning:

1. Clearly state the grade or score that must be earned
2. Allow students to repeat the questions or the quiz until the qualifying score or grade is earned
3. Incorporate the regulations as a link, file, or embedded player
4. Provide explanations for incorrect answers and point them to the passages that provide the correct responses
5. Categorize and classify the questions according to the nomenclature used in the codes
6. Ensure that the form of the questions is similar to that used in the test, which they will be required to take if there are further exams or skills demonstrations that must be performed

Competency Frameworks

Moodle allows you to tie to Competency Frameworks, which are external performance standards. For example, if your organization has an overall rubric that lists types of competencies, you may classify your questions so that they align with the competency categories. Then, when the student correctly performs the tasks in the quiz, a positive score is received and a box checked in the Competency Framework.

It is possible to automate the process so that the Competency Framework is automatically updated for the student. However, it is easier to simply code the questions so that they reflect the competency categories and to independently calculate a score for the competency framework.

Quiz questions can tie to the competency frameworks you may be using. Alternatively, entire quizzes can tie to them and incorporate a single aspect of the framework.

Certificates

Certificates are important for talent management functions (universities, associations, and individual record-keeping). Certificates can be digital, and they can be printable. Moodle has a number of plugins for certificates. Certificates can be generated upon successful completion of a quiz or a series of quizzes.

Badges

Badges are similar to certificates, but they can also be displayed in social media, which makes them ideal for promoting and publicizing courses and programs. Badges are earned upon successful completion of a quiz or series of quizzes.

Moodle's Badge plugin allows you to design your own badge and also to make them portable so that they can be displayed on social media. Instead of having to upload them to all your social media sites, it's possible to utilize the Open Badges project and include the social media in the Open Badges Backpack.

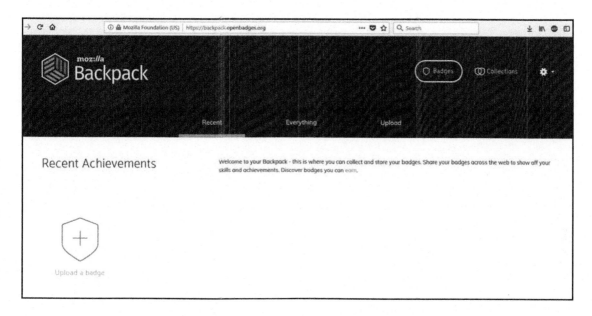

You can know more about them by referring to `https://backpack.openbadges.org/backpack/welcome`.

Summary

Moodle's quiz activity is rich in feedback. The different types of feedback enable you to turn a quiz into a learning activity. Consider using the quiz activity not just for testing but also for teaching. It can also be used for demonstrating competency, mastery learning, and compliance. Accomplishments can be recorded and displayed automatically using plugins such as Certificates and Badges.

The site administrator and teachers should work together to organize questions in the question bank and to give teachers access to the categories of questions they need.

In the next chapter, you'll learn how to make a course more social with forums and chats.

Getting Social with Chats and Forums

9

At the heart of Moodle is the theory of learning that people learn best when they learn from each other, through meaningful interaction. Some of the interaction occurs in collaborative activities. However, bulk of the interaction will occur in social settings, both in synchronous or live chats or in asynchronous discussion board areas, called **forums** in Moodle.

Social course activities encourage student-to-student interaction. Peer interaction is one of the most powerful learning tools that Moodle offers. It not only encourages learning, but also encourages exploration. This tool also makes courses more interesting, because students can share their knowledge, which increases student participation and satisfaction. Peer sharing is part of the social constructionist approach to learning. Moodle embraces this approach. This chapter teaches you how to add communication activities to a course and how to make the best use of them. It includes chats, forums, and other forms of social media.

A forum-based instructional strategy

As you review your learning objectives and seek to map the course materials with the course activities, think about how you can make your course structured around forums and chats.

It may seem hard to envision at first, but in practice it's actually quite simple. As you set up your course, ensure that you include a forum in each of your units. Then you can use the forum for the following purposes:

- Making instructional materials available. The advantage of having them in the forum is that you can let the instructors comment and add more materials, commentary, and so on.

- Asking instructional materials-focused discussion questions. The students can read the materials and immediately comment and share their impressions.
- Posts of drafts and peer reviews. This is a great place to post drafts of papers or comments, and then solicit responses and peer reviews from students.
- Post rubrics, both for peer reviews and final grading.
- Post current controversies, links to articles, and multimedia links.

Learning from one another

You can set up the forum and chat modules so that students have the optimal conditions to learn from one another:

- First, you can ensure that the prompts are engaging and do not result in *yes* or *no* answers.
- Second, you can ask students to share their work and comment in a positive, constructive way.
- Third, you can encourage students to share experiences and things from current events. All of these activities and prompts will be very engaging, and they will serve as excellent motivation.
- Finally, you can remind people of deadlines and include checklists of things to do. They will help students organize their work and manage their time effectively.

The Chat module

Sometimes it is helpful to have synchronous or real-time communication. We often use our smartphones for texting when we need a quick answer or want to ask a rather informal question. The Chat module in Moodle is similar. In certain ways, the Chat module is a bit redundant, because students may be already chatting with each other via social media such as Google Hangouts or Skype. However, the good thing about using the Chat module is that it is a bona fide Moodle product, and it is possible to save the chat conversations within Moodle. Saving the transcripts of chats can be very important for instructors who want to ensure that they are communicating, and also for students who may wish to keep a record of what they have said.

Another advantage of chat is that your students may use speech-to-text applications (Dragon or Google), which automatically inserts a microphone avatar or logo. It is a good way to have students practice speech-to-text, and also can be very helpful for those students who may have limited vision or limited mobility with their hands or fingers.

A chat room can be useful for students who are in a group. However, it's not necessarily a good idea to have a chat with the entire class, because threads can get lost fairly quickly if people are commenting at the same time.

When you add a chat room to a course, by default, any student in the course can enter this chat room at any time. As with other activities, access restrictions can be set to override this default. The **Course Chat Room** can become a meeting place for students in the course, where they can come to collaborate on work and exchange information. If you give group assignments or have students rate other students' assignments, consider adding a chat room to the course and encouraging students to use it. Also, consider saving transcripts of the chat sessions so that they can act as another reference tool for students.

When you schedule a chat session, the scheduled time appears on **Course Calendar** and is also displayed in the **Upcoming events** block:

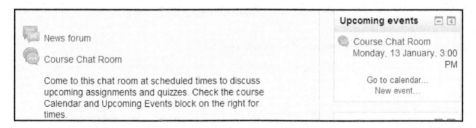

As the chat module is open all the time, when you put a chat on the calendar, you are not restricting access to the chat module. You are just creating a reminder to inform students when they should click on the chat module.

If a group of more than five or six wants to communicate, it's usually much better to use a discussion board rather than chat. That said, if you are launching a webinar, it is always good to have chat available in order to send questions, comments, and to alert the instructor if there are technical difficulties. BigBlueButton and Skype have chat built in so that people can communicate via chat as they also converse with each other via video or pure audio.

When a student selects a chat, they see the **Description** that you entered when you created the chat. You can use this **Description** to instruct the student about the purpose of the chat:

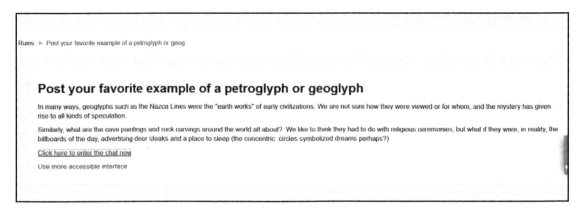

When you enter a chat, it launches a pop-up window. You can choose between two themes: **Bubble** or **Compact**; I've selected **Bubble**. Ensure that your students don't have popups blocked:

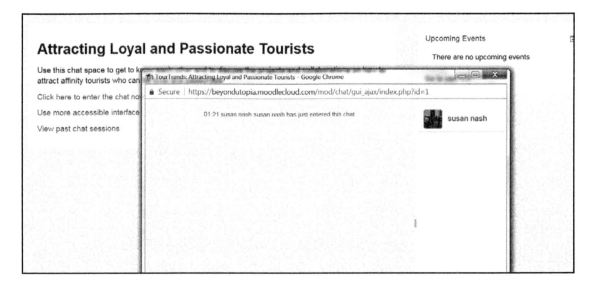

Let's look at the settings that you use to create a chat.

The chat settings page

The **Creating Chat** page is where you create and select settings for a chat. When you first add a chat, you will be taken to this page. To edit the settings for an existing chat, select the chat and then from the left-hand side menu bar, select **Administration | Chat administration | Edit Settings**. This will take you to the same page, but it will be called **Editing Chat** instead of **Creating Chat**. Both pages have the same settings.

Keep in mind that entering a name for a chat room generates a pop-up window. If your students have blocked popups, they'll get a message to unblock their pop-up blocker. Here's a screenshot that shows what the popups look like:

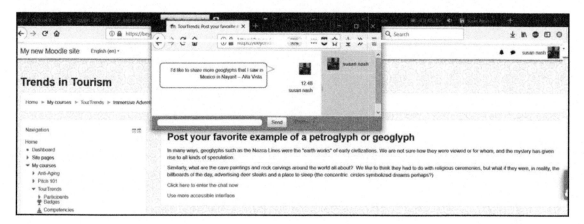

Let's consider the options you have for settings on this page. Note that as in all the activities, you now have a chance to tie the chat so that it fulfills competencies. You can also tag the topics for use in social media, and you can also restrict access so that the chat takes place within groups.

Here's a screenshot that shows how to describe the chat room, and also where to click in order to restrict access:

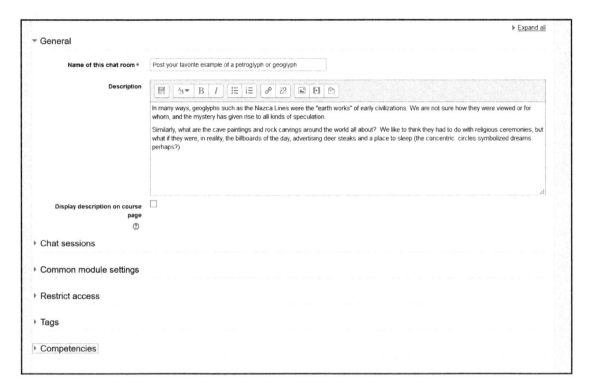

The name of this chat room

This is the name that students will see on the course's home page:

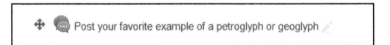

Description

When the students enter the room, the **Description** will appear. Ensure that the **Description** makes sense and does not confuse or distract your students.

When a student selects a chat, they will see the introduction text before clicking on the chat room. Also, you can display the **Description** on the course's home page.

Scheduling *office hours*—it's often a good idea to schedule virtual office hours before a high-stakes test or a big project. One good way to do so is to make a calendar entry for the chat session and then to make it available to all the members of the course. Then, you can be available for questions. Ensure that you save the transcript, because many people may have the same questions but, perhaps, cannot attend at the same time. You can post your chat transcript. Keep in mind that your chat room will be open all the time, not just during office hours. Your office hours notice on the calendar simply means that you'll be there and waiting for questions.

The next chat time and repeat/publish sessions

As stated in the beginning of this section, as long as a chat is visible to the student, they can enter that chat room at any time. Therefore, the settings for **Next chat time** and **Repeat sessions** don't open and close the chat. Instead, these settings put a time and date for the chat on the class calendar.

Chat times are listed in **Calendar** and in the **Upcoming Events** block. Note that chats are not restricted to these times; they are only announced as a way for people in the course to *make a date* for the chat. However, this is a good way for the teacher to announce online office hours.

Spontaneous chats have the best chance of happening if the course has a lot of students who frequent the course's home page. Also, consider adding the **Online Users** block so that when students visit the site, they will know who is online and can invite others to the chat room.

Saving past sessions – Past sessions and everyone can view past sessions

Past chats are automatically saved. The **Save past sessions** setting enables you to choose how long the system saves the chats for. The setting for **Everyone can view past sessions** determines whether students can view past chats (**Yes**) or only teachers can view past chats (**No**).

Preventing students from seeing one another's chats

The only security for a chat room is turning the group mode on so that only students in a selected group can see each other in this chat room. You will find the group settings under **Common module settings**.

Remember that on the **Course settings** page, you can set **Enrolment duration** as **Unlimited**. This means that once a student is enrolled in the course, they are always enrolled until you manually unenroll the student. If you leave the course open to all the students who were ever enrolled, consider segregating your chat into groups. Then, create a group that includes only the currently enrolled students; this prevents previous students from giving away too much in the chat room.

Creating and running forums

Forum is at the heart of Moodle, and it provides you a way to organize student interaction, provide peer review, share information, and disseminate course content. You can also use the forums to provide links to assessments.

Forums are one of Moodle's most useful features. A well-run class forum can stimulate thoughtful discussion, motivate students to become involved, and result in unexpected insights.

You can add any number of forums to a course and to the site's front page. By default, anyone with access to the course will have access to various forums in that course. To separate students, you can use the group mode to ensure that students from different groups cannot see each other's posts in the forum.

You can also create a course that consists only of a forum. The course's home page is the forum. The course will consist of only discussion topics. You perform this using the course type **Social** under the course settings.

In this structure, you will need to plan carefully. The discussion topics will need to correspond to units, and you will need to be consistent as you place the course readings, videos, student responses, and links to assessments.

Forum-based content delivery

A very convenient way to deliver content is to create forums that correspond to the weeks in the course. For example, if you have an eight-week course, you can create eight separate forums. Each one can correspond to specific content (text, blocks, video, audio, presentations, and more) that you will like the students to read. By putting the links in the forum threads, you can ensure that everyone progresses through the course at the same pace and covering the same content. You can then include a few questions in the forum and open threads that allow students to ask questions, and also to reflect on the material. In fact, it's a good place to add a few reflective questions.

Forum-based assignments

By organizing assignments in the forums, you can ensure that you attach the content and reviews to the assignments. For example, you may wish to have students write essays about readings. If you do so, you can open up a forum in which you describe the paper, include expectations, and even incorporate a rubric. You can open threads for students to ask questions, and you can put a link to the Dropbox so that they can, with a single click, submit their assignments.

One advantage of using forum-based assignments is that if you have any changes, you can be assured that most of your students will see the changes because they will occur in the same location that everyone is visiting. It's a "one-stop shopping" point for assignments.

Forum-based peer review

Using the forums for peer review is also a good idea, but you'll need to ensure that you establish good ground rules because the forum is, after all, a public place. If you use the forum as a place for students to start a thread, post a draft, and then respond to each other's drafts, you'll need to ensure that they keep their comments positive and productive. One good way to do that is to provide a checklist of items to respond to. For example, you can ask students to respond to a series of questions:

- What did you like about this post?
- How could the post have been more specific?
- When did you want to know more? What could the author have provided?

The key is to keep the peer review questions brief and avoid having too many. After all, you want to motivate your students to interact, not frighten them into avoiding the forum altogether.

Forum-based review and link to assessments

The forum is a wonderful place to provide a self-contained place for quiz and exam review and practice before they take the full exam. The best way to organize forums for assessment review, practice, and performance is to tie the forum title to the topics covered in the assessment. Then, create a link to the key content covered and describe the learning goals or outcomes. Then, include a few review questions. Ensure that your practice or review questions are in the same format as the ones that they will be taking for their final assessments.

The practice forum is a great place for students to develop self-efficacy and an "I can do it!" attitude. The way to develop self-confidence is to allow feedback in the practice test and allow them to take the test or quiz as many times as they like. Ensure that you always link back to the course content that contains the correct responses or the information they need.

General purpose forum

When a student enters a general purpose forum, they see the description entered during the creation of the forum, as shown in the following screenshot:

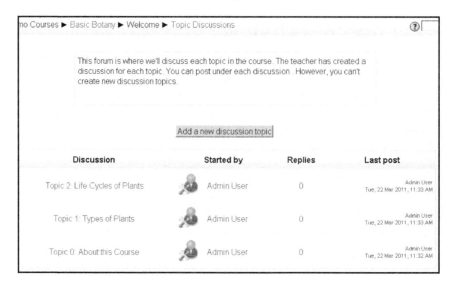

While writing a forum post, the student uses the same online editor you see when creating web pages, resources, and activities in Moodle.

Also, you can allow students to upload files to a forum posting. These files are attached to the forum post.

If you ask students to collaborate on assignments or ask them to review each others' work, consider adding a forum specifically to discuss the assignment. Encourage students to use the forum to preview each others' work and collaborate on various assignments.

Using the news forum to send notifications

Moodle offers several ways to send email announcements to a class. You can use the **People** block to select people in your class and send them a message. Also, when you want to send a message to everyone in a class, you can use the default **News Forum** that is automatically added to every class. By default, in the **News Forum**, **Subscription mode** is set to **Forced subscription**. Also, only teachers have the ability to post messages in the forum.

When the teacher posts a message in the class's **News Forum**, everyone who is subscribed to the **Forum** receives the message. With everyone subscribed, the entire class will receive a copy of each posting.

As **News Forum** is unique for all other forums, it should not be deleted or moved. If you think that you will not need it, just hide it instead of deleting it.

Multiple forums

Remember that a class can have as many forums as you want. If your course uses groups, you can use groups in the forum. Also, you can hide old forums and create new ones. This is useful if you run students through a course on a schedule. Just turning off old forums and creating new ones enables you to refresh parts of the course.

Forum settings

The **Settings** page is where you select settings for a forum. It's accessed from **Administration** | **Forum administration** | **Settings**. Let's take a look at how each of these settings affect the user experience.

General settings

The general settings affect the appearance and function of the forum.

The forum name

This is the name that students will see when a forum is listed on the course's home page.

The forum description

When a student enters a forum, they will see **Forum description** at the top of the forum's page. This text should tell the student what the forum is about. You can also use this introduction to tell the student if they can rate posts by other students. It also tells the student how to link to a document with more extensive instructions on how to use the forum. This is possible because the description is a full-featured web page that can hold anything you put on a web page.

As with other activities, if you check the **Show description** box, the description will display on the course page.

The forum type

On Moodle, you can create several types of forums. Each type can be used in a different way. The types of forums are as follows:

Type of forum	Description
A single simple discussion	The entire forum appears on one page. The first posting at the top of the page is the topic for the forum. This topic is usually created by the teacher. The students then post replies under this topic. A single topic forum is most useful for short and highly-focused discussions.
Each person posts one discussion	Each student can create one and only one new topic. Everyone can reply to every topic. You may need to explain that students only get one new topic, so they should choose their topic wisely.
Q and A	This is like a single topic forum. Here, the teacher creates the topic for the forum. Students then reply to this topic. However, a student cannot see anyone else's reply until they have posted a reply. The topic is usually a question posed by the teacher, and the students' replies are usually answers to this question.

A standard forum displayed in a blog-like format	In a standard forum, anyone can start a new topic. Teachers and students can create new topics and reply to the existing postings. Displaying the discussion in a blog-like format makes the title and body of each discussion visible. This is a great structure for stimulating discussion and sharing of links, images, and embedded social media posts.
A standard forum for general use	In a standard forum, anyone can start a new topic. Teachers and students can create new topics and reply to the existing postings. Only the titles of discussions are visible; you must click on a discussion to read the postings under it.

The maximum attachment size

Students can attach files to forum postings. This sets the maximum file size the student can upload. One of the settings turns off the student's ability to upload files to the **Uploads are not allowed** forum.

The maximum number of attachments

This sets the maximum number of files that can be attached to one post, not the maximum for the whole forum.

The display word count

When set to **Yes**, the forum will show how many words are there in each post. The word count is shown at the bottom of the post, so you will not see the word count until you have clicked on the post.

The subscription mode

Selecting **Force subscription** subscribes all students to the forum automatically (even students who enroll in the course at a later time). Before using this setting, consider its long-term effect on students who took your class.

If you reuse the same course for a later group of students, the previous group will still be enrolled. Do you want previous students to be notified of new postings in the current class's forum? If not, there are several solutions:

- Don't force all students to be subscribed
- Use groups to separate the current group of students in the class from the previous groups
- Create a fresh instance of the course for each new group
- Reset the course, which will unenroll past students
- Create a new forum for a new group of students

If you select **Auto subscription**, everyone in the course is subscribed to the forum, but later they can unsubscribe. With **Force subscription**, the student cannot unsubscribe as long as they are enrolled in the course.

Read tracking

When turned on, this highlights the forum posts that the students haven't read.

Post threshold to block settings

These settings help you prevent the forum from being taken over by a few prolific posters. Users can be blocked from posting more than a specific number of postings in a specific amount of time. As they approach the limit, they can be given a warning.

For the preceding example, you can set a limit of eight posts per day. After a student makes a sixth post for the day, the system will warn them that they are approaching the limit for the number of posts per day. After eight posts, the student cannot post anymore that day.

Ratings

In a forum, a *rating* is really a *grade*. When you enable ratings, you are really allowing the teacher to give each forum posting a grade. In the following screenshot, you can see the first posting in the forum, which was made by the teacher. After this, you can see the reply left by **Student1**. The student's reply was rated by the teacher:

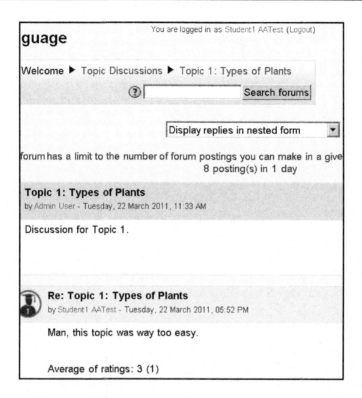

By default, only teachers, non-editing teachers, and course managers can rate forum postings. If you want students to be able to rate postings in a forum, you must enable this for the forum. You do this on the **Permissions** page. Before leaving the **Settings** page, save your work.

To enable students to rate forum postings, perform the following steps:

1. Select **Forum**.
2. Then, select **Settings | Forum administration | Permissions**.
3. From **Advanced role override**, select **Student**.
4. A page listing the student's permissions *for this activity* is displayed. Scroll down to the section labeled **Activity: Forum** and locate the permission for **Rate posts**.
5. Select the **Allow** radio button.
6. Click on the **Save changes** button.

Summary

Moodle offers several options for the student-to-student and student-to-teacher interaction. When deciding which social activities to use, consider the level of structure and the level of student-to-student/student-to-teacher interaction you want. For example, chats and wikis are naturally unstructured with a lot of opportunities for the student-to-student interaction. These are good ways of relinquishing some control of the class to students. A forum offers more structure, because entries are segregated to topics. It can be moderated by the teacher, making it even more structured.

You may want to introduce a chat and/or forum at the beginning of a course to build *esprit de corps* among several students and then move on to a collaborative wiki (such as a group writing project).

In the next chapter, we will see how to encourage collaboration among students using wikis and glossaries. We will learn how to use collaboration as an instructional strategy, develop a glossary and a wiki, and develop collaborative projects.

10
Collaborating with Wikis and Glossaries

Collaboration can be a cornerstone of constructivism and the place where students truly learn from each other. They can share their insights, set goals and targets, and bring prior learning to their collaborations. In addition, collaboration allows students to develop a body of knowledge or a project plan that can be implemented in the real world.

Moodle has incorporated wikis and glossaries in the activities, and while they can be completed individually, they are perfect vehicles for collaboration. The key is to examine the learning objectives and determine how best to implement them.

This chapter teaches you how to develop effective collaborative activities that help achieve learning objectives by adding wikis and glossaries to your course. These activities enable students to work together and build a body of knowledge. The resulting collection of knowledge (the completed wikis and glossaries) can be reused by students in future courses. As the course evolves, the wikis and glossaries that past students created can be retained, edited, referenced, and grown.

Using collaboration as an instructional strategy

In our distributed world, where people move from place to place and still communicate with each other and develop work products together, it is necessary to understand how to collaborate productively in a virtual environment. So, there is a pragmatic side to the emphasis in collaboration.

At the same time, it is important to keep in mind that we use Moodle precisely for its structure, which encourages learning from each other. The ability to contribute to glossaries, wikis, and other collaborative activities allows students to contribute knowledge in a way that reinforces and rewards. Thus, it is an instructional strategy that brings together motivation, self-confidence, and curiosity, which creates conditions for learning. It is also a way to reinforce prior knowledge and build on experience as students recall past learning, add to what they already know, and reflect on what others are contributing.

Thus, collaboration can be a very effective instructional strategy and the glossary, wiki, and other areas where students can contribute can form the cornerstones for the knowledge and skills that they will demonstrate in the future. As you work through this chapter, please refer to Chapter 14, *Features for Teachers* as well. In that chapter, you learn how to connect many different elements in Moodle.

Glossary

The **Glossary** activity is one of the most underrated activities of Moodle. On the surface, a glossary is a list of words and definitions that students can access. However, a course creator allows students to add entries to the **Glossary**. Adding entries transforms the glossary from a static list of vocabulary words to a collaborative tool for learning purposes.

If your learning objectives require individuals to be able to identify, define, and describe items or phenomena, the **Glossary** activity is ideal. For example, you may have a course on tourism, and you may wish to develop a glossary of terms that are specialized in the specific area; for example, terms for *culture tourism*. Students can collaborate and make a customized glossary that can help them in the course and in their careers.

A text filter, called **auto-linking**, creates links to glossary entries in your course. When this is turned on by a site administrator, whenever a word from the **Glossary** appears in the course, it's highlighted. Clicking on the word brings up a pop-up window with the word's entry in the **Glossary**. The entry can consist of text, images, media, and links. It is a miniature page devoted to defining and elucidating the glossary term.

You can use a glossary to build a class directory, a collection of past exam questions, famous quotations, or even an annotated collection of pictures.

Enabling glossaries and auto-linking

There are several places where a site administrator will need to enable **Glossary** and its features.

When **Glossary auto-linking** is turned on, a glossary term appears in the course and is linked to its glossary entry. This is how the link looks:

> *Mechanical energy* puts something in motion. It moves cars and lifts elevators. A machine uses mech system is the sum of its kinetic and potential energy. Levers, which need a fulcrum to operate, are the planes are the basic elements of most machines
>
> Environmental Science Terminology: potential energy

Auto-linking creates links when a glossary term is used in the same course in which the glossary is located.

Enabling glossaries for your site

First, under **Site administration** | **Plugins** | **Activity Modules** | **Manage activities**, the site administrator must enable the **Glossary** activity. By default, the **Glossary** activity is enabled on Moodle. Enabling them is needed only if you do not see glossary in the **Add Resource or Activity...** menu:

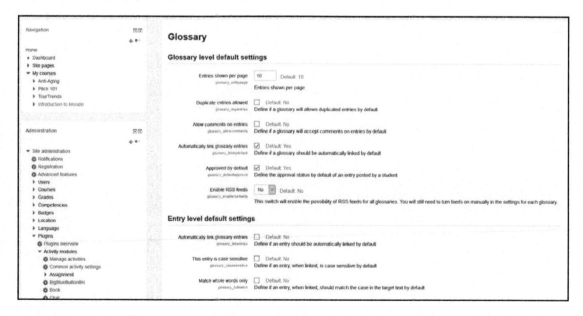

Enabling auto-linking

Auto-linking needs to be enabled in several places at the site, course, and activity level. If you create a glossary term and if it's not being auto-linked in your course, check that glossary auto-linking is enabled at the site, course, and activity/resource level. Each of these is covered in a subsection as we move on.

Enabling auto-linking for the site

Under **Site administration** | **Plugins** | **Filter** | **Manage filters**, the site administrator can turn on **Glossary auto-linking**:

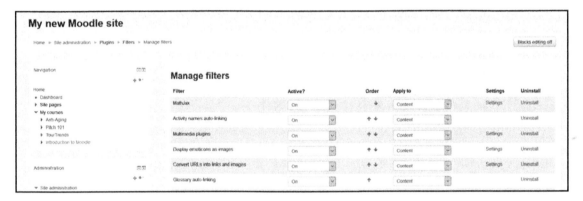

The **Disabled** setting removes the ability for the teacher to turn on auto-linking in the course. The **Off, but available** setting turns off auto-linking by default, but it enables the teacher to turn it on in the course. The **On** setting turns on auto-linking for all courses.

In the right-hand side column, note that the user has chosen to have auto-linking in the **Content** of activities and resources. You can also select **Content and headings**, which will turn on auto-linking for the content of an activity or resource and the words in the heading of that activity or resource.

Enabling auto-linking for the course

If the site-wide setting for auto-linking is set to **On**, you do not need to enable it at the course level. If the site-wide setting is set to **Disable**, it's not possible to enable it at the course level. This setting is available and needed only if the site-wide setting is **Off, but available**.

Under **Administration** | **Course administration** | **Filters**, the teacher must turn on **Glossary auto-linking**. If this is disabled, auto-linking will not work for any of the glossaries in the course.

Enabling auto-linking for the activity or resource

If you have auto-linking enabled for the site and the course and it's still not working, check the auto-linking setting for the activity or resource that you are in. In the **Administration** menu, look for the administration options for the resource or activity that you are in. Select **Filters**, and on the filters page, turn on **Glossary auto-linking**:

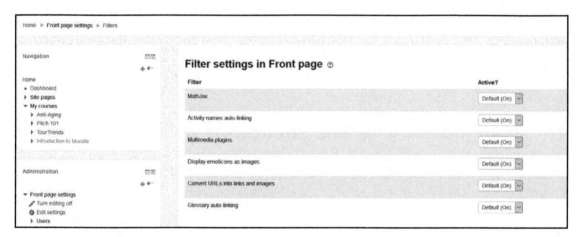

Adding and configuring a glossary

Add a glossary by clicking on **Add an activity or resource** on your course page and then select **Glossary**. When the glossary settings page is displayed, you will need to choose the correct setting to create the kind of glossary that you want for your class. Let's look at the settings that are unique to a glossary.

You will find these settings under **Administration** | **Glossary administration** | **Edit settings**.

The global glossary versus local glossary

By default, a glossary applies only to the course in which it resides. However, you can choose to make a glossary global. In this case, the words from this glossary will be highlighted and clickable wherever they are in your site. The work done in one course then becomes available to all the courses on your site. If your site's subject matter is highly focused, consider using a global glossary. If your site's subject matter is very broad, as in a university-wide learning site, you should use local glossaries to avoid confusion. For example, imagine that you have a course in chemistry and another in statistics. Both use the word *granular*, but chemistry uses it to indicate a powdered substance, while statistics uses it to indicate a fine level of detail.

 Only an administrator can create a glossary in the global glossary. If you have only teacher rights, get an administrator to do this for you.

The main glossary versus secondary glossary

The **Glossary type** setting enables you to designate a glossary as **Main** or **Secondary**. A **Main glossary** is a glossary that will include terms from other glossaries. A **Secondary glossary** is a glossary that stands alone; it does not include terms from any other glossaries.

If you want students to be able to add entries to a **Glossary**, you must make it a **Secondary glossary**. Only teachers can add terms to a **Main glossary**.

You can export terms from a **Secondary glossary** to a **Main glossary** one at a time. So, you can create a **Secondary glossary** to which students will add terms. Then, you and/or the students can export the best terms to the **Main glossary**. Imagine a course with one **Main glossary** and a **Secondary glossary** each time the course is run. The **Main glossary** will become a repository of the best terms added by each class.

You can add a **Secondary glossary** for each section in the course. For example, put a **Secondary glossary** in each topic or week. Then, you can create a **Main glossary** for the course that will automatically include all the terms added to each **Secondary glossary**. Put the **Main glossary** in **Topic 0**, the section at the top of the course's home page. An alternative to using secondary glossaries is to use one main glossary and create categories within that glossary for each section in the course. This keeps all glossary entries in one place.

If you want the course to have only one glossary and want students to be able to add to this glossary, make it a **Secondary glossary**. Although the term *secondary* implies that there is also a primary or main glossary, this is not the case. You can have just a **Secondary glossary** (or more than one) in a course without a **Main glossary**.

Entries approved by default

If you turn on the setting for **Approved by default**, as soon as a student adds an entry to a glossary, this entry will appear in the glossary. If it's turned off, the teacher will need to approve each entry.

If you turn on this setting and students add entries that you think are inappropriate, you can always delete these entries and turn this setting off.

If **Approved by default** is turned off, new terms will await the teacher's approval before being added. In the following screenshot, take a look at the link in the upper-right corner, **Waiting approval(1)**:

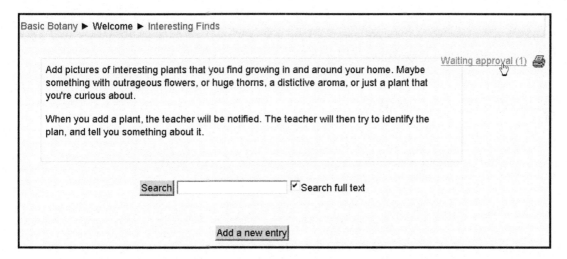

Always allow editing and Duplicate entries allowed

Always allow editing and **Duplicate entries allowed** are two separate settings. However, they can work together in an interesting way.

If you turn on **Always allow editing**, students can edit entries that have already been made. So, if two students have different definitions for a term, they can each contribute their definition to the same entry. In this case, the second student will not need to create a duplicate entry; they can just add their definition to the existing entry.

If you turn off **Always allow editing**, consider allowing duplicate entries. Then, if two students have different definitions for the same term, they can each create an entry for that term.

Allowing comments

If you turn on **Allow comments on entries**, students and teachers can add comments to a glossary entry. These comments will appear at the bottom of the entry. Comments are visible to all the readers of the glossary.

Automatically linking glossary entries

If you turn on **Automatically link glossary entries**, this will not always result in all entries becoming links in your course. Instead, when an entry is created, its editing page will have an option to turn on auto-linking for that entry.

Appearance settings

Under the **Appearance** section, you will find settings that affect the presentation of the glossary. These settings affect the layout of the glossary page, how many entries are shown on a page, the links that users are given, and so on. To determine the best settings for your situation, experiment with the following steps:

1. Log in as a teacher
2. Create a few glossary entries
3. Open another browser, log in as a student, and open the glossary
4. As a teacher, try different settings under **Appearance**
5. Each time you change the settings as a student, refresh the **Glossary** page

Enabling ratings

You can give students the ability to rate glossary entries, just like they can rate forum postings. The question is, what do you want students to rate? The glossary entry's clarity, its helpfulness, or your writing skill in creating an entry? You'll need to consider what you want students to rate and create a custom scale that supports that rating. You determine who can rate glossary entries, and what scale to use on the **Settings** page:

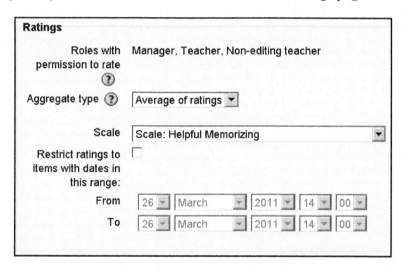

In the preceding screenshot, the teacher applies a custom scale called **Helpful Memorizing** to the glossary. This custom scale was created before the teacher came to this page.

After creating the custom scale, the teacher went to the glossary's **Settings** page and selected it under **Scale**, as shown in the preceding screenshot.

Note that only the **Manager**, **Teacher**, and **Non-editing teacher** courses can rate the entries in this glossary. In the next step, the teacher modifies the permissions to allow students to rate entries.

The process to allow students to rate glossary entries, and it consists of three parts:

1. Creating the rating scale
2. Selecting the scale for the glossary
3. Giving students permission to use the ratings

This is how to create the rating scale:

1. Select **Administration** | **Grade administration** | **Scales**.
2. Click on the **Add a new scale** button.
3. On the new **Scale** page, give a **Name** to the scale. Only the teacher can see this name.
4. In the **Scale** field, enter the values that the user will select when giving glossary definition, a rating. The scale must have more than two items.
5. In the **Description** field, enter a short description. This will help you remember the purpose for this scale.
6. **Save** your changes.

This is how to select the scale for the **Glossary**:

1. Navigate to the **Settings** page of the **Glossary**
2. In the **Scale** field, select the scale that you have just created
3. Modify any other settings that you want on this page
4. **Save** your changes

Giving students permission to use ratings:

1. From the main menu, select **Administration** | **Glossary administration** | **Permissions**
2. On the **Permissions** page, scroll down to the **Activity: Glossary** section
3. Click on the plus sign located next to **Rate entries**:

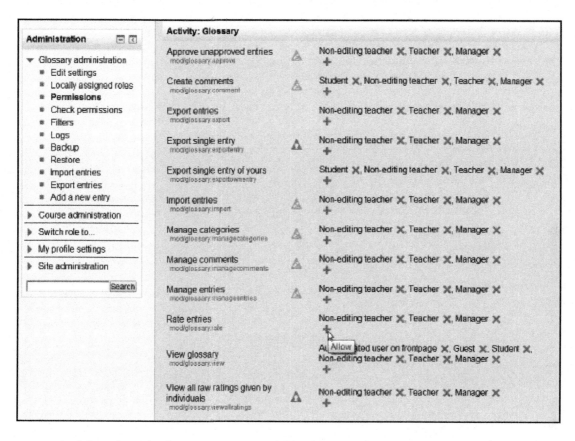

4. Select the role that you want to add to this permission and then click on the **Allow** button.

In our example, students will be able to rate each glossary entry on how helpful it's to memorize the material. From the student's point of view, this is how the result looks:

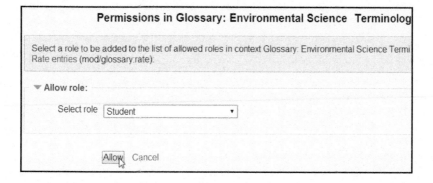

Adding glossary entries

Selecting a **Glossary** from the course menu displays the glossary's introductory page. On this page, you can edit and browse the glossary.

The following screenshot shows the **Add a new entry** button, which appears under every tab in the glossary:

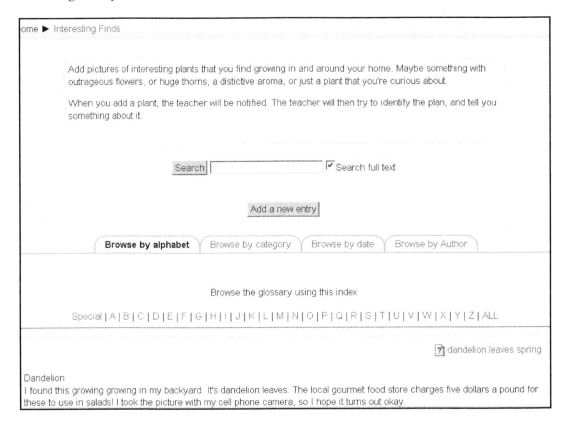

Create new **Glossary** categories by navigating to the **Browse by category** page and then click on the **Add a new entry** button. This button appears under each of the tabs when you browse the glossary, so it's always available.

On this page, **Concept** is the term that you will add to the **Glossary**. Keyword(s) are synonyms, which is equivalent to a *See also* section in an index or dictionary. These terms will link to the same definition as the concept.

Note that you can add a picture or media file to **Description** using the icons in the toolbar: . You can also upload these kinds of files as an **Attachment**, which is what this user chose to do.

If auto-linking is enabled, the bottom half of **Add a new entry** contains the settings, as shown in the following screenshot:

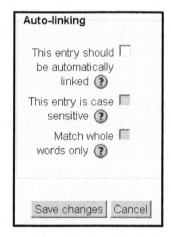

When the glossary term appears in your course, you can have it linked to its glossary entry. The **Auto-linking** option determines whether and when this word should link to its glossary entry.

Importing and exporting entries

The **Import entries** and **Export entries** links enable the teacher to exchange glossaries between courses and even Moodle installations:

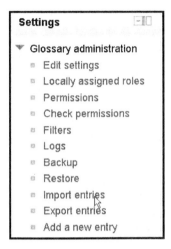

You may want to begin a course with a small glossary and let students add to it as they discover new concepts. If you do this, export the beginning glossary so that you have it available for the next course. The next time you teach a course, you can choose to export everything in the completed course (except the student information and the glossary). In the new copy, just create a new and blank **Glossary** and import the starting **Glossary**.

Also, note that the editing window enables you to include hyperlinks in the definition (the ⚙ icon). This can be used to link to freely available information on the web, such as http://www.wikipedia.org/.

Wiki

The Moodle wiki module enables students to collaborate on a group writing project, build a knowledge base, and discuss class topics. Students can also collaborate on developing ratings criteria for a competition, a team-lead event, or a business plan for a start-up company or organization.

As wiki is easy to use, interactive, and organized by date, it encourages collaboration among its participants. This makes it a powerful tool to create group knowledge. The key difference between a forum and wiki is that when users enter a forum, they see a thread devoted to a topic. Each entry is short. Users read through the thread, one entry at a time. The result is that the discussion becomes prominent. In wiki, users see the end result of the writing. To see the history of the writing, they must select a **History** tab. The result is that the end result of the writing becomes prominent.

The old wiki content is never deleted and can be restored. Wikis can also be searched just like other course material. In the following section, we'll look at the settings on the **Editing wiki** page and how they affect user experience.

Using a wiki for student contributions and explanations of a topic

A wiki can be used to help explain a topic. For example, let's say that a course on entrepreneurship is planning to have a start-up competition. It will be useful to include a list of criteria for judging. It will also be very useful to include a wiki that contains definitions, processes, and procedures. It's a useful tool for instruction because the instructor can provide guidelines and pointers.

Using a wiki to create a list of judging criteria for evaluating a competition

Shark Tank is a popular show on television in which entrepreneurs come before a panel of potential investors and make presentations to entice the panel members to invest. It is an entertaining and informative program, and having a *Shark Tank* as a class project can be equally informative, entertaining, and engaging.

One good way to plan a student *Shark Tank* is to use a wiki. The first step will be to set up a list of judging criteria along with a clear set of guidelines that indicate what is expected in an outstanding *pitch* that will convince the investor to put money in the project or start-up company. Then, the students can also share their evaluations of the start-up pitches in the competition.

Planning collaborative projects – Using the wiki type and groups mode to determine who can edit a wiki

There are several ways to use wikis that focus on a collaborative, actionable project rather than creating a simple repository of knowledge. Two excellent examples are in event planning, and in collaboratively planning a meeting, festival, or activity. Another good example is in developing the business plan for start-ups or in their competition.

Event planning

The wiki can be used to identify the tasks, roles, and resources in the event. For example, let's take the task of planning a wedding. There will be many different elements, ranging from the flowers, the decorations in the area of the wedding ceremony, the reception, the catering, invitations, and more. The wiki can be used to identify the different tasks, and then further define and refine the tasks as they are listed. Then, the wiki can be taken one step further and be used for developing a timeline with action steps.

Business plan for a start-up

As mentioned earlier, a class in entrepreneurship would be the perfect place to have a collaborative business plan. The wiki can contain the following elements:

- Key elements of a business plan
- **Strength Weaknesses Opportunities Threats (SWOT)** analysis
- Financial projections
- Goals and desired outcomes
- Graphics
- Promotions and publicity copy

Using the wiki type and groups mode to determine who can edit a wiki

Wiki content is open to editing by the entire class, a group, the teacher, or a single student. It can also be open to viewing by the entire class, a group, the teacher, or a single student. Note that the teacher determines who can see and edit the wiki content; the settings differ.

The settings for who can edit the wiki content are done using the **Wiki mode** drop-down box.

The setting for who can see the wiki content is done using the **Groups** mode.

Making a wiki editable by only a single student appears to turn the wiki into a personal journal. However, the difference between a single student wiki and a journal is that a journal can be seen only by the student and the teacher. You can keep a single student wiki private, or you can open it to change the setting and make it collaborative for the student's group or the entire class.

The first-page name

The name on the first page of the wiki will be taken from this field.

If there is one wiki for the entire class, when the first student enters the wiki, that student will see the starting page(s). If that first student edits any page, the next student who enters will see the edited version, and so on. If there is one wiki for each group in the class, then each group will get a *fresh* wiki with the starting page(s) that you created. Also, if each student gets their own wiki, each student will see their starting pages when they enter their wiki.

The Default format

The **Default format** setting determines whether wiki authors use standard the wiki markup or HTML code while editing. If you will use the HTML editor for other student activities, setting this to HTML can simplify this activity for your students. They will get familiar with the HTML editor and don't need to learn the wiki markup language. However, if your students are accustomed to wikis, you may want to select **Creole**. This enables them to use a common wiki markup, which is faster for experienced typists.

If you do not select the **Force** format, when a student enters the wiki, they will be able to select the format to use for editing purposes:

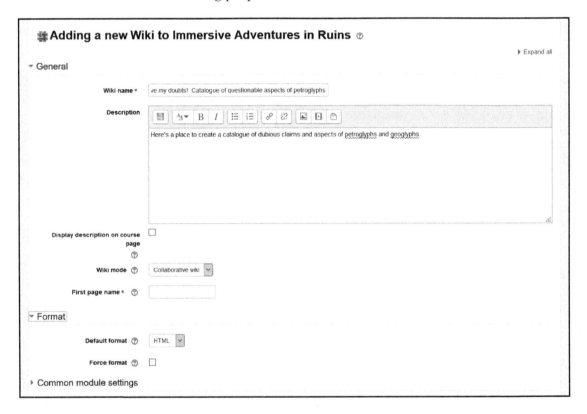

Summary

Moodle offers several options for students to collaborate on building a body of knowledge. A class can work together to build a glossary, which can be imported and reused in future classes. They can work together to write a wiki, which provides an opportunity for them to organize their knowledge into a narrative.

Look at glossaries as a way for students to collect new knowledge, and look at wikis as a way for students to organize new knowledge. You may also look at wikis as ways to encourage students to develop projects that can be implemented after the class is over in real-life applications.

One way to ensure that you keep your students motivated and on track is to ensure that they stay engaged. Monitor these activities and encourage your students to participate.

In the next chapter, you will learn how to use Moodle to run a workshop. In it, we will cover workshops, group projects, combinations of group and individual projects, workshop strategies, and the four phases of a workshop.

Running a Workshop 11

A workshop provides a place for students in a class to see an example project, upload their individual projects, and see and assess each other's projects. When a teacher requires each student to assess the work of several other students, this workshop becomes a powerful collaborative grading tool.

Workshops are ideal for putting into practice a theory or a technique. They allow students to apply the concepts and also to take a building block approach, with guidance and help on each step of the way.

In addition to applying knowledge, workshops encourage group projects and collaboration. The advantage of a workshop over using a wiki or the Glossary as a collaborative project is that the workshops allow more options for bundling materials and activities, and there are also more options for assessment.

Workshops can also be done in conjunction with a face-to-face workshop with corporate or not-for-profit activities and training. Further, the workshop allows one to create a building block approach, which makes it ideal for a hybrid delivery, and also a "flipped" classroom.

In this chapter, we will address how, when, and why to use a workshop and how to develop strategies for group-based projects as well as individual projects. In Chapter 14, *Features for Teachers* you will learn how to set up grade categories.

Why use a workshop?

A workshop is a great way to boost the knowledge and skill level of a group very quickly. Workshops in Moodle, like those held in face-to-face settings, are great for getting students up to speed and functional, with very little downtime. They usually focus on a single outcome, and they pare down the focus to ensure that the specific skill or knowledge set is achievable in a short period of time.

When are group project-based workshops best?

Although students may initially dread having to work in a group, it can be one of the most fruitful learning experiences of their education, and, not only do they learn about a topic or skill, they also practice working in a distributed environment, much like the one we work in today in our cloud-based, global workplace.

To avoid frustration, though, it's important to carefully choose how and when you have students work in groups. If you know your students have widely varying schedules, live in different time zones, and have variable access to high-speed internet, you may need to give them certain guidelines so that they will not lose patience with each other, or with the infrastructure and the course itself.

Group projects work best in the following situations:

- The students need to show competency in the same thing (for example, how to build a tiny home).
- The students do not have a lot of time, and the outcome needs to be very concrete and focused (for example, a market study for building a day spa as a part of a casino expansion).
- The outcome is easily evaluated; for example, the products can include a written report, graphics, maps, a presentation, a video, all of which are uploaded in the cloud and a link is provided (to avoid the problem of file size limitations).
- Individuals are motivated, and they see a concrete value in the ultimate product of the workshop. For example, the workshop product can help individuals land a job, launch a consulting business, or develop social media presence.

Workshop strategies

Workshops can be ungraded, peer-graded, instructor-graded, or a combination of peer- and instructor-graded. Workshops enable you to create very specific assessment criteria for graders to use. Also, workshops let you set due dates to submit grading work. You can use these and other features to build a strategy to make best use of workshops in your courses.

Peer assessment of submissions

One strategy for workshops is to have students assess each other's work before that same work is submitted as a graded assignment. For example, you can create a workshop in which students assess each other's subject matter, outlines, and hypothesis for their term papers, or they can assess each other's photos for specific technical and artistic criteria before they are submitted to the instructor for grading purposes.

The timing of submissions and assessments

Workshops enable you to set different due dates in order to submit work and assess other students' work. If you set both due dates as the same, many students may submit their work just before the submission deadline so that they cannot be assessed at all before the assessment deadline. Consider setting the submission deadline well before the assessment deadline. So, before opening up the assessment ability to students, examine the work submitted and ensure that it's close to what you expected or were trying to elicit from students. You may even want to use the time between submission and assessment to refine your assessment criteria, in response to the work submitted.

The four questions

The fields in the workshop window give you many choices. No matter what you enter in each field, your many decisions can be summed up as follows:

- What will you have each student do? Create a file offline and upload it to the workshop? Write a journal entry? Participate in an online chat? Perform some offline activity and report on it via email or wiki? While the workshop window enables a student to upload a file, you can also expect any other activity from the student.
- Who will assess assignments? Will a teacher assess all assignments? Will students be expected to assess other students' assignments? Will each student self-assess their work?
- How will the assignments be assessed? You can determine a number of criteria on which each assignment is assessed, the grading scale, and the type of grading.
- When will students be allowed to submit their assignments and assessments? The assignment becomes available as soon as you show it. However, you can expect students to assess an example before being allowed to submit their own work; you can also set a deadline to submit the assessment.

All the fields that we cover here are variations of these questions. The online help does a good job of explaining how to use each field. Instead of repeating how to use each field here, we will focus on how your choices affect the student and teacher experience.

The four phases

When you run a workshop, you will go through four phases:

- **Phase 1**: The *setup* phase is when you create a workshop and choose settings for how it will work. These settings are discussed in detail under the edit settings page.
- **Phase 2**: The *submission* phase is when students submit their work. Also, each student will be given assignments to assess the work of some other students. The assessments can be allocated automatically by a system, or a teacher can manually allocate assessments to students. Either way, at the end of the submission phase, each student will have submitted their work and been told to assess the work of one or several other students.
- **Phase 3**: During the *assessment* phase, students will assess each other's work. The teacher will create assessment forms that students will use when conducting their assessments of each other's work.
- **Phase 4**: During the *grading evaluation* phase, students are given grades for how well they evaluated the work of their peers. This is the final phase of the workshop.

We will look at each phase of the workshop.

The setup phase – The edit settings page

The workshop activity is the most complex tool currently available on Moodle. Workshops are designed so that a student's work can be submitted and offered for peer review within a structured framework. Workshops provide a process for both instructor and peer feedback on open-ended assignments, such as essays and research papers. There are easy-to-use interfaces to upload assignments and perform self-assessments and peer reviews of other students' papers. The key to a workshop is the scoring guide, which is a set of specific criteria to make judgments about the quality of a given work. There are several fields under a workshop, which will be explained in the following sections. They provide a place for students as well as teachers in the class to make the best use of Moodle.

Name and description

The settings under **General** partially answer the question—what will you have each student do?

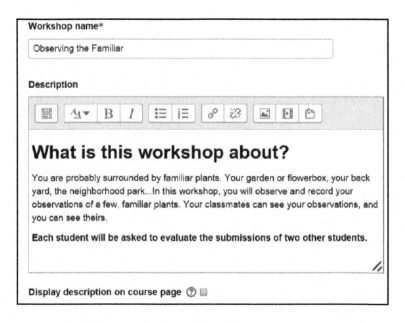

Your students will see and click on the **Workshop name** field. The **Description** field should give instructions on how to complete the workshop.

Grading settings

These fields determine the maximum points a student can earn for a workshop and how to calculate these points, as shown in the following screenshot:

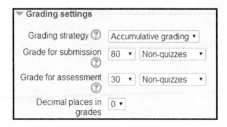

The grading strategy

A workshop assignment is quite flexible in the type of the grading scheme used. This setting determines the overall scheme.

In the **Accumulative grading** strategy, the grade for each element is added to arrive at the accumulated grade. This style of grading enables you to present the reviewer with a numeric scale. You can also present the reviewer with *Yes* or *No* questions. One of the questions is does this workshop meet the requirement? Alternatively, you can present the reviewer with a grading scale, such as *poor, fair, good,* and *excellent.* If you do use a *Yes* or *No,* or a grading scale, you will assign a point value to each response. Consider informing the reviewer of the value of each response. For example, instead of just writing poor, fair, good, excellent, consider writing poor (1 point), fair (2 points), good (3 points), or excellent (4 points).

When **Comments** is selected for **Grading strategy**, students can comment on each assessment element, but they cannot select a grade; however, teachers can grade students' comments. In this case, the workshop is transformed from where students grade each other to where the teacher grades each student's comments.

 A workshop that uses **Comments** may be especially useful when you want to have a structured discussion on material that you present to students.

As a course creator, you can present the students with material that has been uploaded to the workshop or use the workshop's description to direct students to the material they must assess. After the students have viewed the material, they enter the workshop and leave comments according to the elements presented. As the workshop requires that students comment on clearly defined evaluation elements, the students' discussion is structured and kept on track.

When you choose the **Number of Errors** option, students evaluate a workshop with a series of *Yes* or *No* questions. Usually, you create questions to evaluate whether or not the submission met a requirement, such as *does the student have a variety of opinions?*

When writing one of these questions, ensure that it can be answered using only *Yes* or *No*. A sign that you need to revise your question is the presence of the word *or*. For example, don't write *did the student describe the plant well enough to distinguish it from others?* or *is there still doubt as to which plant the student is describing?* Such a question cannot be answered with *Yes* or *No*.

The answer to an evaluation question is sometimes very clear and sometimes subjective. For example, the question *did the student describe the plant well enough to distinguish it from others?* is subjective. One reviewer may think that the student did an adequate job of describing the plant, while another may think otherwise. These questions can be a good way to perform subjective peer evaluations of each student's work.

If the work requires a more objective evaluation (such as *did the student include all five identifying features covered in this lesson?*), you may not need a workshop. This kind of objective evaluation can be easily performed by the teacher, using an assignment.

For a rubric grading strategy, write several statements that apply to the project. Each statement has a grade assigned to it. The reviewers choose the one statement that best describes the project. This single choice completes the review.

You can create several such elements; the reviewers must select a statement for each of them.

Grade for submission is the maximum number of points a student can be given by a grader.

Grade for assessments is the grade that the student receives to grade other submissions. This grade is based on how close the assessment the student completes is to the average of all assessments for the same submission. For example, student A submits work and students B, C, and, D assess the work and give scores of 10, 9, and 5. The average assessment is 8, so students B and C will receive higher marks for their assessments than student D. In essence, the grade for assessments is the grade for grading purposes.

The Submission settings

The **Submission settings** is where you enter instructions for users. You also set limits on how many files students can upload in the workshop and how large these files can be. This is where you partially answer the question, that is, what will you have each student do? The following is the screenshot of **Submission settings**:

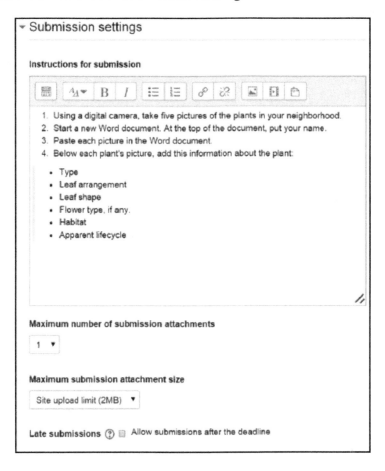

The user will see the **Instructions for submission** label when they click on the workshop.

Maximum number of submission attachments and **Maximum submission attachment size** determine the size of a file and how many files the user can upload.

Late submissions allow users to submit their work after the deadline. The deadline is set further down the page.

It is a good idea to encourage students to upload their work to the cloud and then provide a link. For example, this can work with presentations in Screencast-o-matic, or in a video on YouTube. This will help students avoid hitting the file size limit.

Assessment settings

The settings in this section are used to give the users instructions for how to perform their assessments and determine when to present the user with examples to assess.

The actual criteria used in the assessment are not created on this page. Instead, the criteria are created under **Administration** | **Workshop administration** | **Edit assessment form**.

We will cover the process on how to create the assessment form later. However, on this page, we will just give the user instructions for the assessment:

Feedback settings

If the **Overall feedback** mode is enabled, a textbox appears at the bottom of the assessment form. Students who will perform assessments can enter feedback in this textbox. You can make these comments optional or required.

The settings for feedback attachments determine whether the person who is assessing can upload a file(s) with their assessment. The student who submitted the work will see the attachment(s) with the assessment.

The **Conclusion** field gives the teacher a place to write a message that students can see after the workshop is finished. For example, you can instruct students to produce a new work based on the feedback that they received in the workshop, instruct them to write a blog post reflecting the activity, or just congratulate them on a job well done.

Example submissions settings

If the workshop uses examples, users can assess an examples of work provided by the teacher. The user's assessment of the example is then compared to the assessment provided by the teacher. This enables users to practice assessing work before they assess each other's work.

Users receive a grade for how well their assessment agrees with the assessment provided by the teacher. However, the grade is not counted in the grade book.

Availability settings

The settings under this section answer the question: when will students be allowed to submit their assignments and assessments?

Note that the submissions and assessments can open on the same day. However, assessments cannot open before submissions (there would be nothing to assess).

If you enable the **Switch to the next phase** setting after the submissions deadline, then after the submission deadline, the workshop will automatically switch to the assessment phase. If you do not enable this setting, the teacher will have to manually advance the workshop to the assessment phase.

If you have the workshop automatically advanced to the assessment phase, you should also have the workshop automatically allocate assessments to the students. If you don't have the workshop automatically assign assessments to the students, it will advance to the assessment phase; there will be no assessments for students to perform. Setting up automatic allocations is performed under **Administration** | **Workshop administration** | **Allocate submissions** | **Scheduled allocation**.

The edit assessment form page

On this page, you enter the assessment criteria. The exact contents of this page will change, depending on the type of assessment that you selected on the workshop settings page. In the following screenshot, the workshop grading strategy is set to **Accumulative grading**:

Making the maximum grade a multiple of the number of assessment elements enables students to more easily interpret their grades. For example, suppose a workshop is assessed for five elements. For each element, the assessor will choose from four statements:

- **A**: The workshop does not meet this requirement anyway (0 points)
- **B**: The workshop partially meets this requirement (1 point)
- **C**: The workshop meets this requirement (2 points)
- **D**: The workshop exceeds this requirement (3 points)

You can assign a point value of zero for each A selection, one point for each B selection, two points for each C selection, and three points for each D selection. Then, each element will be worth a maximum of three points. With five elements, the workshop will have a maximum grade of 15. This will make it easy for the student to interpret their grade.

When the student conducts an assessment, this is how the assessment form looks:

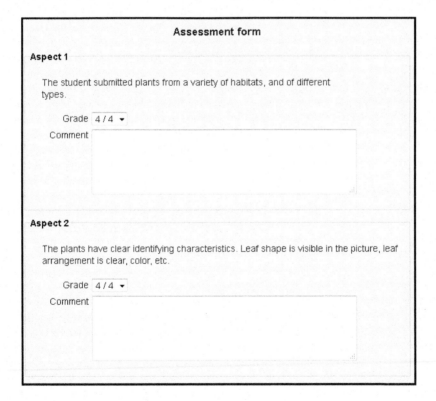

Note that for each assessment criteria, the student can enter comments.

Adding an example to the workshop

After you save the workshop settings and the assessment form, you can add an example to your workshop. Selecting a workshop will give you the following screen:

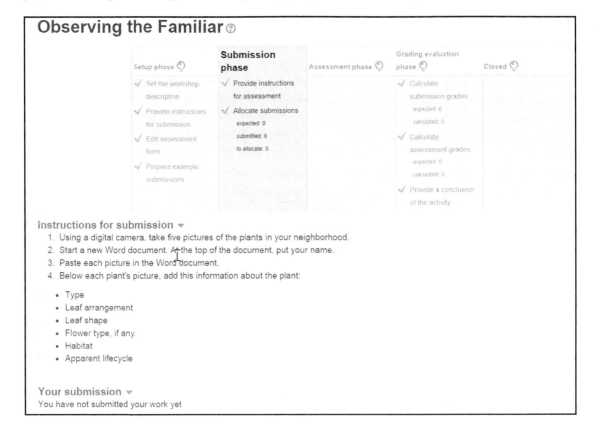

Instructions for submission ▾

1. Using a digital camera, take five pictures of the plants in your neighborhood.
2. Start a new Word document. At the top of the document, put your name.
3. Paste each picture in the Word document.
4. Below each plant's picture, add this information about the plant:

   - Type
   - Leaf arrangement
   - Leaf shape
   - Flower type, if any.
   - Habitat
   - Apparent lifecycle

Your submission ▾
You have not submitted your work yet

To add an example submission, let's begin by clicking on the **Add example submission** button. This brings you to a page that displays the same assessment instructions that your users will see. This is where you can upload the example to be assessed:

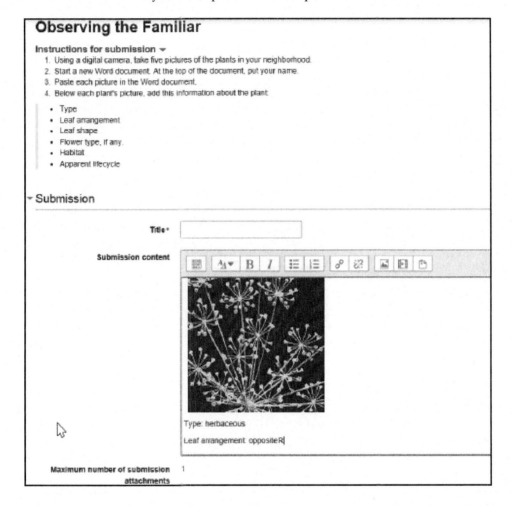

After you save the example, Moodle displays a message to say that you must assess the example, as follows:

After you assess the example, Moodle returns you to the workshop's home page. You will see the progress that you have made, which is indicated on this page:

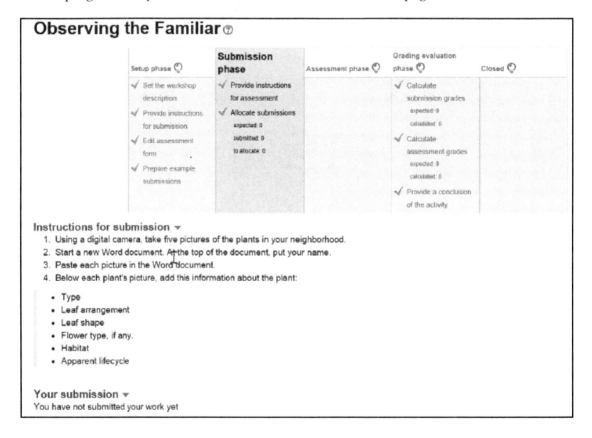

Note that the next step will be for the teacher to allocate the student submissions for assessment. However, no one has submitted anything yet. At this point, the teacher waits for students to submit their work.

The submission phase – Students submit their work

Although the teacher has finished setting up the workshop and is ready for students to submit their work, students may still see this message: **The workshop is currently being set up. Wait until this is switched to the next phase**.

The teacher must manually switch the workshop from one phase to the next. Even if you're done with the setup and are ready to accept submissions, Moodle doesn't know it.

To switch to the next phase, the teacher must click on the light bulb before this phase. In our example, the teacher clicked on the light bulb before the submission phase and saw this message:

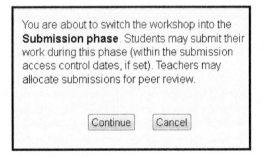

You are about to switch the workshop into the **Submission phase**. Students may submit their work during this phase (within the submission access control dates, if set). Teachers may allocate submissions for peer review.

Continue   Cancel

Now, when the student selects this workshop, they see a prompt to submit work:

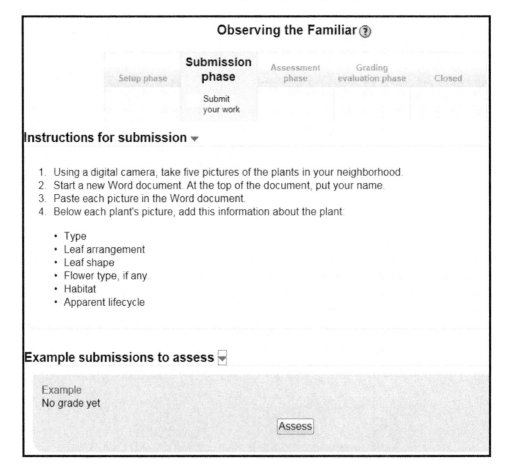

Note that the student can also assess the example at this point. On the settings page for **Mode of examples assessment** in this workshop, we selected **Voluntary**; therefore, this example is not required. If we had made assessing the example mandatory, the student would receive a message that they cannot submit work until the example is assessed.

Allocating submissions

As soon as students begin submitting their work, you can start allocating these submissions to other students for assessment. Do this under **Workshop administration** | **Allocate submissions**. You can allocate submissions manually or randomly.

If you perform a random allocation, all the submissions that were sent up to that point in time will be allocated to other students for assessment. However, submissions sent after the random allocation will not be automatically allocated. You will need to perform another random allocation for the next submission, and so on, until the workshop is complete.

The assessment phase

When you move the workshop to the assessment phase, the allocations that you made during the submission phase become available to students. In this phase, students will actually assess each other's work.

The grading evaluation phase

When you move the workshop to this phase, you can tell Moodle to automatically calculate the grades of students. You can also override these grades and enter your own grades.

Students can no longer modify the submissions that they have sent in.

The closed phase

When you close a workshop, the final grades are written in the course's grade book. These grades can be checked by students as well as students and administrators.

Summary

Moodle offers several options for student-to-student and student-to-teacher interaction. When deciding which social activities to use, consider the level of structure and amount of student-to-student/student-to-teacher interaction you want. For example, chats and wikis offer relatively unstructured environments with lots of opportunities for the student-to-student interaction. These are good ways of relinquishing some control of the class to students. A forum offers more structure because entries are classified on the basis of topics. It can be moderated by the teacher, making it even more structured. A workshop offers the most structure, by virtue of the set assessment criteria that students must use when evaluating each other's work. Note that as activities become more structured, the opportunity for students to get to know one another decreases.

You may want to introduce a chat and/or forum at the beginning of a course to build *esprit de corps* among students and then move to a collaborative wiki (such as a group writing project). Finally, after the students have learned more about each other and are comfortable working together, you can use a workshop for their final project.

In the next chapter, you will learn about groups and cohorts, and the differences between the two. You will see how to segregate students in a course into teams. You will also learn how to manage enrollments in a quick and efficient way using cohorts. You will learn how to use cohorts to enroll and unenroll large groups of students.

12
Groups and Cohorts

Being able to effectively coordinate activities so that groups and cohorts work well together will enable you to ensure that there are ideal conditions for learning, especially the collaborative learning that is so vital to online learning. Groups and cohorts can be one of the strongest elements in your course, and they can be absolutely critical in motivating students and keeping them engaged.

This chapter shows you how to use groups to separate students in a course into teams. You will also learn how to use cohorts to mass enroll students into courses. We will discuss how to use the features of Moodle to make managing enrollments and groups very efficient and pleasant.

Groups versus cohorts

Both groups and cohorts are collections of students. However, there are several differences between them. We can sum up these differences in one sentence, that is, cohorts enable administrators to enroll and unenroll students en masse, whereas groups enable teachers to manage students during a class. So, you can think of a cohort as a collection of students who are staying together in order to complete an entire course or sequence of courses together. Groups are smaller sets of students within the course.

Here's another way to approach it: Think of a cohort as a group of students working together through the same academic curriculum; for example, a group of students all enrolled in the same course. Think of a group as a subset of students enrolled in a course. Groups are used to manage various activities within a course.

Cohort is a system-wide or course category-wide set of students.

There is a small amount of overlap between what you can do with a cohort and a group. However, the differences are large enough that you would not want to substitute one for the other.

Cohorts

In this section, we'll look at how to create and use cohorts. You can perform many operations with cohorts in bulk, affecting many students at once.

Creating a cohort

To create a cohort, perform the following steps:

1. From the main menu, select **Site administration** | **Users** | **Accounts** | **Cohorts**.
2. On the **Cohorts** page, click on the **Add button**. The **Add new cohort** page is displayed.
3. Enter a **Name** for the cohort. This is the name that you will see when you work with the cohort.
4. Enter a **Cohort ID** for the cohort. If you upload students in bulk to this cohort, you will specify the cohort using this identifier. You can use any characters you want in the **Cohort ID**; however, keep in mind that the file you upload to the cohort can come from a different computer system. To be safe, consider using only ASCII characters, such as letters, numbers, some special characters, and no spaces in the **Cohort ID option**; for example, Spring_2012_Freshmen.
5. Enter a **Description** that will help you and other administrators remember the purpose of the cohort.
6. Click on **Save changes**.

Now that the cohort is created, you can begin adding users to this cohort.

Adding students to a cohort

Students can be added to a cohort manually by searching and selecting them. They can also be added in bulk by uploading a file to Moodle.

Manually adding and removing students to a cohort

If you add a student to a cohort, that student is enrolled in all the courses to which the cohort is synchronized. If you remove a student from a cohort, that student will be unenrolled from all the courses to which the cohort is synchronized.

We will look at how to synchronize cohorts and course enrollments later. For now, here is how to manually add and remove students from a cohort:

1. From the main menu, select **Site administration** | **Users** | **Accounts** | **Cohorts**.
2. On the **Cohorts** page, for the cohort to which you want to add students, click on the People icon:

3. The **Cohort Assign** page is displayed. The left-hand side panel displays users that are already in the cohort, if any. The right-hand side panel displays users that can be added to the cohort.
4. Use the **Search** field to search for users in each panel. You can search for text that is in the username and email address fields.
5. Use the **Add** and **Remove** buttons to move users from one panel to another.

Adding students to a cohort in bulk – Upload

When you upload students to Moodle, you can add them to a cohort.

After you have all the students in a cohort, you can quickly enroll and unenroll them in courses just by synchronizing the cohort to the course. If you will upload students in bulk, consider putting them in a cohort. This makes it easier to manipulate them later.

Here's an example of a cohort. Note that there are **1204** students enrolled in the cohort:

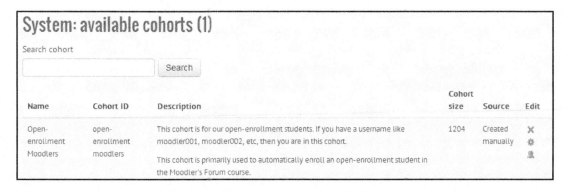

These students were uploaded to the cohort under **Administration** I **Site administration** I **Users** I **Upload users**:

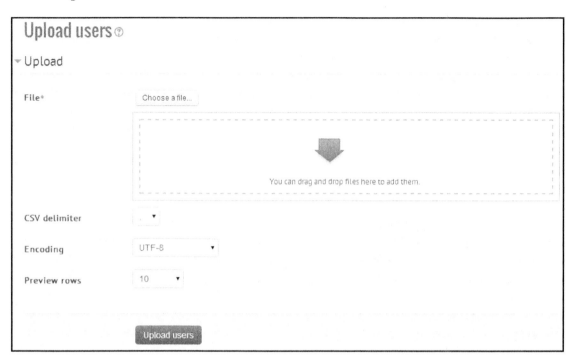

The file that was uploaded contained information about each student in the cohort. In a spreadsheet, this is how the file looks:

```
username,email,firstname,lastname,cohort1
moodler_1,bill@williamrice.net,Bill,Binky,open-enrollmentmoodlers
moodler_2,rose@williamrice.net,Rose,Krial,open-enrollmentmoodlers
moodler_3,jeff@williamrice.net,Jeff,Marco,open-enrollmentmoodlers
moodler_4,dave@williamrice.net,Dave,Gallo,open-enrollmentmoodlers
```

In this example, we have the minimum required information to create new students. These are as follows:

- The username
- The email address
- The first name
- The last name

We also have the cohort ID (the short name of the cohort) in which we want to place a student.

During the upload process, you can see a preview of the file that you will upload:

Further down on the **Upload users preview** page, you can choose the **Settings** option to handle the upload:

Usually, when we upload users to Moodle, we will create new users. However, we can also use the upload option to quickly enroll the existing users in the cohort.

You saw previously, in the *Manually adding and removing students to a cohort* section, how to search for and then enroll users in a cohort. However, when you want to enroll hundreds of users in the cohort, it's often faster to create a text file and upload it, than to search your existing users. This is because when you create a text file, you can use powerful tools—such as spreadsheets and databases—to quickly create this file. If you want to perform this, you will find options to **Update existing users** under the **Upload type** field.

In most Moodle systems, a user's profile must include a city and country. When you upload a user to a system, you can specify the city and country in the upload file or omit them from the upload file and assign the city and country to the system while the file is uploaded. This is performed under **Default values** on the **Upload users** page:

Now that we have examined some of the capabilities and limitations of this process, let's list the steps to upload a cohort to Moodle:

Prepare a plain file that has, at minimum, the `username`, `email`, `firstname`, `lastname`, and `cohort1` information. If you were to create this in a spreadsheet, it may look similar to the following screenshot:

	A	B	C	D	E	F	G	H
1	username	email	firstname	lastname	password	city	country	cohort1
2	moodler000	moodlerstudent@williamrice.net	moodler000	changeme	1234ABCD	New York	US	open-enrollment moodlers
3	moodler001	moodlerstudent@williamrice.net	moodler001	changeme	1234ABCD	New York	US	open-enrollment moodlers
4	moodler002	moodlerstudent@williamrice.net	moodler002	changeme	1234ABCD	New York	US	open-enrollment moodlers
5	moodler003	moodlerstudent@williamrice.net	moodler003	changeme	1234ABCD	New York	US	open-enrollment moodlers
6	moodler004	moodlerstudent@williamrice.net	moodler004	changeme	1234ABCD	New York	US	open-enrollment moodlers

1. Under **Administration | Site administration | Users | Upload users**, select the text file that you will upload.
2. On this page, choose **Settings** to describe the text file, such as delimiter (separator) and encoding.
3. Click on the **Upload users** button.
4. You will see the first few rows of the text file displayed. Also, additional settings become available on this page.
5. In the **Settings** section, there are settings that affect what happens when you upload information about the existing users. You can choose to have the system overwrite information for the existing users, ignore information that conflicts with the existing users, create passwords, and so on.
6. In the **Default values** section, you can enter values to be entered into the user profiles. For example, you can select a city, country, and department for all the users.
7. Click on the **Upload users** button to begin the upload.

Cohort sync

Using the cohort sync enrolment method, you can enroll and unenroll large collections of students at once. Using cohort sync involves several steps:

1. Creating a cohort
2. Enrolling students in the cohort
3. Enabling the cohort sync enrollment method
4. Adding the cohort sync enrollment method to a course

In the previous section, you saw the first two steps: how to create a cohort and how to enroll students in the cohort. In this section, we will cover the last two steps: enabling the cohort sync method and adding the cohort sync to a course.

Enabling the cohort sync enrollment method

To enable the cohort sync enrollment method, you will need to log in as an administrator. This cannot be done by someone who has only teacher rights:

1. Select **Site administration** | **Plugins** | **Enrolments** | **Manage enrol plugins**.
2. Click on the Enable icon located next to **Cohort sync**.
3. Then, click on the **Settings** button located next to **Cohort sync**.
4. On the **Settings** page, choose the default role for people when you enroll them in a course using **Cohort sync**. You can change this setting for each course.
5. You will also choose the **External unenrol action**. This is what happens to a student when they are removed from the cohort.
6. If you choose **Unenrol user from course**, the user and all their grades are removed from the course. The user's grades are purged from Moodle. If you were to read this user to the cohort, all the user's activity in this course will be blank, as if the user was never in the course.
7. If you choose **Disable course enrolment** and remove roles, the user and all their grades are hidden. You will not see this user in the course's grade book. However, if you were to read this user to the cohort or to the course, this user's course records will be restored.

After enabling the cohort sync method, it's time to actually add this method to a course.

Adding the cohort sync enrollment method to a course

To perform this, you will need to log in as an administrator or a teacher in the course:

1. Log in and enter the course to which you want to add the enrolment method.
2. Select **Course administration** | **Users** | **Enrolment methods**.
3. From the **Add method** drop-down menu, select **Cohort sync**.
4. In **Custom instance name**, enter a name for this enrollment method. This will enable you to recognize this method in a list of cohort syncs.

5. For **Active**, select **Yes**. This will enroll the users.
6. Select the **Cohort** option.
7. Select the role that the members of the cohort will be given.
8. Click on the **Save changes** button.

All the users in the cohort will be given a selected role in the course.

Unenroll a cohort from a course

There are two ways to unenroll a cohort from a course. First, you can go to the course's enrollment methods page and delete the enrollment method. Just click on the **X** button located next to the cohort sync field that you added to the course. However, this will not just remove users from the course, but also delete all their course records.

The second method preserves the student records. Once again, go to the course's enrollment methods page located next to the **Cohort sync** method that you added, and click on **Settings**. On the **Settings** page, select **No** for **Active**. This will remove the role that the cohort was given. However, the members of the cohort will still be listed as course participants. So, as the members of the cohort do not have a role in the course, they can no longer access this course. However, their grades and activity reports are preserved.

Differences between cohort sync and enrolling a cohort

Cohort sync and enrolling a cohort are two different methods; each has advantages and limitations.

If you follow the preceding instructions, you can synchronize a cohort's membership to a course's enrollment. As people are added to and removed from the cohort, they are enrolled and unenrolled from the course. When working with a large group of users, this can be a great time saver. However, using cohort sync, you cannot unenroll or change the role of just one person. Consider a scenario where you have a large group of students who want to enroll in several courses, all at once. You put these students in a cohort, enable the cohort sync enrollment method, and add the cohort sync enrollment method to each of these courses. In a few minutes, you have accomplished your goal. Now, if you want to unenroll some users from some courses, but not from all courses, you remove them from the cohort. So, these users are removed from all the courses. This is how cohort sync works.

Cohort sync is everyone or no one

When a person is added to or removed from the cohort, this person is added to or removed from all the courses to which the cohort is synced. If that's what you want, great.

An alternative to cohort sync is to enroll a cohort, that is, you can select all the members of a cohort and enroll them in a course, all at once. However, this is a one-way journey. You cannot unenroll them all at once; you will need to unenroll them one at a time.

If you enroll a cohort all at once, after enrollment, users are independent entities. You can unenroll them and change their role (for example, from student to teacher) whenever you wish.

To enroll a cohort in a course, perform the following steps:

1. Enter the course as an administrator or teacher.
2. Select **Administration** | **Course administration** | **Users** | **Enrolled users**.
3. Click on the **Enrol cohort** button. A pop-up window appears. This window lists the cohorts on the site.
4. Click on **Enrol users** next to the cohort that you want to enroll. The system displays a confirmation message.
5. Now, click on the **OK** button. You will be taken back to the **Enrolled users** page.

Although you can enroll all users in a cohort (all at once), there is no button to unenroll them all at once. You will need to remove them one at a time from your course.

Managing students with groups

A group is a collection of students in a course. Outside of a course, a group has no meaning.

Groups are useful when you want to separate students studying the same course. For example, if your organization is using the same course for several different classes or groups, you can use the group feature to separate students so that each group can see only their peers in the course. For example, you can create a new group every month for employees hired that month. Then, you can monitor and mentor them together.

Groups are excellent for course projects and also for conducting peer reviews.

After you have run a group of people through a course, you may want to reuse this course for another group. You can use the group feature to separate groups so that the current group doesn't see the work done by the previous group. This will be like a new course for the current group.

You may want an activity or resource to be open to just one group of people. You don't want others in the class to be able to use that activity or resource.

Course versus activity

You can apply the groups setting to an entire course. If you do this, every activity and resource in the course will be segregated into groups.

You can also apply the groups setting to an individual activity or resource. If you do this, it will override the groups setting for the course. Also, it will segregate just this activity, or resource between groups.

The three group modes

For a course or activity, there are several ways to apply groups. Here are the three group modes:

- **No groups**: There are no groups for a course or activity. If students have been placed in groups, ignore it. Also, give everyone the same access to the course or activity.
- **Separate groups**: If students have been placed in groups, allow them to see other students and only the work of other students from their own group. Students and work from other groups are invisible.
- **Visible groups**: If students have been placed in groups, allow them to see other students and the work of other students from all groups. However, the work from other groups is read-only.

You can use the No groups setting on an activity in your course. Here, you want every student who ever took the course to be able to interact with each other. For example, you may use the **No groups** setting in the news forum so that all students who have ever taken the course can see the latest news.

Also, you can use the **Separate groups** setting in a course. Here, you will run different groups at different times. For each group that runs through the course, it will be like a brand new course.

You can use the **Visible groups** setting in a course. Here, students are part of a large and in-person class; you want them to collaborate in small groups online.

Also, be aware that some things will not be affected by the groups setting. For example, no matter what the group setting, students will never see each other's assignment submissions.

Creating a group

There are three ways to create groups in a course. You can do the following:

- Manually create and populate each group
- Automatically create and populate groups based on the characteristics of students
- Import groups using a text file

We'll cover these methods in the following subsections.

Manually creating and populating a group

Don't be discouraged by the idea of manually populating a group with students. It takes only a few clicks to place a student in a group. To create and populate a group, perform the following steps:

1. Select **Course administration | Users | Groups**. This takes you to the **Groups** page.
2. Click on the **Create group** button. The **Create group** page is displayed.
3. You must enter a **Name** for the group. This will be the name that teachers and administrators see when they manage a group.
4. The **Group ID** number is used to match up this group with a group identifier in another system. If your organization uses a system outside Moodle to manage students and this system categorizes students in groups, you can enter the group ID from the other system in this field. It does not need to be a number. This field is optional.
5. The **Group description field** is optional. It's good practice to use this to explain the purpose and criteria for belonging to a group.
6. The **Enrolment key** is a code that you can give to students who self-enroll in a course. When the student enrolls, they are prompted to enter the enrollment key. On entering this key, the student is enrolled in the course and made a member of the group.

7. If you add a picture to this group, when members are listed (as in a forum), the member will have the group picture shown next to them. Here's an example of a contributor to a forum on `http://www.moodle.org` with her group memberships:

8. Click on the **Save changes** button to save the group.
9. On the **Groups** page, the group appears in the left-hand side column. Select this group.
10. In the right-hand side column, search for and select the students that you want to add to this group:

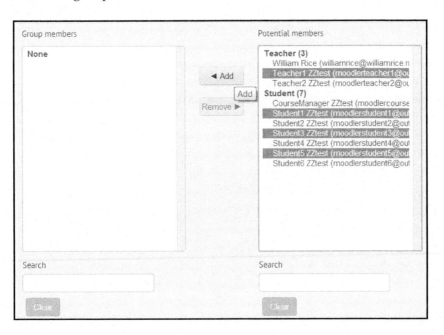

Note the **Search** fields. These enable you to search for students to meet a specific criteria. You can search the first name, last name, and email address. The other part of the user's profile information is not available in this search box.

Automatically creating and populating a group

When you automatically create groups, Moodle creates a number of groups that you specify and then takes all the students enrolled in the course and allocates them to these groups. Moodle will put the currently enrolled students in these groups even if they already belong to another group in the course.

To automatically create a group, use the following steps:

1. Click on the **Auto-create groups** button. The **Auto-create groups** page is displayed.

2. In the **Naming scheme** field, enter a name for all the groups that will be created. You can enter any characters. If you enter @, it will be converted to sequential letters. If you enter #, it will be converted to sequential numbers. For example, if you enter Group @, Moodle will create **Group A**, **Group B**, **Group C**, and so on.

3. In the **Auto-create based on** field, you will tell the system to choose either of the following options:

   - Create a specific number of groups and then fill each group with as many students as needed (**Number of groups**)
   - Create as many groups as needed so that each group has a specific number of students (**Members per group**)

4. In the **Group/member count** field, you will tell the system to choose either of the following options:

   - How many groups to create (if you choose the preceding **Number of groups** option)
   - How many members to put in each group (if you choose the preceding **Members per group** option)

5. Under **Group members**, select who will be put in these groups. You can select everyone with a specific role or everyone in a specific cohort.

6. The setting for **Prevent last small group** is available if you choose **Members per group**. It prevents Moodle from creating a group with fewer than the number of students that you specify. For example, if your class has 12 students and you choose to create groups with five members per group, Moodle will normally create two groups of five. Then, it will create another group for the last two members. However, with **Prevent last small group** selected, it will distribute the remaining two members between the first two groups.

7. Click on the **Preview** button to preview the results. The preview will not show you the names of the members in groups, but it will show you how many groups and members will be in each group.

Importing groups

The term *importing groups* may give you the impression that you will import students into a group. The **Import Groups** button does not import students into groups. It imports a text file that you can use to create groups. So, if you need to create a lot of groups at once, you can use this feature to do this.

This needs to be done by a site administrator.

If you need to import students and put them into groups, use the upload students feature described in the *Adding student to a cohort in bulk – Upload* section. However, instead of adding students to the cohort, you will add them to a course and group. You perform this by specifying the course and group fields in the upload file, as shown in the following code:

```
username,email,firstname,lastname,course1,group1,course2
moodler_1,bill@williamrice.net,Bill,Binky,history101,odds,science101
moodler_2,rose@williamrice.net,Rose,Krial,history101,even,science101
moodler_3,jeff@williamrice.net,Jeff,Marco,history101,odds,science101
moodler_4,dave@williamrice.net,Dave,Gallo,history101,even,science101
```

In this example, we have the minimum needed information to create new students. These are as follows:

- The username
- The email address
- The first name
- The last name

We have also enrolled all the students in two courses: `history101` and `science101`. In the `history101` course, `Bill Binky`, and `Jeff Marco` are placed in a group called **odds**. `Rose Krial` and `Dave Gallo` are placed in a group called **even**. In the `science101` course, the students are not placed in any group.

Remember that this student upload doesn't happen on the Groups page. It happens under **Administration | Site administration | Users | Upload users**.

Summary

Cohorts and groups give you powerful tools to manage your students. Cohorts are a useful tool to quickly enroll and unenroll large numbers of students. Groups enable you to separate students who are in the same course and give teachers the ability to quickly see only the students they are responsible for.

In the previous chapters, you saw how to add content and activities to your course. In this chapter, you learned how to use some tools to manage students in your course. In the next chapter, you will see how to extend your course using the functionality of blocks.

13
Extending Your Course by Adding Blocks

Blocks add functionality to your site or course. This chapter describes many of Moodle's blocks, helps you decide which ones will meet your goals, and tells you how to implement them. In this chapter, you will learn about blocks, their uses, and how to configure and customize them.

Defining a block

A block usually displays information in a small area in one of the side columns. For example, a block can display a calendar, the latest news, or the students enrolled in a course. Think of a block as a small applet or widget.

They can also include links to parts of the course and thus be something like navigation bars. Blocks serve an important function in that they call attention to items and help you point the student to things you do not want them to overlook.

Blocks are also very engaging, and they can be good calendars, or even engaging content or activities.

Uses of blocks

When configuring the site, you can choose to display, hide, and position blocks on the site's front page. When configuring a course, you can also show/hide/position blocks on the course's home page. The procedure is the same whether working on the site's front page or a course's home page. The site's front page is essentially a course. You can also give students permission to add blocks to their personal **My home** page and to their **My profile** page.

Many blocks are available to you in a standard Moodle installation. You can also install additional blocks, available through `http://moodle.org/plugins`.

Examples of blocks in action

There are many blocks that are available in a standard Moodle installation. Perhaps the most popular one is the **CALENDAR** block, which you can position so that it appears prominently in the corner. The **CALENDAR** block is an excellent tool, because it allows you to remind students of deadlines and key milestones.

The **Course completion** block is extremely useful as an engager and motivator, because you can both remind students where they are in the course and also reward them for progressing well through the course.

Blocks such as **Course overview** can help you create a nicely organized page. The **Course description** has a similar function.

Other blocks are very useful as shortcuts to important pages within Moodle. These blocks include **Activities**, **Main menu**, **Courses**, **Section links**, and **Upcoming Events**.

Blocks are wonderful organizational tools. They are also excellent tools for helping students keep on task. However, they can be overused to the point that they can make the page rather cluttered and distracting.

To avoid problems of clutter, ensure that you plan your use of the blocks and prioritize what you'd like your students to do and see.

Configuring where a block appears

You can configure a block to appear on the course's home page and on all the resource and activity pages in the course. You can also configure a block to appear on all the courses in a category.

For example, in the following screenshot, the user is configuring the **Upcoming events** block in the **Intro Enviro Sci** course:

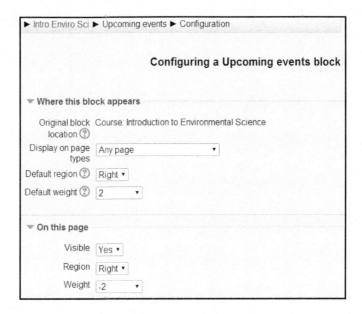

These settings work in combination to determine where a block appears. In some places, some of these settings have no effect. The following is a list of the combinations that you might find most useful.

When you add a block to a page, any display settings that you choose will affect the block from that page on, down through the hierarchy of pages. For example, suppose you add a block to the main page of a course, as the user is doing in the preceding screenshot. Any display settings will affect the block on that page and other pages inside that course.

As this block is being added to a course page, the block will not be displayed on any pages outside of that course.

If you want a block to appear on every page in your site, or on every occurrence of a specific page type, add the block to the front page of your site. Here's a screenshot that shows the drop-down menu, you must click on **Plugins** and it will open another drop-down menu entitled blocks:

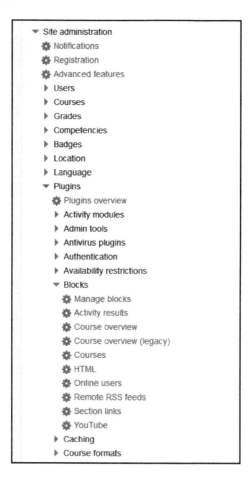

When you do that, under **Block settings**, you will see choices for **Page contexts**:

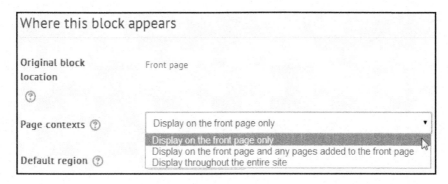

Further down the page, you will see a setting that determines whether the block is displayed on this page (that is, on the front page):

These settings can work together to produce the result that you want. For example, if you are an administrator and want a block to appear on every page in your site except for the front page, add the block to your front page. Choose **Display throughout entire site**, and then for just the front page, set **Visible** to **No**.

You can also add a block to all the courses in a category. From the **Site administration** menu, select **Courses | Manage courses and categories**. Then, select the category. Add the block to the category page. Then, under the settings for **Where this block appears**, choose which pages in the category will display the block.

Many Moodle themes now allow the user to move blocks to a special dock. This dock collapses, saving space on the screen for the main Moodle content. In the next screenshot, you can see that the user has docked the **Search forums** block and is about to dock the **Navigation** block:

In a responsive theme, the docked blocks will be displayed at the bottom of the page on a small screen.

Now that you know how to configure where your blocks appear, let's look at how you use some of the blocks available to you.

Standard blocks

Moodle gives you many standard blocks that you can add to your courses. Some of the most useful ones are discussed in the following sections.

The Activities block

The **Activities** block lists all types of activities that are used in the course:

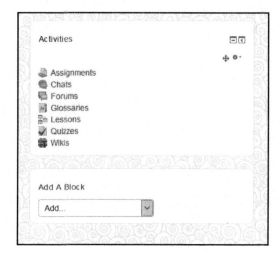

If a type of activity is not used in the course, the link for that type is not presented. The activity type is only shown if your course contains at least one instance of that type. When a user clicks on the type of activity, all those kinds of activities for the course are listed.

In the following screenshot, the user clicked on **Forums** in the **Activities** block, and a list of the resources in the course is presented:

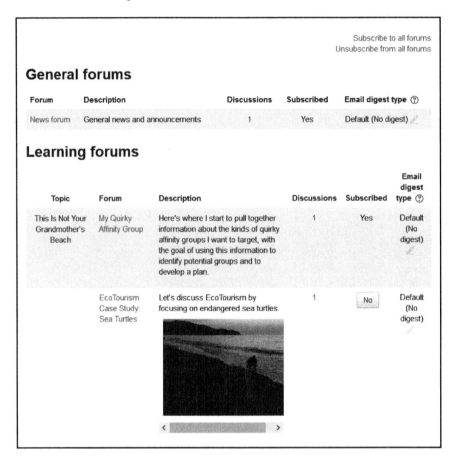

 If this block is on the site's front page, clicking on a type of activity gives a list for the activities on the front page (not for the entire site).

The Blog menu block

By default, every Moodle user has a personal blog on the site. Selecting this block, as seen in the following screenshot, puts the menu into the sidebar of the course:

Note that this block provides shortcuts to blog entries about the course. If blogging will be a part of the course, include this block on the main page of the course.

The Blog tags block

This block displays a list of the blog tags used site-wide. The tags are listed in an alphabetical order. The more blog entries that use a tag, the larger that tag is:

The CALENDAR block

Workshops, assignments, quizzes, and events appear on the **CALENDAR** block:

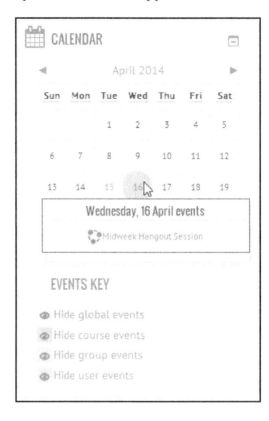

In the preceding screenshot, you can see that the user is pointing to an event that begins on **April 16, 2014**. A pop-up window shows the name of the event. This event was added to this course, so it is a course-wide event.

When the user clicks on one of the four links at the bottom of the **CALENDAR** block, it disables the display of that type of event.

When a deadline is added to an activity in the course, it will automatically be added to the calendar.

The comments block

The **Comments** block enables anyone with access to it to leave and read comments. The comments are all saved, so you can accumulate quite a long list of comments.

In the next screenshot, the **Student1** user is logged in. Note that **Student1** can delete their comment but not the comment left by the course administrator:

Students can delete only their own comments. Of course, the teacher, manager, and site administrator can delete anyone's comments.

As all comments are saved, and the list can get long, you probably want to limit the comment block to a single course, that is, you don't want to add a comment site-wide, or to all the courses in a category. If you do, the block can become crowded with comments (unless this is the effect that you want). The site administrator can decide how many comments are displayed in comments blocks from **Site administration** | **Front page** | **Front page settings**.

Consider adding a **Comments** block to an activity or a resource and using the first comment to encourage students to leave their feedback, as follows:

The Course completion block

This block works with course completion tracking. For this block to function, you must first set the criteria for completing the course, and completion tracking must be enabled at the site level. This is done under **Course administration** | **Course completion**.

When a student views this block, they see the conditions for course completion and the status of each condition. When a teacher views this block, they see a report of the completion status for each student in the course.

Course/site summary

If you add this block to the front page of your site, it will display the front page summary that is found under **Site administration** | **Front page settings** | **Edit settings**. If you add it to a course page, it will display the course description that is found under **Course administration** | **Edit settings** | **Course summary**.

The Courses block

The courses block, like the **Navigation** block, displays the courses that the student is enrolled in.

The FEEDBACK block

On the front page of your site, you can create a feedback activity. This feedback activity can then be used in all or some of the courses on your site. This way, you don't need to recreate the feedback activity for each course, and since the feedback for each course uses the same questions, you can make meaningful comparisons among the courses.

First, you add the feedback activity to the front page and immediately hide it on the front page. That is what we did in the following example. You can see that the feedback activity is grayed out on the front page in the next screenshot:

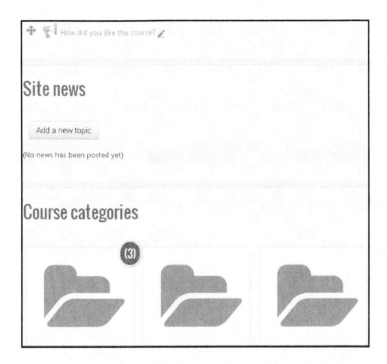

Under the **Settings** for the feedback activity, there is a setting to map the activity to all or selected courses:

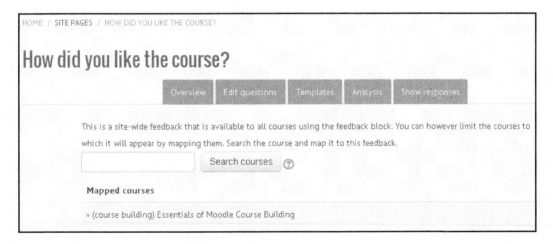

You can see in the preceding example that this feedback activity has been mapped to the course called **Essentials of Moodle Course Building**. When we go to that course and add the feedback block, we see the following:

In short, the **FEEDBACK** block gives the students access to a feedback activity that has been added to the front page and then mapped to the current course. That feedback activity becomes an activity in the current course.

The HTML block

The **HTML** block creates a block in the sidebar that can hold any HTML (or any web content) that you can put on a web page. Most experienced web users are accustomed to the content in the sidebars being an addition to the main content of a page. For example, we put menus and interesting links in the sidebars in most of the blogging software. I suggest that you keep with that standard. Use the **HTML** block to hold content that is an interesting addition to the course, but not essential. For example, you can put an annotated link to another site of interest.

When you edit an **HTML** block, Moodle gives the same full-featured Web page editor that you get when adding a web page to a course.

Think of an **HTML** block as a miniature web page that you can put into the sidebar of your course.

The Latest News block

When you create a new course, by default it has a **News forum**. The **Latest News** block displays the most recent postings from this forum.

Even if the forum is renamed, this block displays the postings. The number of postings displayed in this block is determined in the course settings page, by the **News items to show** field.

Recall that the front page of your site is another course. If the **Latest News** block is displayed on the site's front page, it displays the latest postings from the site-wide news forum, or site news.

If you have set the news forum to email students with new postings, you can be reasonably sure that the students are getting the news, so you might not need to display this block. However, if the news items are of interest to visitors not enrolled in the course, or if the course allows guest access, you probably want to display this block.

The Logged in user block

If a visitor is not logged in, Moodle displays small **Login** links in the upper-right corner and bottom-center of the page. However, the links are not very noticeable. The **Logged in user** block is much more prominent. One advantage to the **Logged in user** block over the small **Login** links is the block's greater visibility.

If you want the **Login** block to be displayed on every page of your site, set **Page context** to **Display throughout the entire site** and ensure that the locks are unlocked and the eye is open:

Logged in user	0	2017111300	👁	🔓
Login	0	2017111300	👁	🔓

After the user logs in, this block displays information about the current user. The information is taken from the user's profile. It also displays a **Logout** link.

The Messages block

The **Messages** block provides a shortcut to Moodle's **Messages center**. It displays the latest messages received. This is a shortcut to the page you will reach by selecting **Administration| My profile | Messages**.

The My latest badges block

This block displays the badges that the student has earned on your site. It can be added to the front page, the user's **My Home page**, and to the main page of a course. It probably makes the most sense when added to a user's **My Home page**.

The My private files block

If the site administrator enables the repository for private files, then when the user is selecting a file to be uploaded into a course (such as when submitting an assignment), the user will be able to choose from files that only they can access. These files are stored under **My profile** | **My private files**. Also, users can upload files to their private files even when those files are not part of a course.

This block gives the user a shortcut to access their private files.

The Online users block

The **Online users** block shows who is in the current course at the present time. If it is on the site's front page, it shows who is on the site. When it is added to a course, it can be a good way to lessen the isolation of e-learning. The block is updated every few minutes.

The quiz results block

The **Quiz results** block is available only if there is a quiz in the course. It displays the highest and/or lowest grades achieved on a quiz within a course. You can anonymize the students' names in the block.

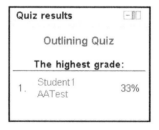

You can add this block to your course multiple times. So, you can have a Quiz results block for each quiz in the course.

The Random glossary entry block

Moodle's **Random glossary** block pulls entries from a selected glossary and displays them in a block. It can pull entries from any glossary that is available from that course. In the following screenshot, you can see how to configure it:

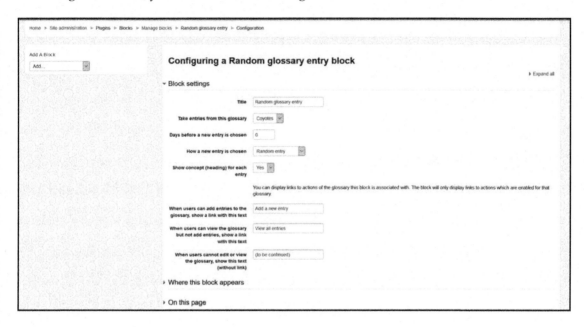

Even though the name is **Random glossary** block, you can control the order in which the entries are pulled from the glossary and how often the block displays a new entry. For example, in the following screenshot, the **Random glossary** block is set to display each entry in order, and to change each day:

Here are some ideas for using the **Random glossary** block for something other than a glossary:

- Highlights from the work that past students in this class submitted. If the class is working on a long-term project, create a glossary that contains the best work submitted by previous classes who completed that project. Display the glossary while the current class is working on that project.
- Inspirational or informative quotes related to the field of study.

- If you're teaching in a corporate setting, consider putting rules and procedures into their own glossaries. You can create a separate glossary for each type of rule or procedure, for example, a human resources policies glossary, a purchase order glossary, and so on. Then, display random entries from these glossaries in the appropriate courses.
- Create a glossary with past exam questions and their answers. Students can use this as another resource to prepare for their exams.
- Funny anecdotes related to the field of study.
- Inspiring or amusing images and audio.
- Common mistakes and their corrections; for example, how to spot software bugs or common foreign language grammar errors.

The recent activity block

When the **Recent activity** block is added to the home page of a course, it lists all the student and teacher activity in that course since the user's last login. The link for a full report of recent activity displays a page that enables you to run reports on course activity.

When added to the site's front page, it lists all the student and teacher activity on the front page, but not in the individual courses, since the user's last login. If someone is logged in as a guest user, this block displays any activity since the last time that guest logged in. If guest users are constantly coming to your site, this block may be of limited use to them. One strategy is to omit this block from the site's front page so that anonymous users don't see it and add it only to courses that require users to authenticate.

The Remote RSS feeds block

When the **Remote RSS feeds** block is added to a course, the course creator chooses or creates the RSS feeds to display in that block.

The following example shows an RSS feed from an adventure racing site. This feed is the result of the configuration that is shown in the following screenshot:

A feed can be added by the site administrator and then selected by the course creator for use in an RSS block. Alternatively, when the teacher adds the **Remote RSS feeds** block, they can add a feed at that time. If **Share feed** is set to **Yes**, the new feed becomes available to all other teachers, for use in all other courses.

The Search Forums block

The **Search Forums** block provides a search function for forums. It does not search other types of activities or resources. When this block is added to the site's Moodle search forums front page, it searches only the forums on the front page.

When it's added to the main page of a course, it searches only the forums in that course. It searches post titles and content.

This block is different than the **Search courses** field that automatically appears on the site's front page. The **Search courses** field searches course names and descriptions, not forums.

Section links

The **Topics** block displays links to the numbered topics or weeks in a course. Clicking on a link advances the page to that topic.

The Upcoming Events block

The **Upcoming Events** block is an extension of the **CALENDAR** block. It gets event information from your calendar. By default, the **Upcoming Events** block displays 10 events; the maximum is 20. It looks ahead a default of 21 days; the maximum is 200. If there are more upcoming events than the maximum chosen for this block, the most distant events will not be shown.

This block is helpful for reminding students of the tasks they need to complete in the course.

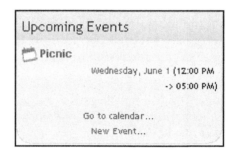

Summary

When deciding which blocks to display, consider the comfort level of your students. If they're experienced web surfers, they may be comfortable with a full complement of blocks displaying information about the course. Experienced web surfers are adept at ignoring information they don't need (when was the last time you paid attention to a banner ad on the web?). If your students are new computer users, they may assume that the presence of a block means that it requires their attention or interaction. Also, remember that you can turn blocks off and on, as needed. The key is to use blocks to enable students to succeed. You can use blocks as signposts and guides. However, avoid the overuse of blocks, because they can be distracting.

In the next chapter, you will learn how to optimize your course for teachers, including how to view course logs and activity reports to determine what students have done, how to view and categorize grades, and how to grade.

14
Features for Teachers

Moodle offers several features that are of special interest to teachers. These focus on determining how well your students are progressing through a course. Reports and logs show you who has done what on your site, or in your course. Also, grades not only tell you how well your students are scoring, but can also be curved and weighted very easily.

Being able to generate student progress reports can be a very useful tool as you prepare documents that detail the kind of work your students are doing, their time spent on tasks, and their completion rates. If you are required to generate statistics for student success or persistence, you will find Moodle's reports and logs a lifesaver.

Also, if you are required to document when students first log in to a course, and when they were last active, you'll find the reports and logs to be extremely helpful. They are also useful in determining whether or not a student merits an *incomplete* rather than a failing grade.

Finally, if your organization must demonstrate competency, being able to generate reports that pinpoint how and where students are succeeding or failing in the assessments and learning outcomes can be vital.

Logs and reports

Moodle keeps detailed logs of all the activities that users perform on your site. You can use these logs to determine who has been active on your site, what they did, and when they did it.

Some reports are available at the course level; teachers can access these reports. Other reports are available at the site level; you must be a site administrator to access these reports. Both are covered in this chapter.

Moodle has a modest report viewing system built into it. However, for sophisticated log analysis, you need to look outside Moodle.

To view the logs and reports for a course, you must be logged in as a teacher or a manager. Then, select **My courses** | **Name of course** | **Reports**.

You can use this page to display three different kinds of information. From the top to bottom, they are as follows:

- Logs
- Live logs
- Activity report
- Course participation
- Activity completion
- Statistics

Let's look at each one separately.

Viewing course logs

Note that Moodle's display of the log files can be filtered by course, participant, day, activity, and action. You can select a single value for any of these filters, as seen in the following screenshot:

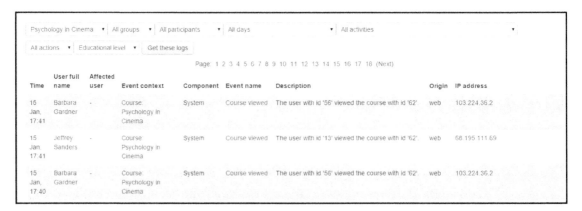

You cannot select multiple values for any of these filters, that is, you cannot look at the logs for two courses at the same time, four participants at the same time, or for a few days at the same time. If you want a more sophisticated view of the logs, you must use a tool other than Moodle's built-in log viewer.

Fortunately, you can download the logs as text files and import them into another tool, such as a spreadsheet. To download the logs, use the drop-down menu at the bottom of the page, as seen in the following screenshot:

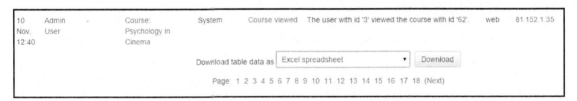

For example, you can use Excel's data menu to format, chart, and analyze the data. A complete discussion of Excel's data functions is beyond the scope of this book, but there are many sources of help for these functions.

The following screenshot is an example of a table created in Excel from imported data. I've sorted the data by participant (full names) so that, at a glance, I can see which users are the most active:

	A	B	C	D	E	
1	Course	Time	IP Address	Full name	Action	Information
2	FreePics	2007 February 24 19:34	82.27.68.16	LisaMarie Alexandria	course view	Free Wild Pictures
3	FreePics	2007 January 16 19:43	82.27.73.24l	LisaMarie Alexandria	course view	Free Wild Pictures
4	FreePics	2007 January 16 19:23	82.27.73.24l	LisaMarie Alexandria	resource view	Common Burdock in the Spring
5	FreePics	2007 January 16 19:23	82.27.73.24l	LisaMarie Alexandria	course view	Free Wild Pictures
6	FreePics	2007 January 16 19:23	82.27.73.24l	LisaMarie Alexandria	course enrol	Deer Habits
7	Debris Huts	2007 February 18 16:43	86.136.132.	Bradford Sorens	course view	Debris Huts
8	Debris Huts	2007 February 18 16:43	86.136.132.	Bradford Sorens	course enrol	Debris Huts
9	Bow Drill	2007 February 18 16:43	86.136.132.	Bradford Sorens	course view	Bow Drill Firestarting
10	Bow Drill	2007 February 18 16:43	86.136.132.	Bradford Sorens	course enrol	Debris Huts
11	Tracking Basic	2007 February 18 16:42	86.136.132.	Bradford Sorens	user view all	
12	Tracking Basic	2007 February 18 16:41	86.136.132.	Bradford Sorens	course view	Tracking Basics
13	Tracking Basic	2007 February 18 16:41	86.136.132.	Bradford Sorens	course enrol	Debris Huts
14	Water's Edge	2007 February 18 16:40	86.136.132.	Bradford Sorens	course enrol	Debris Huts
15	Water's Edge	2007 February 18 16:40	86.136.132.	Bradford Sorens	course view	By the Water's Edge
16	FreePics	2007 February 18 16:31	86.136.132.	Bradford Sorens	course view	Free Wild Pictures
17	FreePics	2007 February 18 16:31	86.136.132.	Bradford Sorens	resource view	Wild Plant Pictures
18	FreePics	2007 February 18 16:31	86.136.132.	Bradford Sorens	course view	Free Wild Pictures
19	FreePics	2007 February 18 16:31	86.136.132.	Bradford Sorens	course enrol	Debris Huts

Note that the preceding table in the screenshot contains information from several courses; you can see that in column **A**. There are two ways to get information from several courses in the same place. First, you can run the report as an administrator, from the administrative interface. This enables you to run a report for all the courses on the site. Second, as a teacher, you can download the data from each course separately and combine it in one Excel sheet or workbook.

Viewing live logs

Live logs show what has happened in the current course, for the past hour:

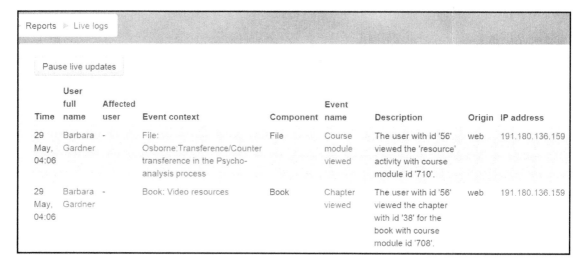

Use live logs if you want to observe the students as they use the course. For example, you might monitor the course while students take a scheduled quiz.

Viewing activity reports

An activity report offers a user-friendly view of an activity in a single course. While the logs show complete information, an activity report just shows the course items, what was done in each item, and the time of the latest activity for that item. When you first select **Activity report** from the menu, you are presented with a list of all the activities in the course, as illustrated:

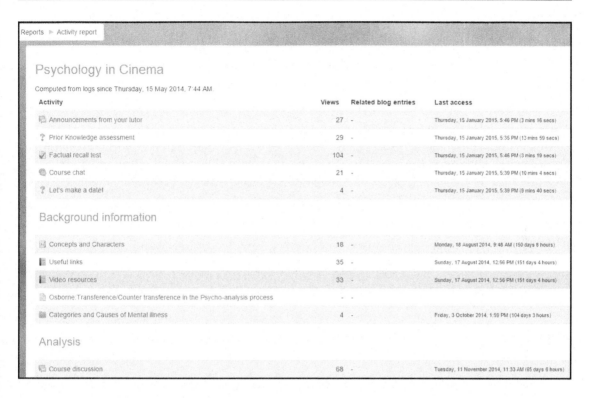

From this list, select the activity for which you want a report, and you are taken to that activity. In this example, the teacher selected **Prior knowledge assessment**, which opened that activity. Then, the teacher can select **View 11 responses** in order to see how the students participated in this activity:

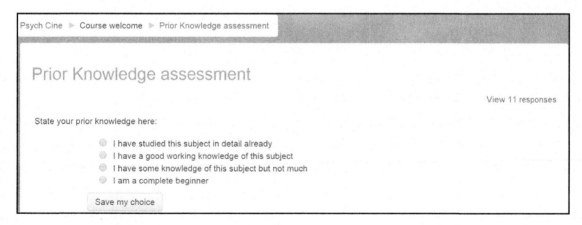

Note that an activity report only acts as a link to the activities in a course. Once you select an activity, you will use that activity's method for viewing a report.

The participation report

The participation report is especially useful for discovering which students need to complete an activity and sending them a reminder to complete it. In the following example, the teacher is looking at the report for a feedback activity called **Psychology in Cinema Evaluation.** The teacher wants to see who submitted their feedback for the course:

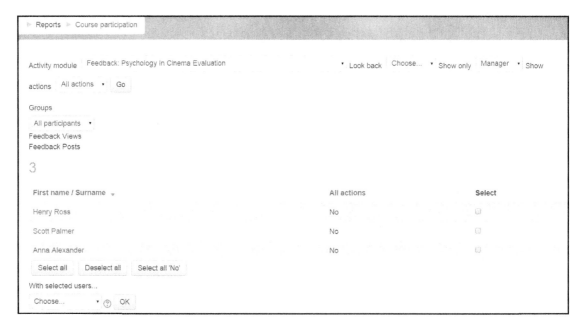

In this demonstration course, the teacher wants all the students to give their feedback. So, the teacher will send a message to the students who have not completed the activity. To do this, they select the students and then, from the **With selected users...** drop-down list, select **Send a message**:

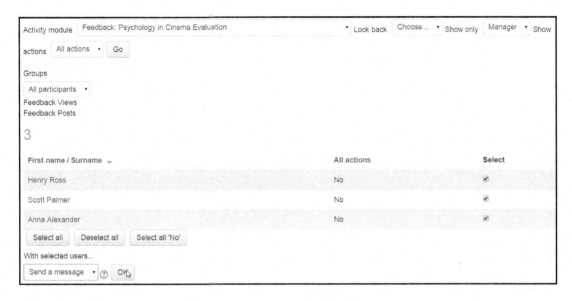

This takes the teacher to a page where they can create and send the message. The message will be sent to the students' email addresses and also be stored in their Moodle messages.

Using activity tracking

You can take the monitoring to a more precise level. If the course has activity tracking enabled, you can view a report showing the completion status of the activities in the course:

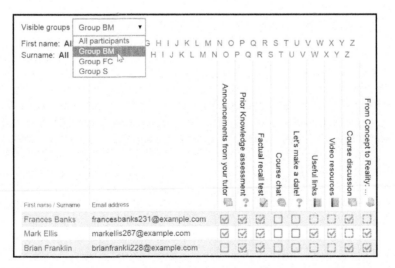

Note that you can show activity for just one group, or for all the students in the course. Also, this report shows only those activities whose completion status is being tracked.

Viewing grades

To access grades, select the course that you want to see the grades of, and then select **Grade administration** | **Grader Report**; this displays a summary of the grades for that course:

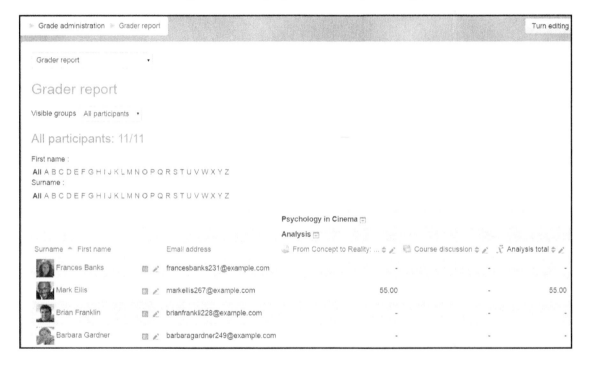

Note that, in the preceding screenshot, some students have not completed the first assignment in this course, **From Concept to Reality....** Also, note the **Turn editing on** button in the upper-right corner of the page; the teacher can use that to override the grades being displayed by entering new ones. When the teacher clicks on that button, the grades on this page become editable.

In our example course, the teacher wants to investigate the lack of grades for the **From Concept to Reality...** assignment, so they will click on the name of the assignment, which takes the teacher out of the **Grader report** and into the assignment itself. In the following screenshot, note that the Navigation bar at the top of the page now shows that we are viewing the assignment:

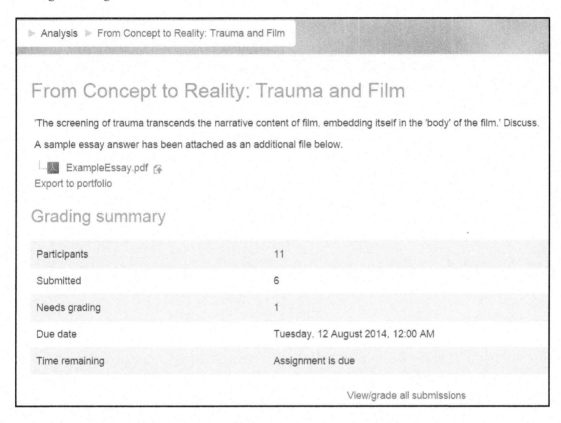

The **Grader report** is the teacher's starting point for examining the grades in a course. It also enables the teacher to enter updated grades. From there, you can click into individual activities and investigate or modify the grades.

Categorizing grades

Each of the graded activities can be put into a category. Note that you put activities into categories, not students. If you want to categorize students, put them into groups.

Viewing grade categories

Categorizing the graded activities in a course enables you to quickly see how your students are doing with various kinds of activities. If you do not assign an activity to a category, it will then belong to the **Uncategorised** category, by default. The next screenshot shows a course that uses the **Quizzes** and **Non-quizzes** categories. These were created by the teacher in order to compare the students' performance in tests on other activities, because they were concerned that some student may have test anxiety.

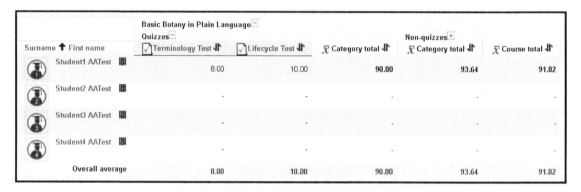

Note that in the category labeled **Quizzes**, the grades are displayed for two quizzes, that is, **Terminology Test** and **Lifecycle Test**. The page also displays the **Category total** for **Quizzes**.

In the category labeled **Non-quizzes**, it displays only the **Category total**. Grades for individual activities under **Non-quizzes** are not displayed. If the user clicks on the **+** sign located next to **Non-quizzes**, the individual grades in that category will be revealed.

In this example, the teacher can see that the scores of **Student1** in the quizzes are consistent with their scores in the non-quiz activities. Categorizing the activities made it easy to see the comparison.

Creating grade categories

Categories are created and items are moved into categories, in the same window.

To create a grade category

1. Select **Administration | Grade administration | Setup | Categories and items**
2. At the bottom of the page, click on the **Add category** button. The **Edit category** page is displayed
3. Fill out the page and save your changes

To assign an item to a grade category

1. Select **Settings | Grade administration | Categories and items**
2. Select the item(s) that you want to assign to the category
3. From the drop-down menu at the bottom of the page, select the category to which you want to move the item(s):

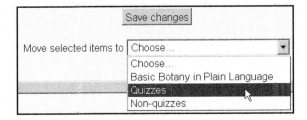

4. Click on the **Save changes** button

The most important point here is to determine what kind of question you want to answer when you examine student grades, and create categories that enable you to answer that question. For example, *How do my students do on quizzes versus more interactive activities, like workshops and forums?* To answer that question, create a category just for quizzes, and you can answer that question just by viewing the grades. Alternatively, *How do my students do on offline activities versus online activities?* To answer that question, create online and offline grading categories.

Remember that these categories are not written in stone. If your needs change, you can always create and assign new grading categories, as needed.

Using extra credit

When using the simple weighted method of calculating the final grades, you can designate any activity as extra credit. When an item is extra credit, its points are not added to the total possible points for the category.

First, navigate to **Grade administration** | **Setup** | **Categories and items**. From there, select the extra credit item for editing:

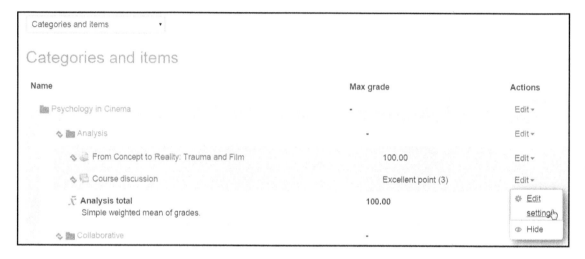

Once you are on the editing page for the item, you can designate it as extra credit just by clicking on the checkbox labeled **Extra credit**.

You can also create a category just for extra credit activities. Alternatively, you can use the extra credit setting on selected activities. Both approaches will work.

Weighting a category

You can, and probably should, assign a weight to a grade category. By default, a weight of **100** maximum grade is applied to every category. This means that each category contributes equally to the course total. In the following screenshot, you can see that the **Collaborative** and **Individual** categories are assigned a weight of **100**. The **Analysis** category has a weight of **200** as the maximum grade:

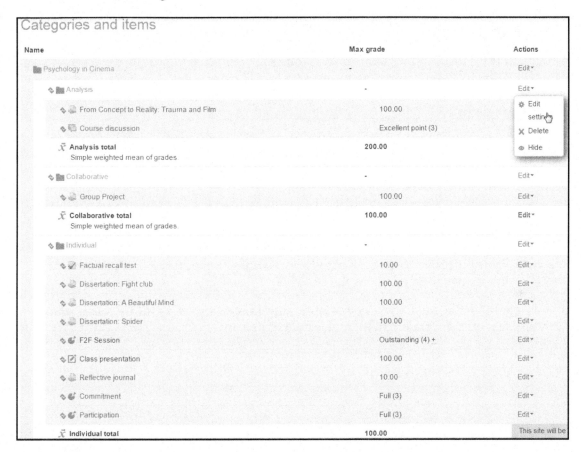

The weight for the category is set by selecting **Edit settings** for that category. On the **Edit settings** page, you can enter the total number of points possible for the category.

No matter what numbers you enter for category totals, you can enter any number for the course total. The category totals will contribute proportionately to the course total. For example, suppose two grade categories are worth four and six points, respectively. The course total is 20 points. The final grade of one category will be worth 40 percent of the course total (eight points), and the final grade of the other category will be worth 60 percent (12 points) of the course total.

Compensating for a difficult category

You might want to add extra points to everyone's grade in order to compensate for an especially difficult assignment. The easiest way to add extra points to everyone's grade for that specific assignment is to add an extra grade item to a category and then give everyone points for that item.

In the following screenshot, you can see that the teacher has added a grade item worth two points to the **Quizzes** category and designated it as **Extra credit**.

At the bottom of the **Categories and items** page, click on the **Add grade item** button. This brings you to a page where you can create an item that has the sole purpose of holding a grade in the grade book.

When you add a grade item instead of an activity, you must enter the grade for the students manually. This is because there is no activity in Moodle for the students to perform, so Moodle cannot calculate a grade for the students.

To add grades to the grade item, go to **Course administration** | **Grades** | **Grader report**. On this page, for the extra credit item, select the Edit icon:

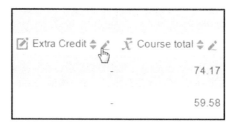

This brings you to a page where you can manually enter a grade for each student, or you can update the grade for all the students at once, as the teacher is about to do in the following screenshot:

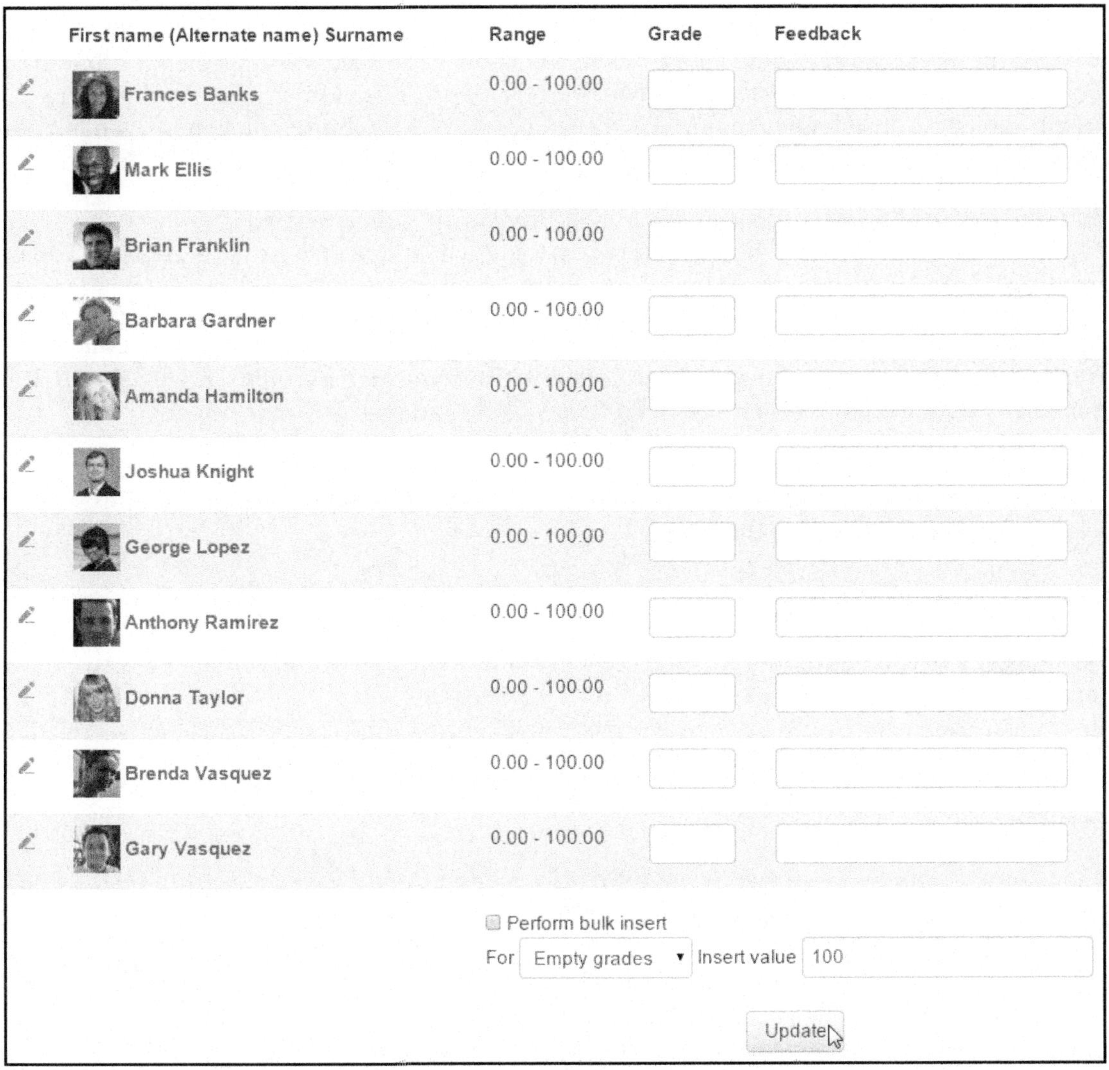

	First name (Alternate name) Surname	Range	Grade	Feedback
✎	Frances Banks	0.00 - 100.00		
✎	Mark Ellis	0.00 - 100.00		
✎	Brian Franklin	0.00 - 100.00		
✎	Barbara Gardner	0.00 - 100.00		
✎	Amanda Hamilton	0.00 - 100.00		
✎	Joshua Knight	0.00 - 100.00		
✎	George Lopez	0.00 - 100.00		
✎	Anthony Ramirez	0.00 - 100.00		
✎	Donna Taylor	0.00 - 100.00		
✎	Brenda Vasquez	0.00 - 100.00		
✎	Gary Vasquez	0.00 - 100.00		

☐ Perform bulk insert

For [Empty grades ▾] Insert value [100]

[Update]

Summary

Whether in a classroom or online, managing a successful course requires two-way communication between the teacher and students. Constantly monitoring the course logs and grades gives you an early indication that a class may need a mid-course correction. You can use questions, surveys, and chats to discover specific problems and challenges that the students are facing. After bringing the course back on track, custom grading scales, extra credit, and curves can help you equalize the grades. When teaching online, make a habit of checking the logs and grades often.

You can use the reports and logs for administrative purposes as well, to comply with requirements to document when students first logged in and also their progress for student success and student academic progress.

Now that you have worked your way through this entire book, you have a basic toolkit for creating, delivering, and managing a successful online course in Moodle. However, you don't need to do it alone! When you need help with Moodle, there are many good resources.

First, the Moodle community at http://moodle.org is an excellent resource. The forums contain plenty of accumulated wisdom.

Second, you are welcome to visit my site at http://www.beyondutopia.com and click over to my blog at http://www.elearningqueen.com for longer how-to articles about online learning. Leave comments and join the conversation. Also, feel free to contact me via LinkedIn at https://www.linkedin.com/in/susannash/.

Third, check out other Moodle books by Packt Publishing. They deal with specific topics in more detail, such as Moodle security, administration, and using Moodle in a corporate environment.

Thank you for taking a journey through Moodle with me, and I look forward to seeing you online with the rest of the Moodle community.

Other Books You May Enjoy

If you enjoyed this book, you may be interested in these other books by Packt:

Moodle 3.x Developer's Guide
Ian Wild

ISBN: 978-1-78646-711-9

- Work with the different types of custom modules that can be written for Moodle 3.x
- Understand how to author custom modules so they conform to the agreed Moodle 3.x development guidelines
- Get familiar with the Moodle 3.x architecture—its internal and external APIs
- Customize Moodle 3.x so it can integrate seamlessly with third-party applications of any kind
- Build a new course format to specify the layout of a course
- Implement third-party graphics libraries in your plugins
- Build plugins that can be themed easily
- Provide custom APIs that will provide the means to automate Moodle 3 in real time

Learn to Create WordPress Themes by Building 5 Projects
Eduonix Learning Solutions

ISBN: 978-1-78728-664-1

- Simple and advanced themes – covers basic syntax and files along with archives and search pages
- Photo Gallery – add simple animation and use the W3.CSS framework to design a photo gallery theme
- Wordstrap – incorporate Twitter Bootstrap into the theme and use the WP_NavWalker Class
- E-commerce Theme – build an e-commerce theme using the Foundation framework

Leave a review - let other readers know what you think

Please share your thoughts on this book with others by leaving a review on the site that you bought it from. If you purchased the book from Amazon, please leave us an honest review on this book's Amazon page. This is vital so that other potential readers can see and use your unbiased opinion to make purchasing decisions, we can understand what our customers think about our products, and our authors can see your feedback on the title that they have worked with Packt to create. It will only take a few minutes of your time, but is valuable to other potential customers, our authors, and Packt. Thank you!

Index

Printed in Great Britain
by Amazon

79680566R00249